Patents and Strategic Inventing

The Corporate Inventor's Guide to Creating Sustainable Competitive Advantage

NICHOLAS J. NISSING

New York   Chicago   San Francisco   Lisbon   London
Madrid   Mexico City   Milan   New Delhi   San Juan
Seoul   Singapore   Sydney   Toronto

This publication is designed to provide accurate and authoritative information in regard to the subject matter covered. It is sold with the understanding that neither the author nor the publisher is not engaged in rendering legal, accounting, securities trading, or other professional services. If legal advice or other expert assistance is required, the services of a competent professional person should be sought.
— *From a Declaration of Principles Jointly Adopted by a Committee of the American Bar Association and a Committee of Publishers and Associations*

McGraw-Hill books are available at special quantity discounts to use as premiums and sales promotions or for use in corporate training programs. To contact a representative, please e-mail us at bulksales@mcgraw-hill.com.

This book is printed on acid-free paper.

CONTENTS

ACKNOWLEDGMENTS

I've had the opportunity to work with a large number of attorneys and inventors over the years, and I owe a debt of gratitude to each one. The intellectual challenge of both inventing and patent strategy has provided both frustration and elation over the years. My colleagues have educated and encouraged me in these endeavors.

In particular, I am indebted to the contributors of several chapters: Byron Olsen, Jeff Lindsay, Mark Mondry, and Elvir Causevic. I've had the pleasure of working with Byron on several inventions, and I look forward to the next opportunity to collaborate with him. I gained tremendous respect for Jeff while he was a competitor and read many of his patents to learn more about his strategic thinking. Mark is a rare attorney with a firm grasp of innovation, business, and legal strategy. And Elvir, a fellow engineer, inventor, entrepreneur, and IP strategist, would be an asset to almost any endeavor.

I would also like to thank two of the reviewers who have significantly improved the book's content—in particular, Cliff Lawson, whose "aircraft carrier" concept remains my favorite unpublished strategy, and Vlad Vitenberg, a true Renaissance man in addition to being an unparalleled patent attorney. And I would like to thank Paul Trokhan, a mentor and friend who has been extremely influential in my understanding of inventing and patent strategy. Paul is easily the most strategic inventor I know, and he provided the greatest quantitatively verifiable piece of advice I've ever received.

Finally, thanks to my wife for her support of my umpteenth simultaneous project, and to my daughter and her beautiful smile every time I get up from the keyboard.

Introduction

Most inventors assume that a granted patent is a valuable asset. Rarely is this actually the case. The vast majority of patents are never licensed or enforced. Simply put, most patents are nearly worthless. This book is about how to create new inventions and products that have powerful patent positions, from basic terminology to advanced techniques like strategic inventing.

Corporations are focused on creating value, and value is created through establishing a competitive advantage. Patents are one form of competitive advantage, but most patents are not very valuable—if they are valuable at all. It may seem strange to highlight this point in a book about patents, but the fact remains that most patents describe inventions that are never commercially marketed, never result in licensing revenues, and never create a meaningful competitive advantage.

If you are in a new product development (NPD) or research and development (R&D) organization, you've probably been exposed to patents a few times already. You may even be the inventor of a new product or technology. However, if you're like most corporate inventors, you probably haven't received much formal training related to patents. Perhaps you've been through a presentation or two about corporate policies and were issued a lab notebook. Maybe you even had a brief overview from a lawyer—but left with more questions than you came in with.

Now what?

Unfortunately, most scientists and engineers find the patent system to be complex and illogical. They may not admit it, but so do most attorneys.

I started out as a corporate inventor myself, working in new product development for Procter & Gamble. After being named an inventor

on a number of patents, I realized that I enjoyed the intellectual challenge of combining new product development with the elements of
patent strategy. I eventually left and started a consulting company with
a focus on innovation and intellectual property. This new venture gave
me the opportunity to work on a variety of projects in diverse fields, and
broadened my view of patents and invention. Seeking further challenges,
I eventually went back to a corporate position as a patent agent, and
I currently focus on competitive strategy in the biotechnology industry.
And no, I'm not a lawyer.

Along the way, I had some excellent mentors and worked with some
great lawyers. However, I discovered something interesting: a little
knowledge goes a long way. When an inventor knows something about
patent law, it becomes easier to identify inventions, and those inventions
also become more valuable. That having been said, there is no need to
dwell on the details. In fact, I have good news: you need to know only a
little about patents to improve your inventive productivity and the competitive advantage of your new products significantly. That's what this
book is about: creating new products with powerful patent positions.

But don't worry, first we'll address the fundamentals. Patents
involve lots of strange words and sometimes even strange definitions
for words that you already know. There are caveats to nearly every rule,
and exceptions to the caveats. The entire process can be quite confusing. In reality, however, there is a relatively short list of basic terms and
concepts that the inventor needs to know in order to be effective—
enough to direct a project and communicate effectively with attorneys
and executives.

In less-than-ideal situations, patent strategy will be relegated solely
to the patent attorney. NPD personnel will develop a new product
and then send some paperwork (e.g., an invention disclosure form) over
to the attorney to file a patent application. Developing a product that
has the most significant competitive advantage requires a more integrated approach: first the patent strategy is defined, and *then* the product is developed. Most books on innovation and product development
emphasize creativity, marketing, or business strategy. While these are
all legitimate elements of the innovation process, other tools are needed
as well: an understanding of patents, patent strategy, and strategic
inventing.

If you're like me, you spent most of your time in school studying a
particular discipline—perhaps one of the sciences or engineering.
Patents and intellectual property didn't even come up more than once
or twice. Though they may have done tremendous research, few of your

professors were inventors. Upon entering the industrial arena, you probably found that patents became more important—especially in R&D and NPD functions. They are visible symbols of productivity for individuals and projects. Often, an individual's reputation is influenced by the number of patented inventions that he produces. However, little time is devoted to training the corporate inventor in the subjects of invention, patents, and strategy. This lack of patent training for those who don't specialize in intellectual property has led to some unfortunate misconceptions.

MISCONCEPTION 1: "WE HAVE A PATENT FOR THAT"

This is one of the most common phrases heard in NPD and R&D organizations when discussing new products. Many scientists, engineers, and managers assume that having a patent related to a product means that there is a useful amount of competitive space that is protected. Unfortunately, this is rarely true. If you'd like to test this out for yourself, take a trip to the supermarket. Pick up a product and look for patent numbers stamped on the package. Once you've found one, look at the products to the left and right. Do they provide the same function? If the answer is yes, you're probably looking at patents with relatively low value. Having a patent, or even a portfolio of patents, doesn't create value for the corporation unless they help to establish a meaningful form of competitive advantage.

MISCONCEPTION 2: "WE LET THE LAWYERS HANDLE IT"

In some companies, attorneys are treated like a black box—inventors hand over an invention disclosure document and eventually get back a notice saying that it is or isn't being pursued. Many times I've heard researchers complain about this process because negative replies are rarely followed by thorough explanations. To the uninitiated, the process is a mystery.

Attorneys are great resources, but they are not omniscient. It would seem strange that your attorneys understood business strategy better than your executives, or that they understood the technical development options better than your engineers. A more integrated process involving technical, business, and marketing input will result in a better strategic focus and greater value in the resulting patents.

Leaving patent strategy in the hands of attorneys can create another significant problem: they frequently do what they are asked to do. Attorneys spend much of their time getting patents granted for their clients. After a while, it can almost seem as if having patents granted is the objective. It is not. Patents create value indirectly—by establishing a competitive advantage, defining ownership rights, ensuring freedom to operate, and so on. If the patent doesn't address one of these objectives, it doesn't create value. Inventors who understand the basics of patent strategy can improve the process and the quality of the output. The number of strategically valuable ideas will increase, and the throughput of the process as a whole will accelerate—while also improving the efficiency of your patent attorneys.

MISCONCEPTION 3: "THE PRODUCT COMES FIRST, THEN THE PATENT STRATEGY"

In most NPD and R&D organizations, the emphasis is on coming up with new product ideas or discoveries. That's why these organizations exist, of course. As a result, the default methodology is to create the new product or discovery first, then go to the patent attorney for help in developing a patent strategy. This could be called a "discovery-driven" approach to patent strategy. For many projects, this approach is sufficient. In more competitive industries, however, the development of the patent strategy should be integrated into the product development process from the very beginning. It may even be worthwhile to develop the patent strategy *before* research is started. Furthermore, there are often times when it will be advantageous to create inventions specifically based on the patent strategy, even if there is no product directly related to the invention.

Does this sound crazy? Perhaps it does. However, recall that the purpose of patents is to create a competitive advantage. Patents act to keep others from making, using, selling, or importing your invention. In other words, they can directly influence your business and your competitors' business by protecting the best features of your product. The emphasis is on competition. A good patent strategy is always focused on how the patents will affect the competition. In fact, a patent may be valuable even if you never actually turn it into a product. If you can predict where your competitor is headed, you can use this knowledge to improve your patent strategy, even if the invention isn't related to *your* next product.

Furthermore, the patent system can be extremely valuable for many things that aren't related to filing patents on your products. Patents and the information they contain can be extraordinarily valuable for activities like competitive intelligence, predictive invention, building protective fences, avoiding potential legal troubles, and guiding long-term development strategy.

ABOUT THIS BOOK

This book is designed to give you tools to improve your results through a more complete understanding of patents and related strategies. The tools discussed here are specifically related to patents and inventions, and are designed to be most beneficial to corporate inventors and managers in NPD and R&D organizations. However, it should be noted that this information is incomplete. I have chosen not to include detailed explanations of many topics in this area (e.g., international patent law, patent prosecution, and contracts). This is for a very specific reason: there are some things that are best left to attorneys. The corporate inventor needs an understanding of the objectives and terminology, a toolbox of techniques, and a way to apply her creative genius. Corporate inventors don't need to know everything about patent law; that's why there are patent attorneys.

Throughout this book, you will notice that I frequently emphasize the role that researchers should play in the patent process. While I advocate an active role for the inventor, you should always involve an attorney for answers to specific legal questions. There are many nuances and exceptions in the patent laws, and don't forget that the laws are constantly changing. This book is not intended to replace the attorney, but to improve the overall coordination of effort between inventors and lawyers, and to increase the value of the resulting intellectual property.

My goal is to provide the principles and basic information that will help you increase the quality and impact of your inventions. Despite the overall complexity of the patent system, the basic principles are really quite simple and rarely change. A little time and effort can be tremendously enlightening for the nonspecialist.

The first part of this book will cover the key concepts, terminology, and tools that you will need if you are to find, review, and discuss your inventions and your competitors' patents. Some of the language related to patents can be intimidating, but it doesn't have to be. Terms like "statutory subject matter," "best mode embodiments," and "nonobviousness" can be confusing at first, but they actually have relatively simple meanings. You can find hundreds of *pages* explaining each of these terms in detailed legalese, but what you need to know as an inventor can be distilled into hundreds of *words*.

The second part of the book will begin our foray into patent strategy. Strategy is all about the allocation of resources: Where is the best place to focus your inventive efforts? How does your invention fit into the competitive landscape? How do you know if a particular invention will be valuable? What kind of patents should you pursue? We'll also talk about how a good patent strategy can be used to organize multiple filings over time to create the strongest overall portfolio, the most significant competitive advantage, and the longest overall duration of protection.

The third part of the book will focus on strategic inventing. This term describes a process of developing an invention with a specific focus on maximizing the value of the related patent strategy. We'll discuss the benefits of differentiation, and how to know when you have a truly great invention. For example, a great scientific discovery isn't necessarily a great invention; conversely, a great invention doesn't necessarily require a scientific discovery.

There are also four chapters written by authors with specific expertise to provide some additional perspective on important topics: Chapter 9, written by Byron Olsen; Chapter 15, written by Elvir Causevic; Chapter 17, written by Mark Mondry; and Chapter 20, written by Jeff Lindsay. Each of these authors has a unique background and experience that make him well suited to write on these important topics.

As you will notice, I frequently refer to the "product" as if it were a physical thing that you hand to the "consumer." This isn't always accurate, of course. You may work in a business-to-business (B2B) environment, and there may be several companies further along the value chain before the product gets to the end consumer. Or perhaps your product is actually a service. In general, similar principles apply to both products and services, even though the terminology may differ.

I will also be using the word *consumer* from time to time. This may not be a common word in your industry, particularly if you're in a commodity chemical business, B2B, or some other field where consumers are significantly removed from your operation. Or you may be in an industry like software or electronics where the consumer is often referred to as the "user."

Your accommodation of my use of these terms is appreciated and will minimize my having to write and your having to read about the "product or service that you supply to the consumer, customer, end user, or other intermediary" throughout the text.

PART 1

KEY CONCEPTS

CHAPTER 1

Intellectual Property: The Real Estate of Your Mind

One of the most confusing aspects of patents and intellectual property is the terminology. This is one area in which attorneys really do have a language of their own, which can make it difficult for those who aren't legal specialists to understand the issues. One goal of this book is to introduce you to the words and phrases that you'll need to understand in order to recognize opportunities and issues related to patents and inventing.

The phrase *intellectual property* refers to a group of legally defined categories of things that would be difficult to own in the traditional sense of ownership. In particular, you can think of intellectual property (IP) as defining the boundaries of the real estate created in people's minds. For example, if you have a great idea that you created and developed using your intellect, the boundaries of what you own (your intellectual property) are defined in a manner similar to the way in which the boundaries of a piece of physical property are defined.

For a section of land, the boundaries are defined as geographic locations using an agreed-upon system, perhaps using latitude and longitude coordinates. Once the edges of a property have been defined, a deed is written to register the ownership of the property. The deed contains the name of the owner, when he took possession of the property, and where the boundaries are located. If there is a dispute over the location of one of the edges of the property, a surveyor is called in to locate the boundaries according to the specifications described in the deed. Your neighbor may claim to own part of your backyard, but the boundaries defined in the legal document determine who really owns that piece of land.

This is a reasonable analogy to how intellectual property works, but with one big exception: intellectual property usually deals with things that are hard to define in a meaningful way using purely physical limitations.

For example, the supply of intellectual property is not limited. Your neighborhood has only a certain amount of space that can be divided among the residents. On the other hand, a song or invention can be duplicated many times without running into any physical limitations. Nonetheless, the creator of the intellectual property invested significant resources—money, time, and creativity—in the development of this intellectual property. To encourage such endeavors, the creators of intellectual property are granted limited ownership rights to their creations.

The founders of the United States included these concepts in the constitution, Article 1, Section 8, where they describe basic powers of the government:

> The Congress shall have Power To lay and collect Taxes, Duties, Imposts and Excises, to pay the Debts and provide for the common Defence and general Welfare of the United States; but all Duties, Imposts and Excises shall be uniform throughout the United States;
>
> To borrow Money on the credit of the United States;
>
> To regulate Commerce with foreign Nations, and among the several States, and with the Indian Tribes;
>
> To establish an uniform Rule of Naturalization, and uniform Laws on the subject of Bankruptcies throughout the United States;
>
> To coin Money, regulate the Value thereof, and of foreign Coin, and fix the Standard of Weights and Measures;
>
> To provide for the Punishment of counterfeiting the Securities and current Coin of the United States;
>
> To establish Post Offices and post Roads;
>
> To promote the Progress of Science and useful Arts, by securing for limited Times to Authors and Inventors the exclusive Right to their respective Writings and Discoveries. . . .

While our primary interest is the form of intellectual property involving inventions (i.e., patents), there are several other categories with which you should be familiar: copyrights, trademarks, and trade secrets. Even within the category of patents, there are several distinctly different types of intellectual property. Note that this book focuses on intellectual property issues from a U.S. perspective. While these general categories are relatively common, IP laws in other countries differ significantly.

COPYRIGHTS

This category describes works with a creative or artistic element when they are fixed in a tangible form. Copyright can be used to protect original works, including literary, dramatic, or musical compositions; computer software; architecture; and just about anything else that you could consider an artistic work. Copyright does not protect the facts or ideas contained within the work, but only the work itself. In other words, the form of the work defines the boundaries of what the creator owns. For example, if you create a painting of the Golden Gate Bridge, you own that specific painting—not all paintings, nor even all paintings of the Golden Gate Bridge. Generally, copyright is intended to prevent copying (surprise!), so it would prevent someone from copying your painting without your permission. These days, copyright is extremely important in electronic works like software, digital images, music, and movies that can be easily copied and distributed over the Internet. Works subject to copyright are protected as soon as they are created—they can be registered with the federal government to help substantiate ownership, but this is not required.

The term of a copyright can be tough to figure out because the law has changed over the years, and when the work was created will affect the length of the copyright. The creator of the work can also affect the length of the copyright. For example, for works created after January 1, 1978, copyright usually lasts for the life of the author plus 70 years. However, the copyright on an anonymous work lasts for 95 years from its publication or 120 years from its creation, whichever comes first.

Interestingly, at the time of this writing the government's copyright website includes "How do I protect my sighting of Elvis?" in the copyright FAQ (http://www.copyright.gov/help/faq/faq-protect.html#elvis). As the FAQ points out, you can protect only a photo of the event or some other fixed work based on the event.

TRADEMARKS

This category describes words, phrases, symbols, or designs that identify a particular source of goods and services in commerce in order to distinguish them from similar products from a different manufacturer. For example, if you buy a soft drink, you'd like to be sure that you're buying an actual Coke made by the Coca-Cola Company, not an imitation made by a local start-up in the owner's garage. Because Coke is a valid trademark, no one else is allowed to use that name for a soft drink. In other words, trademarks are designed to prevent confusion in the marketplace by allowing a particular manufacturer or service provider to own distinctive names or symbols that people associate with its product. Trademarks can include more than just names and logos, though; they even include "trade dress," or a distinctive product or packaging appearance. As with copyrights, registering the mark with the federal government is not required. However, doing so strengthens your claim of ownership and will be a significant advantage if there should ever be a dispute over ownership or over other similar marks that competitors might use. Trademarks last as long as the mark is being used in commerce—if you stop using a mark for a significant period of time, you may lose your right to it.

TRADE SECRETS

This category of intellectual property describes information that is known to you or your company and has economic value but is not known by others. Trade secrets can include technical information like formulas or design specifications, but they can also include nontechnical information like customer lists or business plans. The key aspects of a trade secret are that it provides economic value and that it is in fact a secret. Consequently, not all secrets are trade secrets. For example, information about your health may be secret or otherwise "confidential" information, but it doesn't have economic value, so it isn't protected as a trade secret (it is protected by privacy and HIPAA laws, however). On the other hand, if you accidentally spill your marketing plans during an interview on TV, those plans are no longer secret, so they aren't protected. Unlike copyrights and patents, trade secrets can last forever—or at least as long as you can keep them secret. Any invention that you hope to get patented should generally be kept as a trade secret at least until the patent is filed (we'll talk more about this later).

UTILITY PATENTS

This category of intellectual property is what people usually mean when they refer to patents. As mentioned earlier, there are other types of patents, so it's important to be aware of this distinction if there is ever any question as to the topic of interest. Utility patents are used to protect inventions for the inventor's exclusive use for a limited time. Specifically, "Whoever invents or discovers any new and useful process, machine, manufacture, or composition of matter, or any new and useful improvement thereof, may obtain a patent therefor, subject to the conditions and requirements of this title" (35 U.S.C. 101). We'll spend plenty of time discussing this category in more detail later, so for now just think of these patents as protecting what you would typically call an *invention* in the common usage of the word.

DESIGN PATENTS

Design patents can be used to protect the ornamental or aesthetic design of an otherwise functional item. For example, design patents can protect designs of bottles, containers, packaging, furniture, car parts, shoe soles, and even tire treads. The only thing protected by the design patent is the appearance of the device—not its material or function. That being said, there are usually opportunities to get both design patents and utility patents related to a new product. The design of computer icons and graphical user interfaces (GUIs) can also be protected using design patents.

PLANT PATENTS

There is a separate category for plant patents that can be used to protect new and unique varieties of plants. Plant patents are limited to new varieties that have been asexually reproduced (by grafting, for example). Sexually reproducing plants (i.e., in general, those that reproduce through seeds) can also be protected by "plant variety protection" (PVP) and standard utility patents.

INTELLECTUAL PROPERTY IN THE REAL WORLD

As you can see, there are many different concepts that are lumped into the basket of intellectual property. As mentioned earlier, they generally have in common an assignment of rights to the creator; the relative lack of physical limitations on copying, distribution, or disseminating; and the establishment of boundaries for what defines the property. Furthermore, it is important to recognize that several of these categories will often be used simultaneously to maximize the competitive advantage of a particular product in commerce.

Consider your mobile phone, for example. There are probably hundreds of utility patents on the technology employed in the device, additional design patents on the case and the user interface, trademarks on the brand of phone, and copyrights on the software. Even more intellectual property will be involved when you consider the packaging (potential trade dress, design, and utility patents), sales and marketing materials (trademarks and copyrights), and even the instructions and user's guide (trademarks and copyrights). While this book will focus on patents and related strategies, it is worthwhile to note that every product has multiple opportunities for intellectual property protection in many different categories. Furthermore, the intersection of these categories can often be an interesting area for establishing a competitive advantage. For example, can you use a design patent to protect against knockoff replacement parts for your technological invention? Could you use a copyrighted limerick as a device identifier to prevent competitive hardware from being recognized? Should your device have a peculiarly shaped plug instead of a more common rectangle to provide differentiation and potential design protection? Should you intentionally create inventions to maximize your patent protection? We'll talk more about these concepts in Part 3 of the book, when we discuss strategic inventing.

Some readers may be asking why the government should create new forms of ownership for things like intellectual property—things that aren't limited by physical exclusion like most other forms of property. The Constitution provides a straightforward answer: to promote the progress of science and useful arts. However, there continue to be differences of opinion on this issue. A discussion of these differences could easily take up the rest of this book, so I will offer only a few brief thoughts and leave the philosophical wrangling to others. Many of the most valuable aspects of our society couldn't be "owned" in any meaningful way without creating propertylike attributes by legal statute. The benefit of ownership is primarily the economic incentive provided by limited or controlled availability. Why should we provide an economic incentive to authors, inventors, and purveyors of goods? Time, effort, and resources are required to create these contributions, and some degree of ownership is rightfully ascribed to those who have invested in their creation. If something isn't really an improvement, as is often highlighted by fanciful or pointless patents, for example, then who cares? What is owned is of no value. On the other hand, if it is a valuable improvement, shouldn't we encourage such developments?

In short, a bargain is struck between society and the creator/owner so that the owner enjoys some form of exclusivity in exchange for contributing to the general knowledge and information available to society—that is, in order to "increase the store of public knowledge." Many people argue against patent rights, citing drugs as an example. If there were no patent rights, drugs would be cheaper, they say. And they are most likely correct—existing drugs would get cheaper. On the other hand, companies that are doing research into new medicines would make less profit or even go out of business. With little incentive for investing in costly research, there would be fewer new drugs in the future.

CHAPTER 2

WHAT YOU NEED TO KNOW ABOUT PATENTABILITY AND INVENTORSHIP

O ur friends and colleagues in the legal profession have many wonderful talents and contribute immensely to our discussion of patents. Unfortunately, simple language and ease of understanding are not hallmarks of legal discussions. Many peculiar words are used when writing patents. It's even acceptable to make up new words or assign new meanings to words that are in common use. Many new inventors are discouraged by these complications—such as when their attorney tells them their idea "isn't nonobvious enough." As it turns out, there are a few words and definitions that you do need to know, but not as many as you might think. Learning these words can greatly improve your ease of communication with your attorney and your overall effectiveness as an inventor. This is an area where the Pareto principle is definitely in play—most of the things you need to know can be enumerated with a short list of key terms.

The first of those words is *patentability*. This is a fancy way of describing the likelihood that a potential invention will actually be granted a patent. For example, a breakthrough new technology is more likely to be patentable than a minor variation. Also, an attorney might ask for a "patentability search" to determine how similar the potential invention is to what has been done before. When you ask about patentability, you're asking whether or not you can get a patent.

In order to determine whether or not your invention is patentable, your attorney will probably ask you about any specific *embodiment* of the invention that you have tested. An embodiment is a specific instance of a product or process. This is usually different from the scope of the entire invention, because the invention will usually cover many possible embodiments. Your invention may be any toothpaste that includes Component X, while an embodiment would be one specific toothpaste formula that contains Component X. Many different toothpaste formulas (specific embodiments) could be made that all fit within the definition of the invention.

While we often use the term *invention* loosely for the purpose of patentability, the invention is defined by the *claims* of the patent, a precise description in the form of a numbered list. In some ways, the claims are analogous to a mining claim, which specifically states the location and boundaries of the mine. Patent claims specifically define the boundaries of the invention. The claims can be found at the end of a patent or application and are always numbered, starting with Claim 1. We'll discuss claims in more detail in later chapters, but for now it's important to recognize that the invention is defined by how it is characterized in the claims of the patent.

Another important phrase to know is *prior art*, which is a fancy way of saying "anything that is already known to the public through some form of public disclosure." Prior art can include patents, scientific literature, physical products, speeches, a website, or anything else that has been publicly available. If the activity has been done in secret and not disclosed to the public, that doesn't count as prior art.

Importantly, the inventor's own work is often cited as prior art. For example, if you were to create a new invention and describe that invention in a scientific paper before filing for the patent, it could be considered prior art. I say "could be" because in the United States, special exceptions exist that give the inventor up to one year to file for a patent after public disclosure. In general, however, the best principle to follow is to minimize any public disclosures related to an invention before filing an application for a patent.

Whether or not a specific publication or event can be considered prior art is often a complex legal issue that must be investigated by an attorney. The following are a few general rules to keep in mind:

- The disclosure must be available to the public in order to be used against the patentability of your invention (i.e., presentations inside your company, anything kept as a trade secret, and other confidential materials don't count).
- Prior art will count against your invention only if it is published before the earliest priority date your invention is entitled to (we'll talk more about priority dates later, but this is usually the first date a related patent application is filed).
- Your own disclosures, including previously filed patent applications, count as prior art. There is a one-year grace period for filing an application in the United States, but this does not apply in areas

outside the United States, therefore, it should generally not be relied upon without first consulting your attorney.

• Whether or not a particular document will count as prior art, especially if it's close to your filing date, is a matter for an attorney to determine. Inventors should understand the general concept, but all specific issues should be brought to an attorney.

Prior art matters for patentability for one very important reason. Remember that bargain we discussed in the previous chapter? If your invention was already in the public domain, you haven't earned the exclusivity that a new contribution would warrant, and so your invention hasn't contributed to society. If it's in the prior art, you should not be awarded a patent.

FUNDAMENTAL REQUIREMENTS FOR EVERY PATENTABLE INVENTION

There are four fundamental requirements for every patentable invention. The invention must be novel, be nonobvious, and have utility. Furthermore, the invention must be within an acceptable category of statutory subject matter.

Novel

Simply put, the invention must be new to the public. It can't exist in the prior art. However, novelty is narrowly applied to the invention itself—is the same invention already found within the prior art? Has this invention invented before? Has it been described in public? If not, then it is novel.

On the other hand, if the invention has been patented or published before, it can't be patented now. Prior art isn't limited to printed publications though, so presentations, public use, pictures, or sales of the invention could all be a problem. As mentioned above, the inventor's own disclosures can count against the patentability of an invention. These are often *novelty destroying* disclosures because the invention itself is used, sold, offered for sale, or described in public.

Nonobvious

The invention also cannot be an obvious variation or combination that would be expected based on the prior art. A good way to think about this requirement is that some aspect of the invention should be at least a little bit surprising. If the invention creates surprising results, that's good. If other researchers doubt the results, or even "teach against" your method, that's even better. Simply put, the more unusual and peculiar your invention is, the more likely it is to be granted a patent. The closer it is to being considered normal or ordinary by someone in your field, the less likely it is to be considered nonobvious. How a particular invention ranks on this criterion is often described by the unfortunate term *nonobviousness*.

The requirement that an invention be nonobvious is a much higher obstacle than novelty. Novelty asks whether or not the invention *exists* in the prior art. Determining whether or not something is nonobvious involves asking whether or not something *similar* to the invention exists in the prior art. Here are some important questions to consider when deciding whether your invention is likely to be considered nonobvious:

- How unexpected is your invention?
- Would someone who is skilled in this field find your invention to be predictable?
- Is there an unexpected synergy in the results (i.e., where $2 + 2 = 5$)?
- Does the prior art suggest a different result from your invention? This is sometimes called *teaching against* and is a great indicator of patentability.
- Have other researchers tried and failed to achieve this result? The failure of others is also a good indicator.

It's often difficult to predict what the patent office will grant. I've had attorneys tell me that XYZ application will never be granted . . . only to have it granted a few months later. On the other hand, attorneys who get nearly all of their applications granted may not be obtaining the broadest claims possible. In general, surprising and unexpected results are easier to patent, while incremental improvements and combinations of known elements are more difficult. Unfortunately, it can be hard to know for sure what will or will not be granted. I find that it helps to think of this requirement not as precisely defined criteria, but as a probability curve.

As shown in Figure 2.1, the probability of getting a patent granted is a function of the creative distinctiveness of the invention. Some might label this axis "inventiveness," or the inverse of obviousness. However, inventions that deliver distinctly different results are usually easier to protect—the more unexpected and unusual the invention, the more likely it is to be deemed nonobvious. Please don't take these percentages as accurate representations of real data; they are simply intended to illustrate the probabilistic nature of the patenting process.

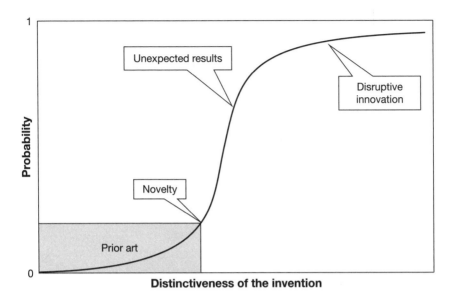

Figure 2.1   Effect of distinctiveness of the invention on the likelihood of a patent's being granted

As you can see from the figure, some patents are granted even though they claim subject matter that is not novel. We can consider these to be mistakes by the patent office, and they probably would not stand up to a challenge in court. As the invention becomes more distinctive, we reach a point when one might say that the results are "unexpected." It still isn't a sure thing that a patent will be granted, but it is a good indication. Finally, we reach a category that might be described as "disruptive innovation" or "brilliant" research. Here we would find significant breakthroughs that deliver readily apparent advantages over the prior art. Not all research is patentable, but from the perspective of nonobviousness, if your peers consider it brilliant, it is very likely to be patentable.

A limitation of this illustration is that the likelihood of an application being granted is also inversely proportional to the breadth of the claims. In other words, if you're attempting to patent a very broad class of technology, that is likely to be more difficult than patenting a narrowly defined invention. Another probability curve could be drawn to illustrate the likelihood of claims being granted based on the breadth of the claims—broad claims are substantially more difficult to obtain, as shown in Figure 2.2. However, the value of the claims increases in proportion to their breath. In short, the most valuable claims are usually the most difficult to obtain.

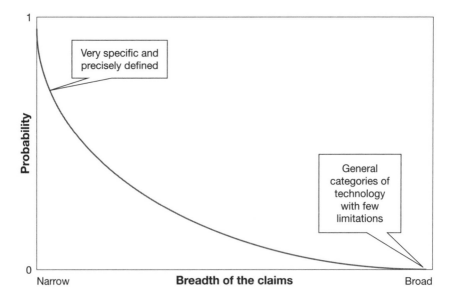

Figure 2.2   Effect of breadth of claims on the likelihood of a patent's being granted

Obviousness is a term that is difficult to define quantifiably, so here are some examples of claims that are usually considered obvious:

- Changes in size for mechanical devices are generally considered obvious unless there is a particular challenge involved. For example, making a taco that is twice as large is obvious, but making a microchip that is 10 times smaller is not.
- The color of the invention and other nonfunctional aesthetic variations are considered obvious.
- Combinations that are suggested within the prior art are considered obvious, even if they haven't actually been made.
- Substitution of elements for other known elements having the same function is considered obvious (for example, the product was previously made with nails, and now it is being made with screws).
- A matter of simple optimization using components that others would be likely to try is considered obvious.
- Combinations that result in additive effects are considered obvious. Each part contributes about what would be expected to the total result. If Component X makes the product 10 percent stronger, Component Y makes the product 15 percent stronger, and X + Y yields a 25 percent increase in strength, the combination is probably obvious.

Here are a few examples of things that are usually considered nonobvious:

- Specific nucleotide sequences are usually considered nonobvious (but must be connected with some function to provide utility).
- Solving a problem that others have tried, but failed, to solve is usually considered nonobvious.
- Solving a problem in a way that others have suggested will not work (i.e., "teaching against") is usually considered nonobvious.
- Solving the same problem with fewer negatives than previous solutions (for example, reduced materials, fewer discrete parts, or easier to make) is usually considered nonobvious.
- Solving a new technical contradiction, as defined by TRIZ, is almost always considered nonobvious (see Chapter 23 for more discussion on this topic).
- Synergistic effects that exceed additive expectations are usually considered nonobvious. If Component X makes the product 10 percent stronger and Component Y makes the product 15 percent stronger, but the combination X + Y yields a 35 percent increase in strength, it's probably nonobvious.

Utility

An invention must also have some useful function. Usually this isn't a particularly tough requirement. After all, if there weren't some use for the invention, why would anyone bother getting a patent for it? It does come into play, however, in some fields in which a discovery contributes useful information that hasn't quite been turned into an invention yet—the sequence of a particular gene, for example. This is helpful information, but without knowing what the gene does, it can't be "used" until more is added. A process for testing for the presence of a particular gene sequence as an indicator of disease, on the other hand, would be an invention because the sequence is used to perform a useful function (i.e., predicting a disease state).

Conversely, it is possible to create useful information that is not an invention. If you sample a prior art compound and measure a property that has never been measured before, that would be potentially useful information. However, because the underlying material already existed in the prior art, characterizing this material isn't patentable.

Statutory Subject Matter

Not everything can be patented, even if the invention meets the criteria outlined so far. The subject of your invention should include a process, machine, manufacture (i.e., product), or composition of matter. These are all recognized categories of patentable subject matter. For the most part, these are broadly construed categories and include nearly "anything under the sun that is made by man." Some things that are *not* patentable include laws of nature, natural phenomena, abstract ideas, information, mathematical algorithms, perpetual motion machines, and mental exercises.

In many fields, statutory subject matter is rarely an issue—typically, mechanical devices, food products, manufacturing methods, drug compositions, and other such manufactured products are all within the bounds of statutory subject matter. However, there are some areas where this criterion can be very important. Two important areas should be mentioned: biotechnology and software. In biotechnology, there is some debate as to what should be patentable. In the United States, newly developed organisms (a bacteria expressing a nonnative gene, for example) are patentable. Likewise, methods of using biological information to create a useful medical test (for example, a genetic cancer screen) are also patentable. However, both are common subjects of debate.

Software and the closely related topic of "business methods" are also patentable in the United States, although much debated. In general, when a process creates a useful transformation of one thing into another thing, it is considered a patentable process. But what if both things are virtual and exist only inside a computer? As long as the other criteria for patentability are met, these can still be patented. An additional guideline is that the invention should produce a concrete and tangible result, in order to differentiate it from unpatentable algorithms that simply change numbers into other numbers.

When the Internet was first being developed, a lot of patents were granted for inventions that covered relatively simple processes, but happened to involve the Internet. At the time, doing almost anything over the Internet was unexpected—but not anymore. For example, Amazon was granted a rather famous patent for a system of purchasing something over the Internet using one click (U.S. 5,960,411). These types of inventions are now much more difficult to patent. However, software and business methods are patentable subject matter.

What Is Not Required for Patentability?

As you read through the requirements for patentability just discussed, you may have noticed that there are no requirements that the invention be *better* than previous inventions. Nor are there requirements for it to be cost-effective, practical, scientifically relevant, or based on significant research. This is why there are many patents granted for weird but industrially insignificant inventions. It's also an important distinction for new inventors, who frequently feel that the hurdle for having a patent granted is extremely high. In reality, the emphasis is on doing something different from what has been done before. Some inventions are significant improvements; some are not.

TECHNICAL REQUIREMENTS NEEDED FOR BEING GRANTED A PATENT

In addition to the requirements for what your invention actually is, there are also requirements that must be met when you file a patent application. While the previous list dealt with the substance of the invention, these involve the contents of the application. There are many detailed requirements that must be followed in order to get a patent granted, but most of these will be handled by your attorney. However, the inventor needs to be aware of the following two requirements, because the attorney will need your input in determining whether or not the requirements have been met.

First, a patent must *enable* others to practice the invention (often referred to as the *enablement* requirement). Remember that bargain with society? In exchange for exclusivity, the inventor must contribute to the public knowledge. In order to be a useful contribution, the invention must be described at a level of detail such that the invention can actually be created and used by other members of society once the period of exclusivity (i.e., the patent term) has expired. In other words, the patent application must enable others to practice the invention.

This generally means that the invention needs to be described in enough detail that someone who is skilled in this area of science could replicate the invention using the description you provide in the patent application. You don't have to start from scratch, however. Any commonly available materials or parts can be used in the description, as can references to other publicly known methods, equipment, standards, or processes. You do have to include enough detail about the steps used so that practicing the invention doesn't require unreasonable experimentation. Usually this means that any important details need to be included, but industry standard practices can simply be referenced as such. Frequently, specific details are included in one or more examples of actual experiments, although this is not required.

Furthermore, a patent application must include the *best mode* of practicing the invention as known to the inventor. Again, in reference to the bargain with society, this prevents the inventor from holding back important information that would be useful to society after the patent expires. It is certainly possible to include other ways of using the invention, and there is no requirement that the inventor label the best mode as such. However, the patent application must include the best information you can provide about the best way to make and use the invention. If you feel that you're holding something back, you probably aren't including enough detail.

Interestingly, the new patent law passed in 2011 removes the lack of best mode as a reason for finding a granted patent invalid. It does not, however, remove the need to include the best mode at the time of filing. This is a peculiar dichotomy, but it leads to the same conclusion: inventors should always work with their attorney to make sure that the best mode is included in any filed applications.

INVENTORSHIP AND AUTHORSHIP

Another important concept to discuss is how we determine who is the actual inventor of the invention. In short, an inventor is a person who contributed to the conception of the invention, that is, the person or persons who came up with the idea. Sometimes it's easy to figure out who the inventor is, but often it's a lot more complicated and may involve personal and professional differences of opinion. Furthermore, there are often multiple inventors with differing contributions to the overall invention. There is no limit to the number of inventors attributed to a single invention, and the collective group is sometimes referred to as the "inventive entity."

Importantly, an inventor does not have to be the person involved in *making* the invention (sometimes called "reduction to practice"), but anyone who contributes to the conception of what goes into the invention is an inventor. For example, if an inventor comes up with a new idea about which compounds to test in an experiment, and a lab technician runs that experiment, the lab technician is not an inventor. On the other hand, if the lab technician has to make changes beyond what the inventor originally described (adding an additional reactant, for example), she may be considered an inventor even if her contribution is relatively minor. The key questions are whether or not any additional improvement or changes were required to make the invention work, and whether or not any of those changes show up in the claims of the patent application. To reiterate, the inventor or inventors are those who contribute to the conception of the invention—it's the ideas that matter, not the reduction to practice.

Furthermore, the standards for determining inventorship are significantly different from the standards for determining authorship.

Many researchers are familiar with the publication standard for authorship, which is generally relatively inclusive. This is not the same standard as for inventorship, which tends to be more narrowly defined. For example, neither the researcher who runs the lab, the project lead, nor your boss should be listed as an inventor unless they contributed to the conception of the invention. This can be a complicated issue, particularly when there are large numbers of people involved in the process of creating an invention.

Inventorship can often result in disputes because researchers may have been intimately involved in a project or perhaps spent innumerable hours in building the invention, but are still not considered inventors. The inventor may be someone who simply made a suggestion and described the components of the invention (i.e., conceived of the invention). However, it is worth pointing out that incorrect inventorship is one reason that a patent can be invalidated, so this is much more important than including friends and colleagues just to be nice. Furthermore, inventorship is a legal determination, so it should always be left up to your attorney. You will probably be involved, however, so work with your attorney to make sure that the appropriate inventors are included, even if that requires some uncomfortable discussions.

KEY POINTS TO REMEMBER

1. Patentability is evaluated based on the claimed invention.
   a. *Patentability.* Whether or not a potential invention is likely to be granted a patent. This is evaluated based on the scope of the claims.
   b. *Claims.* The part of a patent that specifically defines the invention.
2. There are four basic requirements for patentability in the United States.
   a. *Novelty.* The invention must be new in comparison with the prior art.
   b. *Nonobviousness.* The invention must be different enough from the prior art that it is not just a minor variation or obvious combination of known features. Unexpected results and nonadditive effects are usually good indicators of nonobviousness.
   c. *Utility.* The invention must be in a form that does something useful.
   d. *Statutory subject matter.* Almost any process, machine, manufactured product, or composition can be patented, including living things, software, and business methods. However, patents are not granted for information, mathematical algorithms, natural phenomena, mental concepts, or perpetual motion devices.

3. What is *not* required for patentability?

   a. Being "better" than the prior art; economic feasibility; demonstrating that the invention works; practicality; scientific relevance; technical complexity.

4. The required content of a patent application includes the following:

   a. *Enablement.* The invention must be described so that someone with ordinary skill in the relevant technical disciplines can make and use the invention without undue experimentation.

   b. *Best mode.* The patent application must also include the inventor's best known method of practicing the invention.

5. Who is an inventor?

   a. Whoever comes up with the conception of the invention—the original idea—is an inventor.

   b. Constructing and testing the invention does not make one an inventor.

   c. Setting general goals or defining abstract objectives for a project is not considered conception.

CHAPTER 3

CLAIMS AND YOUR FREEDOM TO OPERATE

Another important topic—perhaps even more important than patentability—is determining whether or not you are able to practice your own invention—that is, whether you would have *freedom to operate* (FTO) with respect to this invention. FTO is the ability to do something without infringing on someone else's patents.

Wait a minute . . . don't patents grant the inventor the exclusive right to practice his invention? Nope. Patents grant the inventor the right to *exclude others* from practicing the invention. Specifically, you can exclude others from making, using, selling, offering to sell, or importing the invention as described in the claims of your granted patent. In other words, when your patent is granted, you can stop others from practicing your invention, but that doesn't affect whether or not you can practice it yourself. This can be a confusing point, so it's worth reiterating: it is possible to obtain a granted patent for an invention that you do not have the right to practice. Patentability and freedom to operate are entirely different concepts.

PATENT CLAIMS

When discussing a particular invention, we need to be specific to make sure we know exactly what the invention is. In patent terms, the precise description of the invention is called the *claims*. For practical purposes, the claims can be found at the end of a patent or application and are always numbered, starting with Claim 1. Other parts of the patent are important in order to support the claims, but the claims describe the limits of the actual invention.

The claims are required to specifically point out the elements of the invention in definite terms, and the invention as described by the claims must meet the requirements for patentability. However, the claims do not necessarily need to include all the details of the actual product. For example, if you invent a new breath-freshening compound (Compound X) and would like to claim as your invention a toothpaste containing your compound, the claim does not need to include all of the other components that could possibly be used in toothpaste. To avoid having to list all of these other possibilities, attorneys use the word *comprising*, which in this context generally means "includes the following, but might also include other things." So, for example, you might write your first claim as, "1. A toothpaste comprising Compound X." This claim would cover any compositions of toothpaste that include Compound X, even if they have additional components—even components that you aren't aware of, such as future inventions.

Another word that comes up a lot is the word *said*. Frequently, attorneys refer to a previously mentioned element as the "said element," to reinforce that they are referring to the one that was previously mentioned and not to something new. For example, "a mixture of water, oil, sand, and dirt, wherein said sand comprises at least 10 percent silica sand."

There are many different ways to write patent claims, but it is important that the public be able to read the claims and know whether or not they are violating the exclusive rights granted to the patent holder (i.e., infringing on the patent holder's property). As a result, the claims cannot be indefinite or ambiguous. However, they may be complicated and may include unique definitions or even made-up words. The entire text of the patent can be used to help explain what the claims mean, which may be particularly important for defining key words. However, if the claims are too confusing or vague, they may be too indefinite to enforce, which would make the patent invalid. For example, if you invent a new paper towel, a claim that describes the product as, "A paper towel comprising A and B which is soft" would most likely be considered indefinite. How do you measure "soft"? What I consider soft is probably different from what you consider soft.

Furthermore, attorneys are allowed to include words like *about* and phrases like *at least about*, which start to sound fuzzy after a while. These words and phrases are generally not considered indefinite from a legal perspective, even though common sense would suggest that "about" is intended to be indefinite. These are included to give a small amount of wiggle room in order to prevent someone from avoiding your claims by using slightly more or less of an element than you claimed. A strict reading of a numerical value would put their product outside of the claim, even though it is still "about" the same. This should not be of significant concern, but it does show up quite frequently when reading claims and often makes for peculiar-sounding prose when strung together with other legalese.

Product and Method Claims

In general, there are two basic types of patent claims: *product claims* and *method claims*. Product claims describe a thing that is made, whereas method claims (sometimes called *process claims*) describe a series of steps. Product claims are usually things you could hold in your hand or point at, while method claims are actions that occur in time. Product claims usually sound a bit like a grocery list, while method claims sound more like a baking recipe.

Here's an example of a product claim, abridged from US 3,878,938:

I. A toothpaste containing
   A. Glycerine in an amount of about 15% to about 40% by weight of the toothpaste
   B. Water in an amount of about 8% to about 30% by weight of the toothpaste
   C. Chloroform in an amount of about 0.5% to about 4% of the toothpaste; and
   D. A corrosion inhibitor in an amount of about 0.1% to about 10%.

Note that each of the components listed is provided with numerical ranges that could be easily tested and verified by competitors to determine whether or not they are infringing. It is true that the word *about* introduces some uncertainty, but this is considered acceptable and is actually common.

A method claim might look like the following, which is abridged from US 4,795,630:

1. A method for manufacturing a toothpaste containing an abrasive, a humectant, a binder, a surfactant, and water comprising the steps of:
   a. Mixing said binder, a glycerol selected from the group consisting of propylene glycol, polyethylene glycol and polypropylene glycol as a component of said humectant, and a portion of said water to prepare a liquid dispersion where the binder is slightly swollen,
   b. Mixing the thus prepared liquid containing the slightly swollen binder with an abrasive, said surfactant, the remaining humectant, and the remaining portion of said water, and
   c. Performing a final stage wherein the binder is completely swollen and dissolved to prepare a toothpaste.

Note that the elements of the method claim are written as actions. Importantly, the steps listed in a method claim don't necessarily have to be performed in the order listed unless that is explicitly specified (e.g., in part c of the methods claim example, it indicates that this is the "final" stage).

Another possible type of claim is a *product-by-process* claim. This is used to describe a product that might otherwise be difficult to characterize directly. Frequently, this type of claim will show up as something like the following: "2. The product made by the method of claim 1," where claim 1 is a method claim. However, the product must still be patentable on its own—water made by a process of XYZ is still unpatentable, no matter how inventive the XYZ process is. The XYZ process itself may be patentable, but that would be a standard method claim.

Independent and Dependent Claims

Another important distinction can be made in the relationship of various claims within the same patent or application. The first claim of a patent is always an *independent claim*, which is a claim that can stand entirely by itself and doesn't incorporate elements of any other claims. Any claim relating to Claim 1 would be called a *dependent claim* and would describe additional elements that are added to the invention described in Claim 1. Dependent claims will always make reference to a specific preceding claim. Let's consider the following example:

1. A toothpaste comprising Compound X.
2. The toothpaste of Claim 1, further comprising Compound Y.
3. The toothpaste of Claim 2, further comprising compound Z.
4. The toothpaste of Claim 2, further comprising compound W.
5. A process for making a toothpaste comprising the following steps: mixing Compound X with Compound Y, and homogenizing the mixture comprising Compound X and Compound Y until a stable emulsion is formed.

As a quick review, Claim 1 is a product claim describing toothpaste containing Compound X. Claim 2 describes a toothpaste containing Compounds X and Y; Claim 3 describes a toothpaste containing Compounds X, Y, and Z; Claim 4 describes a toothpaste containing Compounds X, Y, and W. In this example, Claim 1 is an independent claim, and Claims 2, 3, and 4 are dependent claims. Claim 5 is an independent method claim.

It is also possible to write a "multiple-dependent claim," which is essentially a dependent claim that refers to multiple previous claims. For example, a claim could be written as "the toothpaste of Claim 2, 3, or 4, further comprising Compound Q." This is interpreted as if there were separate dependent claims referring to each of the claims in the list, and is mostly just a shorthand way for attorneys to write claims.

Reading claims can be complicated, but it's extremely important for inventors to understand what their patents (and competitive patents) actually protect. It may seem like an unnecessarily convoluted way of doing things, but understanding a little bit about the way claims are written can make it much easier for you to read competitors' patents and also help your attorney to construct the best claims to describe your own inventions. For example, the broadest claims will always be the independent claims. If you're interested in freedom to operate, these are the most important ones to read.

FREEDOM TO OPERATE

The phrase *freedom to operate* or *freedom to practice* generally refers to the ability to do something without being within the claims of any patents that have been granted and are currently in force. In other words, you have the freedom to operate with respect to a particular product or invention if you are not infringing on someone else's claims. If you are infringing on someone else's claims, then you do *not* have FTO.

To infringe on a patent claim, you must be practicing each and every element of that claim. Conversely, to have the freedom to practice an invention, what you are doing must be missing at least one component from any related claims. For example, a claim may describe "a new composition comprising Components A, B, and C." A competing product that includes Components A, B, and C would infringe on this claim, of course. A competing product that includes Components A, B, C, and D would also infringe (remember, *comprising* includes anything else). However, a product that includes A, B, and D would not—it's missing Component C, which is part of the claim. What about a product that includes A, B, C, D, E, F, G, H, and even I? This is clearly a very different product—but it still infringes because it includes all the elements of the claim.

We'll talk about "design-around" inventions again later, but an important thing to remember is that in order to avoid patent infringement, you need to remove at least one element of a previous claim from your product or process.

The Coffee Cup Example

Let's walk through a specific freedom-to-operate example. Imagine that you have discovered a way to improve the insulating properties of ceramic by incorporating a small amount of an unusual ingredient, Component X. Instead of conducting heat readily, the ceramic is now a very good thermal insulator. After spending months in research, you finally conclude that the best application for this invention would be in manufacturing coffee cups that will stay warm longer than any other coffee cups on the market. You contact your local patent attorney, and you file for and are granted a patent with the first claim being "A coffee cup comprising Component X." You immediately quit your day job and start a business manufacturing your insulating ceramic coffee cups, which quickly take the market by storm.

But a competitor is also developing a coffee cup—one that heats more efficiently in the microwave. Adding Component Y to the ceramic material cuts the heating time in half. Eventually, this competitor files a patent application on ceramic coffee cups comprising Component Y.

Without knowing this, you begin developing the same feature in combination with your thermal insulator—a cup offering great thermal insulation *plus* fast heating in a microwave. You're convinced that you have designed the ultimate coffee cup that will be on everyone's must-have list next Christmas. You work with your attorney to file a patent application on "A coffee cup comprising Component X and Component Y."

Assuming that all three patents are granted, your patents protect ceramic coffee cups with Component X and with Component X and Y, while your competitor's patents protect ceramic coffee cups with Component Y.

Can your competitor make a cup with Component X? No. That's within the scope of your granted claims.

Can you make a cup with Component Y? No. That's within the scope of your competitor's granted claims.

Then who has the right to practice the combination of Component X + Y?

Nobody.

Even though you may have a valid granted patent on this composition, you will infringe on your competitor's patent related to Component Y when making the combination. Likewise, another competitor's X + Y cup would infringe on both of your patents.

Patents frequently have overlapping claims, which results in multiple patents covering different aspects of the same product. If the inventions are significant enough, they may lead to cross-licensing discussions, or perhaps the companies will seek to invalidate their competitor's claims by challenging them in court. With the recent changes to patent law, there is also an opportunity for challenging the validity of a patent for nine months after it is granted (or even longer, based on printed materials).

Who Does What

Another important thing to remember about FTO is that whether or not a particular product or process is infringing on a patent is a legal opinion, and not something that should be directly addressed by an inventor. As you have probably figured out already, there are a lot of complex issues at play, and this is not an area in which you should dabble as an inventor. Leave the FTO questions to your attorney.

One of the most common mistakes that corporate inventors make is admitting to infringement in written correspondence. For example, let's say you find one of your competitor's patents, review the claims, and believe that it describes exactly what your company is doing. *Do not* send an e-mail to your boss that says, "I think we're infringing on this patent." Rather, send an e-mail to your attorney (CC: your boss) and ask her to review the claims. Better yet, call your attorney (or your boss) on the phone. In addition to the legal complexity involved in interpreting claims, there is another reason why inventors shouldn't be writing about claim interpretation or FTO: all of these documents could be used against the corporation in court. Sooner or later you may find yourself having to explain to a courtroom why your e-mail says you're infringing when your company's attorneys are arguing that you aren't.

Furthermore, communications with your attorney can be protected by an *attorney-client privilege*, which means that questions that you pose directly to your attorney cannot be used against you in court. Your attorney will be able to communicate about these matters without creating the same risk that you might create, even when using the exact same words.

If this is such a complicated issue, why does the corporate inventor need to be able to understand what claims mean? This is another one of those times when a little bit of understanding can answer most of the important questions. In particular, a basic understanding will help you to know what *isn't* important. If you are reading up on your competitor's patents, for example, you may have to read 10 or 20 patents on a particular topic. Your attorney will not be happy if you ask for his opinion on each one. On the other hand, if you can quickly determine that 18 of the 20 are entirely unrelated to the product you'd like to make, your attorney will be much more willing to help with the 2 that might be relevant.

Keep in mind that every organization has a different approach to how directly researchers should be involved in this process. In some companies, nearly all patent questions are handled by intellectual property specialists—searchers, agents, paralegals, or attorneys. In other organizations, the inventors do 90 percent of the work. In my experience, corporate lawyers are usually overworked and don't always have the time to answer all of the inventor's questions and thoroughly explain concepts and processes related to the patent system. Having patent-savvy researchers can greatly improve the efficiency and effectiveness of a corporation's overall patent strategy. Furthermore, most attorneys will welcome a sophisticated inventor, as it will usually make their job much easier. However, it is important to recognize that it is the attorney's job to come up with the official legal answer, especially on FTO.

KEY POINTS TO REMEMBER

1. The right that is granted to the owner of a patent is the right to exclude others from making, using, selling, or importing the claimed invention.
   a. However, a granted patent does *not* confer rights to practice the invention. Patentability and freedom to operate are two entirely different issues.
   b. Your FTO has nothing to do with your own patents, but everything to do with the patents of others.
   c. The scope of the patent is defined by the claims. As a result, the claims are the most important part of a patent.
2. Infringement occurs when someone who does not have the rights to a patent practices each and every element of the claimed invention without the permission of the patent holder.
   a. Adding an element to the invention will usually still result in infringement (assuming that the claims use open-ended descriptors like "comprising").
   b. Avoiding infringement requires removing at least one element of the claimed invention from the product or process that you would like to practice.
3. Types of claims:
   a. *Product and method claims.* A product claim describes an invention that is a thing, while a method claim describes an invention that is a step or series of steps.
   b. *Independent and dependent claims.* This distinction refers to the structure of the claims, as opposed to the type of invention. Independent claims can stand on their own and don't refer to other claims. Dependent claims refer to one or more other claims and will always be narrower than the claims to which they refer.

CHAPTER 4

A Simplified View
of the Patenting
Process

Now that you know what a patentable invention is, it's worthwhile to talk about the process of obtaining a granted patent. Like most topics discussed in this book, this can be very complicated. However, we'll be covering only the key details that a corporate inventor needs to know. While this chapter may not seem simplified, we're actually leaving out a lot of complex issues. The following should be sufficient to illustrate the key steps in the process and familiarize you with the related documents terminology.

First, let's talk about one of the most important attributes of a patent or patent application: its priority date. The *priority date* is the earliest filing date that your patent application is entitled to use. Priority dates will have a significant impact on whether or not you can be granted a patent because they stop later public disclosures from being used as prior art against your invention. Recall that the novelty and nonobvious requirements for getting a patent granted are both evaluated based on the prior art, which means everything that is in the public domain prior to your invention's priority date.

The priority date is usually the same as the filing date for the first application filed. However, most inventions involve filing at least a few different types of applications, especially if patents on the invention are pursued in foreign countries. These later-filed applications may have different *filing* dates, but they will have the same *priority* date because they will refer back to the first application.

While we're talking about patent applications, let's discuss some important types of patent-related documents that are frequently involved in the patenting process:

- Provisional patent applications
- Nonprovisional patent applications

- Granted patents
- Information disclosure statements
- Assignments
- Oaths and declarations

Provisional patent applications are usually the first step in the patenting process in the U.S. system. However, they are not required—in fact, they are entirely optional. Provisional patent applications are placeholders in the system that can be used to establish a priority date while delaying the filing of a "regular" patent application (sometimes called a *nonprovisional* application) for up to one year.

There are three key reasons to file a provisional patent application: they require less initial paperwork, they can be used to delay the entire patenting process without sacrificing the priority date, and they can be used to delay the effective term of a patent application. Delaying the overall process may be useful when you are trying to save money—you might, for example, file ten provisional applications and after more research find that only three of those are strategically relevant. By waiting an extra year, you've saved the additional expenses of the seven unimportant applications. On the other hand, you may also want to delay the effective term of the patent because your invention will require many years of research or regulatory approval before it can be launched.

The provisional patent application is not examined per se; it's just a placeholder. As a result, there aren't very many requirements for filing with regard to either content or format, unlike regular patent applications, which have many detailed requirements and a great deal of associated paperwork. However, most attorneys prefer to file provisional applications as if they were regular applications because they still have to support the key requirements for patentability, including enablement and best mode. In other words, you still have to put enough thought into the application to make sure that the invention is adequately described or you won't be able to rely on it for a priority date when the regular application is filed. For example, if your provisional application describes an invention containing Compounds A and B, you would not be entitled to the earlier priority date if your regular application claims an invention containing Compounds A, B, and C. The invention containing A, B, and C may still be valid, but it was not described or enabled by the provisional application, so it is not entitled to the priority date of the provisional application.

It is important to note that a provisional application is never published unless a related nonprovisional application is filed. If you decide that you'd rather keep the information contained in the provisional application a trade secret, you can. The document will never be published unless it is referred to by a nonprovisional application.

Nonprovisional patent applications are the "real" applications that start the examination process when they get to the front of the examination queue. Like the provisional application, a nonprovisional application must meet all of the requirements for patentability. Your attorney will help to make sure that these as well as other technical and formatting requirements are all met when drafting the application.

Once the nonprovisional application is filed, it will be published 18 months from the earliest claimed priority date. Generally, this will be 18 months from the filing date of the provisional application if there was one, or 18 months from the date the nonprovisional application was filed if there wasn't a provisional. If you did file a provisional application and claim its priority date for the nonprovisional filing, that means that the nonprovisional application will be published about six months after it is filed (assuming that the regular application was filed about one year from the date of the provisional filing). This isn't quite as complicated as it sounds—just remember that the application is published 18 months from the earliest claimed priority date, no matter what the first application is.

Nonprovisional applications require more paperwork and are generally prepared using specifically formatted documents and carefully curated information. Minor mistakes can be costly—if parts of the patent application are missing, it may not be counted as having been filed on the date on which it's actually submitted. Your attorney or agent will prepare all of the formal documents, so we don't need to spend much time on these now.

Granted patents are issued after the nonprovisional patent application has been examined. The patent office reviews the claims and usually requires the applicant to make certain revisions, often resulting in narrowing of the claim scope. The examiner's job is to make sure that the inventors are granted rights only to what they are entitled to—enough, but not too much. The claims of a granted patent are frequently significantly different from the claims of the initial patent application. The term of a granted patent usually extends until 20 years from the filing date of the nonprovisional application (in other words, 21 years from the filing date of a provisional application).

The three documents just described are central to the overall patenting process. However, there are a few other documents that you need to understand because you will be personally responsible for their content: specifically, information disclosure statements, assignments, oaths, and declarations. These documents are often signed when the application is filed, but they can be filed at a later time depending on your attorney's preferences. You should always read through these documents and make sure you understand what they mean before signing off on the application. These documents have significant legal consequences, including personal legal consequences to you—ask your attorney to explain anything you don't understand.

Information disclosure statements (IDSs) are documents that list all of the related art that you, as the inventor, are aware of that might weigh *against* the patentability of your invention. This might include results from patent searches, literature references, convention presentations, or any other information that might be used to argue against your invention's being granted a patent. Now, you might be thinking, "Why should I help the examiner argue against my patent?" It's far better to have all of the relevant documents in front of the examiner so that you can have greater confidence that your patent is valid when it is granted. Furthermore, this is actually a requirement for filing the application—called the *duty of candor*. It's also one of the legal requirements that your attorney should explain to you in detail, because intentionally holding back information is something that you can be held personally accountable for and that may compromise the validity of your patent. Talk with your attorney to make sure you understand which documents would be relevant to your particular invention, and to make sure you're comfortable with your role in contributing to the information disclosure statement.

Assignments are documents that transfer the ownership of the invention from one legal entity to another. This is usually in the form of a short contract that lists the invention in question and transfers ownership from the inventors to their employer, for example. If you're an inventor who has created something hugely valuable, you may be tempted to hold on to your invention and not assign it to your employer. However, nearly all employment contracts for employees working in research and development or new product development will include a clause called an "agreement to assign" or something similar. You may not have paid much attention to this when you first got your job, but take a look and you'll probably find that you've already agreed to transfer rights to your corporation. The assignment document that you will be signing when the application is filed just formalizes this transfer.

Oaths or *declarations* are documents that inventors are also required to sign to formally claim inventorship of the invention and formally state that they are aware of their duty of candor in disclosing relevant information to the patent office. In addition to the disclosure requirements described in the IDS discussion, the inventors also declare under threat of perjury that they are in fact the actual inventors of the invention. In other words, if you stole the invention from your neighbor, you will be committing perjury when you file this form. Furthermore, if the wrong inventors are intentionally named, the patent may be invalid—even when the other parties work for the same organization.

GETTING STARTED

When you start the process of obtaining a patent, there are a number of choices that you can make. You could file a nonprovisional application right away and start the examination process as soon as the application reaches the front of the queue at the U.S. Patent and Trademark Office (USPTO), which usually takes about two to three years. You could even file a request for accelerated examination or prioritized examination to speed up the whole process. On the other hand, you could file a provisional application and do nothing for up to a year. At the end of the year (or at any time in between), you could choose to file a nonprovisional application, which claims the priority date established by the provisional application. Or, you could just let the provisional application lapse.

Generally, it is better to file a provisional application first and claim priority back to that application with a later-filed nonprovisional application. This is preferred because it has the effect of delaying the examination process and the eventual patent term by up to one year. Delaying is often another way of saying "saving money" when it comes to the patent process. By delaying, you may find out that your invention isn't as important as you thought it was—perhaps it fails in consumer testing, for example. Or perhaps your company's priorities have changed and the entire project is canceled.

The most significant benefit of filing a provisional application is that the patent term and filing expenses will also be delayed. When a patent is granted, the length of its validity is described as the *patent term*. Usually, the patent term is defined as 20 years from the filing date of the first nonprovisional patent application. This can be adjusted slightly as a result of delays in examination, but it's generally close to 20 years from the nonprovisional filing date. By filing a provisional application, you have the ability to claim an earlier priority date and delay the nonprovisional filing date by up to one year, resulting in a corresponding delay in the patent term. This can be extremely important in industries in which products take a long time to develop and may be on the market for many years, such as pharmaceuticals and biotechnology. Keep in mind, however, that this is a delay and not an extension—the patent term (i.e., the time that the patent is in force) will be the same either way.

Conversely, if you need to enforce a patent quickly or if you work in an industry with extremely short product cycles (software or electronics, for example), you may benefit from having the patents granted quickly. With short product cycles, it might be preferable to file a regular application as soon as possible. You might even request an accelerated examination or prioritized examination, which are two procedures for speeding up the process at the USPTO. If having a patent granted quickly is important to your project, these are additional options to discuss with your attorney. However, because these approaches have additional costs and requirements placed on the applicant, they are relatively uncommon unless there is a particular strategic need.

Your attorney will help you make the best choice concerning how the applications should be filed. However, it's important for inventors to be aware of these options to help develop the most effective overall patent strategy and coordinate with research and commercialization plans.

Examination

Once a nonprovisional application is filed, the examination process (sometimes called *prosecution*) will start. More accurately, the application will sit in the patent office until it makes it to the front of the examination queue. When the patent office does respond, it will be in the form of an "office action," which usually states the patent examiner's reasons why your invention should not be granted a patent. It's up to you and your attorney to come up with arguments that will change the examiner's mind. Perhaps the examiner found a prior art reference that you weren't aware of—if it's very similar to your invention, you may not be able to get a patent after all. On the other hand, you may be able to explain why this new prior art really isn't like your invention. Hopefully, you can illustrate some unexpected results that differentiate your invention from anything that the examiner has found.

During this process, the claims of your invention may need to be modified to overcome some of the patent examiner's rejections. For example, the examiner may reject Claims 1 through 5, while allowing

Claim 6. If your arguments fail, your attorney can remove or edit any claims that the examiner rejects. This is one of the main reasons why patents often have many claims. Each claim gives you a slightly different position with respect to patentability, and having a number of them should increase the likelihood that at least a few of your claims will be granted.

Occasionally, however, the examiner will find that the claims are too different from one another and are really describing more than one distinct invention. The examiner will then make a *restriction requirement* and ask you to choose one of the inventions to prosecute in this application. Generally, a restriction requirement isn't much of a problem except that it increases the fees. The other inventions can be prosecuted in separate applications, called *divisionals*. A divisional application is one form of a *continuation* application, in which additional claims are filed based on an earlier application. The original application is usually called the *parent* application, and divisional or continuation applications are sometimes called *daughter* applications; the entire group is often referred to as a *family*.

The examination process can be quite complicated. As with the filing of the application, details are very important. Your attorney will normally prepare the arguments, although inventors are frequently asked to contribute.

Eventually, the invention will either be granted a patent or be rejected by the patent office. If granted, it will be published on the USPTO's website (www.uspto.gov) and in the patent databases.

Now, let's look at a few examples. At the top of Figure 4.1, we have an approximate timeline for prosecution, starting with a regular nonprovisional U.S. application. Next is a timeline for a provisional application. Note the delay of the patent term by about a year. At the bottom of Figure 4.1, we have an illustration of the process when you are starting from a PCT application, which we'll discuss next.

PCT Applications and International Patent Families

In addition to the U.S. process just described, most large corporations will also be interested in obtaining patent protection in other countries. Unfortunately, each country has slightly different patent laws. The typical corporate inventor does not need to be familiar with all of these. However, you should discuss any particular geographies of interest with your attorney so that you understand any significant differences in what inventions are likely to be granted, the length of the patent term, and the statutory subject matter.

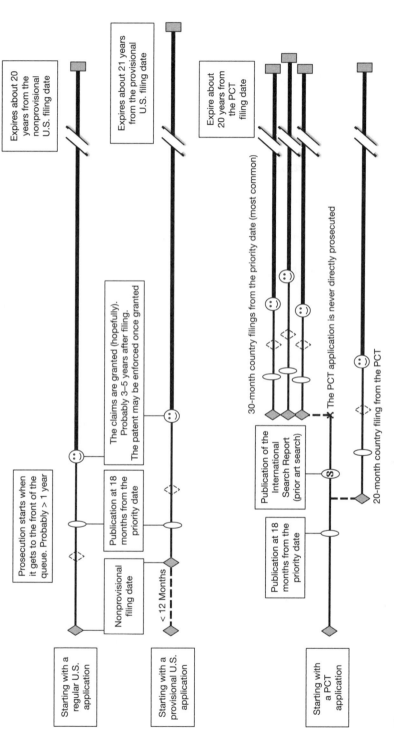

Figure 4.1 Approximate timelines for different filing procedures

Corporations will generally use a process defined by the Patent Cooperation Treaty (PCT) to pursue patent applications in multiple countries around the world. Currently, more than 100 countries have agreed to use this process as a starting point for filing an application in their country (the full list can currently be found at http://www.wipo. int/pct/en/pct_contracting_states.html). In general, an inventor can file one document in a single language and preserve the right to later file applications in many countries. It is important to note that the PCT application does *not* result in the granting of a global or international patent—there is no such thing.

Then why is this so important? Using the PCT process allows the inventor to delay filing applications in each country by up to 30 months from the priority date. This has the potential to postpone enormous amounts of money needed for translation costs and individual filing fees until a later time. Hopefully, during the intervening 30 months, the inventor will get a better idea of whether or not the invention will actually be important enough to protect. If it is not, the PCT application can be abandoned, and no more money needs to be spent. If you do decide to seek protection in certain foreign countries, you will still need to pay for translations and examination in those countries. The important thing about a PCT application is that it simplifies the filing process on the front end and delays the large costs of international filing until a significantly later date.

From an inventor's perspective, the contents of a PCT application are generally the same as those required for a U.S. application. However, it's important to emphasize the local nature of patent laws—each country has its own standards for what is patentable, and each examiner is likely to reach slightly different conclusions. You probably *won't* get the same claims granted in different countries.

When a PCT application is pursued in multiple countries, the resulting patents are considered to be part of the same *international patent family*, generally describing the same invention. However, it's important to recognize that the claims are likely to be different in each country simply because of differences in the examiners, statutory subject matter, and other differences among legal systems. Also, just because something is granted in one country doesn't mean that it will be granted in any others. As mentioned earlier, only individual countries grant patents—the PCT process simplifies filing applications, but it does not lead to an international patent.

One other multicountry system is worth a mention. The European Patent Convention (EPC) allows the European Patent Office (EPO) to grant patents that may be valid in multiple countries in Europe. Interestingly, the patent is granted by one examining body, but it is independently enforced or revoked by individual member countries. The EPO also has a unique "opposition" procedure, through which third parties can "oppose" a patent after a notice of grant has been published. As with other individual countries, a PCT application can be used to start the process when pursuing a European patent.

As one final example, large corporations frequently combine the benefits of the U.S. provisional application with foreign filings via the PCT, as well as non-PCT applications. There are many decisions along the way that can have a significant impact on the timings for each geography. However, a representative example can be found in Figure 4.2. And yes, it gets very complicated.

I THOUGHT YOU SAID SIMPLIFIED

Believe it or not, the diagrams given here are greatly simplified, given all of the possible options and choices that need to be made when filing for patent protection in multiple countries. I've tried to highlight what the common options are, but you'll need to discuss the overall patent strategy with your attorney before you settle on a definite filing plan.

And don't forget, all this complexity isn't free. Writing the application will probably cost at least $10,000 to $20,000 worth of attorney time. Patent office fees in the United States are usually a few thousand dollars. However, each country where you plan to obtain a patent is likely to cost another $5,000 to $25,000. Part of this cost is for attorney time and filing fees, but a large portion of the cost is also for translation services. Precisely translating the content of a patent is often very expensive.

As an inventor, you do not need to understand all of the potential alternatives. However, it will be helpful to understand the key steps in the process as well as the types of documents involved.

KEY POINTS TO REMEMBER

1. *Priority date. The earliest filing date that your application is entitled to.*
    a. Priority dates are used to establish which references are considered "prior art"—if something was in the public domain before your priority date, it is considered prior art.
    b. Earlier priority dates are always better for the sake of patentability.
    c. Unfortunately, an earlier priority date also means an earlier expiration.

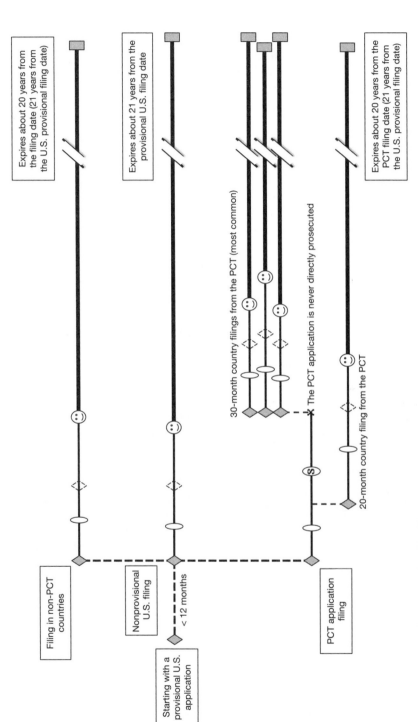

Figure 4.2 Approximate timelines for filing in multiple countries

2. *Key types of applications.*
   a. Provisional applications are optional and serve primarily as place-holders to establish a priority date while delaying prosecution of the application and the eventual patent term.
   b. Nonprovisional applications (a.k.a. "regular" applications) can be filed with or without the benefit of an earlier filed provisional application. Filing this application starts the examination process.
   c. Patent Cooperation Treaty (PCT) applications are applications that can delay decisions on whether to apply in an individual country up to 30 months from the priority date. PCT applications simplify the process for obtaining coverage in multiple countries and further delay the costs.
   d. Continuations and divisionals are applications filed based on earlier applications that contain similar inventions. The priority date of the continuation will be the same as that of the parent application, which will usually result in the same expiration date.
3. *Publication of the application.*
   a. Nonprovisional and PCT applications are published about 18 months after their priority dates.
   b. Provisional applications are never published unless a related nonprovisional application is filed.
4. *Patent term.*
   a. The length of a patent term usually extends up to 20 years from the filing date of the nonprovisional application.
   b. If a provisional application is used, the term will be up to 21 years from the filing date of the provisional application.

CHAPTER 5

THE CORPORATE INVENTOR'S ROLE

Earlier we discussed how inventorship is determined—whoever contributes to the conception of the invention is an inventor. No one else is an inventor, no matter how important she is or how much she has been involved in your project.

There are many pieces that have to come together to make a great product, however, and coming up with ideas is only part of the inventor's role. For one thing, most important products require numerous patents if they are to be adequately protected, so don't turn off your creativity just yet. We'll talk more about how to improve upon ideas in order to build better and more strategically important inventions in Parts 2 and 3.

Every researcher has responsibilities related to being an inventor—or even potentially becoming an inventor in the future. These actions may not seem important at the time, but years from now, they may be critical to establishing the ownership or validity of your patent claims. Hundreds of millions of dollars have changed hands as a result of the contents of a single lab notebook page. Your research may not seem that important now, but some research certainly is—and it's almost impossible to know one from the other at the early stages of the invention process.

FIRST TO INVENT VERSUS FIRST INVENTOR TO FILE

Until March 16, 2013, the U.S. system is still a *first-to-invent* system, which means that the first inventor to conceive of the invention is actually the rightful owner, even if someone else files an application on the same invention first. Some would argue that the first-to-invent system protects the inventor from having someone else steal his idea and obtain a patent, since the original inventor could show from witnessed notebooks or other evidence that he had conceived of the invention at an earlier date. However, this system is significantly different from the one used in the rest of the world, and we will soon be changing to a new system.

After March 16, 2013, under the new *first-inventor-to-file* system, whoever files a patent application first will be the owner of that invention. Furthermore, the earlier you file your application, the earlier your priority date will be.

For example, if you filed your patent application on July 7, 2011, and your competitor described a very similar invention at a trade show on July 8, 2011, it could not be used as prior art against your invention because the public disclosure was after your priority date. On the other hand, if your competitor went to the trade show on July 6, 2011, its disclosure would count against the novelty and nonobviousness of your invention. With respect to patentability, having an earlier priority date is *always* a good thing. There are, however, strategic reasons why you might delay filing, such as maximizing the useful patent term. We'll talk about these strategic issues in more detail in Parts 2 and 3.

Inventor's Notebooks

This change makes the law in the United States more aligned with the laws in most other countries. It also has the potential to change some aspects of the inventor's role.

Under the old system, most corporations required researchers to keep detailed notebooks that were used to record the ideas and activities of the potential inventor. These notebooks were even signed and witnessed by a third party. The information they contained would be used to prove the date on which the inventor conceived of an invention. However, since the date of conception will no longer be used to establish ownership, inventor's notebooks are no longer required, right? Wrong.

While I'm sure there will be a variety of changes in practice as a result of the new laws, it is still important to know who came up with what ideas so that inventorship can be appropriately determined. Disputes concerning inventorship are actually relatively common. Within a corporation, a dispute may be the result of misunderstandings about who should be an inventor, personal pride, competitive careers, and other such factors. But issues may also arise in other situations, such as after an employee leaves a company, if there is a need to determine the ownership of inventions resulting from a collaboration, or when patents are bought and sold. If a potential inventor disputes the ownership of a patent, it can be very damaging to the value of that patent. Having good records is essential to determining who the inventors are.

Your corporation will probably have specific policies concerning what records you need to keep. It's important to recognize that these are not trivial exercises. Also, don't fall into the habit of recording only data. Make sure you record any ideas that might become potential inventions some day. The standard for inventorship hasn't changed—if you come up with the ideas behind an invention, you are an inventor.

INVENTION DISCLOSURE FORMS

Most companies have a system for submitting potential inventions that asks the researcher to provide a basic set of data to management and the legal staff so that the information can be appropriately evaluated and queued for filing. These forms can go by different names and may even have significantly different content. This is because invention disclosure forms (IDFs) are not part of the legal process for getting a patent. They are simply internal paperwork that helps the firm manage the flow of information and answer basic questions about the invention. This is not to say that they aren't important, because they will probably be used to determine whether or not a patent gets filed. However, they aren't a legal requirement.

If you haven't done so already, I'd suggest tracking down a copy of your company's IDF. While your corporation's form will have some unique features, there are some basic things that are generally included: a summary of the results, a list of the researchers involved in generating the results, information about the related art, whether or not the potential invention has been disclosed outside the corporation, whether or not any outside collaborators were involved in generating the results, and anything else that might be relevant to establishing the strategic importance of these developments.

In most corporations, the number of patents that can be filed is limited by resources—not every invention will be turned into a patent application. The IDF is likely to play a role in communicating to the decision makers (1) whether or not this is a patentable invention, and (2) whether or not it is strategically important enough to invest the resources in patenting it. Hopefully, with regard to Question 1, the contents of the IDF will make sense in light of our previous discussion of patentability. With regard to Question 2, this will usually depend on whether or not the invention is directly related to a project and/or the priority of that project. Sometimes really exciting research doesn't get turned into a patent application simply because the product has a low net present value (NPV).

Your company probably has a formal process for deciding how much legal support is provided to each area, and perhaps even a committee to decide on whether or not to file each application. It will be important to understand the process for these decisions, as well as any criteria that have been established, since this can help guide your writing and filing of invention disclosure forms.

SEARCHING THE PRIOR ART

It is essential that potential inventors be capable of doing basic patent searches themselves. Every great inventor I have worked with reads lots of patents—in the same way that great researchers read academic literature. Other patents can be used for inspiration for new inventions, and your competitors' patents can be used to gain significant insight into their potential products, resource allocation, and strategic objectives. For example, the best guidelines for what is patentable in your field are the previously granted patents from your company and its competitors.

Patent searching seems relatively difficult to most researchers. It's true that doing a comprehensive patentability or freedom to operate search can take an enormous amount of time and expertise. However, you don't have to be an expert to do basic searching, which can still provide significant insights. You probably already know a handful of companies and key words that you could use to create a basic search. You will quickly see the benefits as your understanding of the prior art and the competitive landscape grows. More advanced strategies discussed in Parts 2 and 3 will also rely heavily on information gleaned from published patents and applications.

WRITING THE PATENT APPLICATION AND CLAIMS

In general, your attorney will be responsible for the "filing strategy"—drafting the patent application, writing the claims, and determining the best sequence in which to file applications (provisional, U.S. nonprovisional, PCT, or something else). The attorney will be focused on creating an application that will support broad claims and help establish a significant competitive advantage.

However, this process should also involve the inventor directly. The inventor is more likely to fully understand the technology behind the invention, the amount of disclosure required to enable the invention for others, ways in which competitors might try to get around the claims, and even methods for describing the invention (for example, by developing measurement techniques that could be used to quantify aspects of the claims). Drafting the application and claims should be a collaborative effort between the attorney and the inventor—the attorney will handle all the arcane legal details, of course, but the inventor should certainly stay involved throughout the process.

For the most part, this process will be managed directly by your attorney, so we don't need to discuss this in detail. However, if you feel as if you're sending your inventions over a wall (via the IDF, for example), with a finished application being handed back to you for your signature, there is probably something wrong with the process. The inventor should always be interacting with the attorney who is drafting the applications and claims.

In particular, here are some questions to bear in mind when considering the contents of the applications and claims:

* Are there other testing methods that could be used to characterize the invention?
* Have we included all likely alternatives?
* How are our competitors' standard processes different from ours? Have we included their processes as well as ours?
* Does the claim construction make sense from a technical perspective?
* Are the numerical ranges reasonably broad? Are they overly broad? Do they encompass the prior art?
* What would be our competitors' most likely route to design-around these claims? Can we protect against potential design-around attempts in this application or another related application?
* Do the examples work as they are written? Could another researcher of "ordinary skill" replicate my invention from the application?
* Have we included experimental data that are unfavorable to our claimed result?
* Have we included the best mode of practicing the invention?

DEVELOPMENT OF THE OVERALL PATENT STRATEGY

Many researchers and managers believe that the attorneys should be responsible for the patent strategy for a project. In my opinion, development of a good patent strategy requires substantial involvement from the inventor and the project leadership.

First, a brief word on what defines a patent strategy: the patent strategy for a project should include how you're planning to establish a competitive advantage, an overview of the current intellectual property (IP) landscape (yours and your competitors'), the types of claims you expect to be granted, the geographies for which you plan to pursue protection, identification of key competitive technologies, approximately how many applications you expect to file, the resources at your disposal, and when the key steps of the process should take place. There is plenty more to developing a good patent strategy, but this should be enough to whet your appetite for Part 2.

If your attorney understands your project, your competitors, your value-capture strategy, and your strategic objectives as well as you do, then he is qualified to manage the overall patent strategy. But, if that's true, what does he need you for? Just kidding, of course. The patent strategy for a project needs to involve a variety of strategic, competitive, and business perspectives that most attorneys don't have the time to establish on their own. Certainly, the attorney should be involved in every step of the process and should provide a legal perspective to direct the overall effort. However, if you're simply leaving everything up to your attorney, you're probably relying too heavily on him. In fact, most corporate attorneys appreciate the involvement of inventors and leadership—particularly when everyone has a basic understanding of patents and related strategic issues.

WORKING WITH OUTSIDE COLLABORATORS

Innovation is being integrated across corporate boundaries with increasing frequency. Researchers may be involved in everything from traditional research collaborations, to university projects, to joint ventures, and even to "open innovation" such as crowdsourcing for new ideas. These outside collaborations provide significant opportunities to develop new technologies, but they may also create problems for intellectual property. Importantly, most collaborations have specific ownership and payment provisions based on what gets created and by whom. The identity of the inventors can be extremely important to the costs and revenues. For example, there may be one royalty percentage if a development occurs jointly, and another percentage if it occurs solely within the collaborator. Keep the following in mind whenever you're working with people outside of your corporation:

What is our contractual relationship? You will probably have a confidentiality agreement, along with a defined ownership of inventions resulting from this relationship (if you don't, please check with your attorney to understand why not). Make sure that your actions are appropriate for your relationship. This may mean withholding information that would be helpful to your collaborator (if, for example, joint inventorship is substantially disadvantageous to royalties).

What does the collaborator need to know? Most collaborations are limited to a subset technology area. The final product may have 20 components, with this collaboration involving only 1 of them. Your collaborator may not need to know everything about the other 19 components of the final product. Importantly, confidentiality agreements often limit the scope of the protected information to the scope of the collaboration. In other words, if you tell your collaborator about Component 14 when the collaboration agreement extends only to Components 1 and 2, that collaborator may be the sole owner of anything it develops related to Component 14—with or without the benefit of your information.

Can we document our actions? If inventorship is important to the collaboration, you'll need to be extra careful about documenting who comes up with specific ideas. Did you send the idea to your collaborator fully formed, or did your collaborator contribute significantly to the conception? Make sure all information transfer is conducted in writing, if possible. In fact, many confidentiality agreements have a specific provision that confidential information will be recorded in written form and specifically marked as "confidential." Are you following the requirements of your own contracts?

Always make sure that your interactions with your collaborators fall within the bounds of the contract. Small mistakes can be extremely costly—especially if the joint research turns out to be successful!

A FEW THINGS THE CORPORATE INVENTOR SHOULD AVOID

Writing About Patents

Even though I'm very supportive of corporate inventors being actively involved in searching, helping to write patent applications, and developing the patent strategy, it is extremely difficult to fully understand the legal consequences of words and discussions related to patents. Even attorneys won't always be able to predict the consequences ahead of time.

As an inventor, always be careful when you write anything that might have legal implications, because your comments will not have the benefit of privilege and you may cause significant harm in ways that you wouldn't expect. For example, if you find a competitor's patent that you may be infringing, you could write, "This looks like it's invalid." How could that be bad? Well, perhaps your corporation is in the process of acquiring this company for its IP portfolio. A few years later, your company will be trying to use this patent against an infringer in court—and your comment may go a long way toward invalidating the patent.

Interpreting Claims

Claim interpretation is definitely something that should be left to attorneys for any significant decisions. It is important that inventors be able to read and generally understand claims, but don't assume that your general understanding is the same as a legal interpretation. There aren't many things that are more complicated than patent law, and you may be surprised at how peculiar definitions or case law could affect the meaning of what sounds like a straightforward claim.

Disclosing Potentially Patentable Research Before Filing

Hopefully, you won't publish a paper on your new invention before you file a patent application. However, there may be situations in which disclosure is a bit more subtle. For example, perhaps the invention relates to enabling tools that are described in the testing methods section of your paper. Or perhaps the information is disclosed in a regulatory submission. Maybe the information is disclosed by a collaborator who didn't think it was confidential. Conversely, perhaps you're considering licensing a technology and find that the inventor at the outside company has already published the invention.

In the United States, there is a one-year grace period for filing an application after a public disclosure. In other words, if you go to a conference and disclose your invention, you have up to a year in which to file a patent application for the related invention without the disclosure being used against you as prior art. However, this grace period does not exist in countries outside the United States, so it generally shouldn't be relied upon unless necessary. Disclosures can create a benefit under the new America Invents Act (AIA) law in some instances, which we'll discuss in more detail later. In general, however, public disclosure prior to filing is not something that inventors should be doing without first consulting with an attorney to make sure that all potential options (and consequences) have been considered.

CHAPTER 6

PRACTICAL TOOLS FOR
PATENT SEARCHING
ONLINE

W hy should an inventor bother to spend time on patent searching? Once a great invention has been created, aren't the rest of the details up to the attorney or other intellectual property (IP) specialists? Actually, no. Reading other patents can be extremely valuable for inventors. In particular, corporate inventors will learn about how the competition is pursuing similar problems, see how others have solved these problems in the past, and even find examples of how similar inventions have been claimed.

I consider it extremely important that, as a corporate inventor, you be conversant with finding and reading patents, because it will help to make you a better inventor and a more strategic thinker. It's also not nearly as hard as it seems at first. You are the technology expert, and you'll discover things that paid searchers won't understand. In my experience, searching can be a powerful tool for invention, much like brainstorming: instead of building on ideas from a group of people, you're building on ideas from previous inventors and even your competition.

These days, there is an enormous amount of patent-related information available online. Searching has become so easy that many patents are even available from Google. However, there are some important limitations to the readily available tools. It's also important to know a little bit about what you're looking for and how searching will affect what you find.

Here's a short list of searches that will be invaluable to you as an inventor:

• *Searching for inventors.* Who are your competitors' top inventors? Did the author of an interesting paper file an application related to this discovery?

- *Searching for assignees.* Which companies are investing in a particular technology? Which technologies are *not* being pursued by your competitors?
- *Identifying related art for something you're working on.* Will this be prior art against our own inventions? Will we have freedom to operate (FTO)? Should we consider making changes in our research plans? Can we improve our product by incorporating known solutions? Do we need an attorney's opinion on this?
- *Finding key dates.* When was this application filed? Approximately when will this patent expire? Or, is it already expired?
- *Identifying new solutions.* Can we use part of an existing solution to solve a current problem?
- *Understanding patentability and claims in your technology area.* What kinds of inventions are patentable in this technology field? What styles of claims are frequently used?
- *Identifying trends in filing rates.* Is this technology area heating up or cooling down?

We will not be going through step-by-step instructions, primarily because there are so many different tools available for searching, and the exact steps will be dictated by the tool you're using. However, general concepts are important, and you may not realize how useful this information can be or how readily available it is.

FREE WEBSITES

Here's a brief list of some free websites that are helpful. (*Note:* I have not included the exact URLs simply because the web changes so quickly. You should be able to find the search pages within a few clicks of the main URL.)

Google.com/patents. Nearly everyone is familiar with Google's simple interface, and this can be a significant bonus when you already know what you're looking for (for example, a specific patent number). However, Google does not return comprehensive results in the same way that other services do and is not generally used by serious searchers. If you don't currently have access to a paid database, you can probably get at least some insight using this service. This database currently includes only U.S. patents and applications, as well as PDF downloads.

USPTO.gov—patents. The U.S. Patent and Trademark Office (USPTO) has searchable databases for all U.S. patents and applications. Note that the applications and patents are contained in separate databases (PatFT and AppFT) that can be searched only from two separate pages. These are robust search engines, but they do not have the most user-friendly interfaces. Importantly, the output is a text-only inter-face unless your browser is equipped to display TIFF images. (Generally this isn't worth the effort—just find somewhere else to download the PDF, such as Google or Pat2PDF.org.) I usually sug-gest that people start with the "Quicksearch" page, although there are more advanced options.

USPTO.gov — assignments. When doing a patent search, it's very impor-tant to know who owns the patent or application that you're read-ing. Usually, an assignee will be listed on the patent document. However, this assignee information is not updated for later changes and isn't required to be included when the application is filed. In other words, *never put too much trust in the assignee name listed on a patent document* without verifying this information at the USPTO. Unfortunately, there is no absolute requirement that patent assign-ments be recorded, so even the assignment database may not be entirely correct. Nonetheless, it is a very useful database that often includes little-known information about mergers and acquisitions, financing with IP as collateral, or other deals that may never make the news media.

Espacenet.com. This is the European Patent Office website, which offers the ability to search European patents (EP) and applications in addi-tion to Patent Cooperation Treaty (PCT) and other countries' patents. It also includes the ability to export search results into CSV and XLS files for importing into your favorite spreadsheet application.

WIPO.int. This is the website for the World Intellectual Property Organization (i.e., the organization that is responsible for PCT applications), and it includes PDFs as well as international search reports and other documents related to the PCT process.

Patentlens.net. In addition to text searching of U.S., PCT, and European Patent Office (EPO) patents and applications, this site offers sequence-based searching (BLAST) for biological inventions.

FEE-BASED WEBSITES

Each of the free websites just listed has its uses, but none of them will be as helpful as a fee-based alternative. There are a variety of fee-based services for patent searching—you can even hire someone else to do your searching for you. Of the many fee-based search tools available,

I'll mention three: Thomson Innovation (thomsoninnovation.com), Innography (innography.com), and Questel Orbit (orbit.com). There are also numerous others and the features are constantly evolving, so don't necessarily limit your consideration to these three. Furthermore, different packages are offered by these suppliers with more extensive features that may be available for a larger fee.

Thomson Innovation is a very robust online search tool that includes the ability to set up search alerts that e-mail you new results as they happen, and also "work files" that allow you to save results from searches on the web to be analyzed or reviewed later. Results from searches can easily be graphed online or exported to be analyzed further using offline tools. Family members can be grouped to reduce the number of similar results returned.

Innography has many similar capabilities, but it also excels at exploratory searching (when you don't really know what you're looking for) and alternative visualizations. Innography has some tools that are particularly helpful because of their fuzzy logic. For example, "semantic searching" describes searching within large blocks of text (from a research paper, for example) to generate a search query instead of using specific Boolean logic. This can be very helpful when the topic of interest is not easily defined by a few keywords.

The term *Boolean* generally refers to a type of searching that uses AND, OR, NOT, or other operators to create a math-like search query. Boolean operators can usually be nested, so that a search query might include something like "cats AND dogs AND (fish OR horses OR sheep OR cows)" to find references that include both cats and dogs and at least one of fish, horses, sheep, or cows. The operators and syntax do vary by database providers, but all the major suppliers have Boolean searching capabilities.

Moving on to the next product, Orbit offers sophisticated search tools as well as built-in graphical output for landscaping and entity networks. It may be of particular interest if you are doing frequent landscape analysis, investigating inventor or corporate relationships, analyzing adjacent technology space, and identifying technology transfer opportunities. On the other hand, it may be more than you need if you are a typical scientist or engineer in a research or new product development (NPD) organization.

While I'm sure some people would disagree, I believe that Thomson is more likely to be favored by those who like precise Boolean queries, while Innography may be favored by those who are comfortable with fuzzy search methods. Innography's strengths lie in exploring information, but it may not be as popular with experienced searchers who are accustomed to precisely formulating their own queries. Orbit is most likely to appeal to those who spend an above-average amount of time focused on patent landscapes.

For genetic sequence information, a sequence-searching database will also be extremely helpful. Check out GenomeQuest for a paid service with all the bells and whistles.

PRACTICAL SUGGESTIONS

- Practice by searching for things that you know. Find a particular example document and search for it by inventor, by assignee, by title, by claims, and by title + abstract + claims. If it doesn't turn up in your search, figure out why.
- Be conscious of the location of the term within the application. A search term that is located in the title will yield very different results from the same term located in the claims or in the specification.
- Always try to use the most distinctive words possible. When text searching, for example, look for the most industry-specific terminology. Use peculiar and unique words—those that are common only in your industry. For example, "SEQ ID" can be used to find references with genetic sequences.
- Once you find an example reference that is close to what you're looking for, search forward and backward citations (if other patents have found this reference relevant, they will probably also be relevant to you). Search for other work by the same inventors and/or other filings from the same company.
- To start, limit the search databases to only the United States and the PCT (unless you're interested in a specific other country, of course). Most significant technologies will appear in at least one, if not both, of these databases, and this will dramatically reduce the number of duplicate results. Always be sure you understand which geographies you're searching at any given time.
- Make sure you know the format that the search engine is expecting, particularly for publication numbers. This can be extremely annoying at first, but it should be relatively easy to learn with a bit of practice. Full names are written first then last in some databases, while in others they may be written last then first. Publication numbers often have peculiar formatting, and it may take you a few tries to get them right (especially with PCT publication numbers, for example).

- Use multiple fields to narrow down your results. Most good searches involve some key words combined with at least one other category, such as assignees, inventors, time frame, or classification. Or perhaps, you can create a better search by using the same key words in different locations (e.g., claims versus abstract). It's these combinations that are key to creating a really good search.
- For the database you are using, be sure to know what the symbols are for "wild cards" (symbols that can be any letter or any word, or can be used to truncate a word). These can be very helpful when there are lots of variants of similar words. For example, in some databases, entering "frank*" would find documents with "frank," but also "frankenstein," "frankincense," "frankfurter," and other variations.
- Does this database cut off any letters at the end of a word, sometimes called "stemming"? (For example, is "chocolate" the same as "chocolates"?)
- Be careful with the NOT operator. You may be surprised at how many key references you are accidentally excluding. If you do use a NOT operator, limit it to a particular location in the document (e.g., title/abstract/claims) rather than "all."
- As you learn more about the art in your area of interest, continue refining your search. Creating a good search strategy is an iterative process. Don't get frustrated if your first few attempts don't yield the results you were expecting.

Classifications

It's worth pointing out that searching wasn't always done by computer. Surprisingly, when the U.S. patent office was established, the president of the United States had to sign off on each granted patent. Apparently, they weren't expecting very many to be filed. At that time, searching was presumably fairly simple: you just flipped through the stack of patents until you found what you were looking for. Eventually, the stack got big enough that the patent office needed a classification system. There were still stacks of patents, but now there was one specifically for farm implements, one for chemical compositions, and so on. These days, there are thousands of different virtual "stacks," which are now called *classification codes*.

Patents are classified according to what technology areas are expected to be relevant. Since everything is virtual these days, a single invention can be classified in numerous categories—usually half a dozen or more. For example, the U.S. patent number 8,000,000 for a "visual prosthesis" (i.e., a camera with image processing designed to stimulate neurons) is listed in the following classes: 607/17, 607/5, 607/53, 607/54, 607/55, 607/56, 607/57, 607/60, 607/62, and 623/6.63. To give you an idea of what topics these represent, here are some of the descriptions:

607/53: Surgery; Light, thermal, and electrical application; Promoting optical function

607/57: Surgery; Light, thermal, and electrical application; By partially or wholly implanted device

607/60: Surgery; Light, thermal, and electrical application; Telemetry or communication circuits

623/6.63: Prosthesis, parts thereof, or aids and accessories therefor; Retina

If you are particularly interested in inventions that involve devices that are surgically implanted and that also involve telemetry, 607/60 would be a great class to browse or combine with key word or assignee searching. (*Note:* The USPTO has a handy database for classification codes at www.uspto.gov/web/patents/classification.) The international patent classification (IPC) system works on the same principle, but with different categories. You can find information on the IPC at www.wipo.int/ipcpub.

Classifications can be useful for narrowing down your search, particularly if there are class codes that are close to describing your area of interest. Unfortunately, the U.S. and PCT systems have different classification codes, so using them isn't always as easy as it sounds. While many professional patent searchers use classification codes extensively, they can be difficult to use well without a lot of experience.

My suggestion is this: don't try to be an expert on classification codes. Always start by searching with other techniques (e.g., inventor, assignee, or text). However, when you do find a reference that is particularly interesting, do some searching with the classification codes on that reference. Try using a classification code in combination with text terms (particularly if the terms are in common use in two different industries). If you can identify a handful of classification codes that are relevant to your industry, they will greatly accelerate your searching, without your having to spend too much time understanding the entire system.

Search Alerts

Another great feature of most fee-based services is their ability to save searches to run at periodic times as "alerts." These services will usually send you an e-mail with a summary of results. This can be an easy way to keep an eye on the competition without devoting a significant amount of time each week to patent searching.

When setting up an alert, make sure that the search criteria are narrow enough that you won't be getting large numbers of false hits. Otherwise, you're likely to tire of the irrelevant e-mails quickly. I usually use key words found in the title, abstract, or claims in combination with assignees or inventor names to help make sure that the references I receive are in the ballpark. Remember, this isn't intended to keep you abreast of everything that is going on in your industry, only the important filings that you definitely don't want to miss.

I also use these alerts to keep track of developments that I'm expecting to see published, but that haven't shown up yet. For example, let's say your competitor has issued a press release about a new technology, from which it is predicting dramatically improved results. You do a patent search and find that your competitor doesn't have any published applications that mention this technology. It could be that the applications just haven't been published yet, so you could set the search as an alert and forget about it. Someday you'll get an e-mail that highlights the competitor's new activity, and you'll be glad to have it as soon as anyone. A similar approach can be used if you see a presentation or paper that is of interest. Do a search for the key researchers, and if nothing shows up, set an alert, then sit back and wait.

DON'T TRY TO FIND EVERYTHING

One final word of advice: it's usually not worth your time to try to find every reference related to a particular technology. That kind of searching is extremely difficult, which is why there are professional searchers who do nothing but patent searching. But even they won't find *everything*. Patent applications aren't published for 18 months from their priority date, so those unpublished applications will *never* be found. Never assume that you've found everything that's out there, no matter how good your search is.

CHAPTER 7

THE JOY OF READING
PATENTS

Now that you've found some patents that you're interested in, how do you go about reading them without losing your mind? There are a few tricks that might help. First, and most important, don't try to read the whole thing.

Hopefully, your search has turned up a small pile of patents and applications that are of interest for a more detailed review. The size of the pile will determine how much time you can afford to invest in each one. I use the term *pile* loosely, of course, since you'll presumably be doing all but the most detailed review electronically, either with a text file or using a PDF of the patent.

As a quick exercise, download a PDF of the patent US 8,000,000, "Visual Prosthesis." We'll use this as the primary example throughout this chapter. It might also be worthwhile to download a copy of a published application, such as US 2011/0012345 A1 ("Pivot Rings for Coupler Devices"), to contrast a published application with a granted patent. The front page of US 8,000,000 is reproduced in Figure 7.1.

What about provisional applications? A provisional application is not published by the U.S. Patent and Trademark Office (USPTO) except in the file histories of applications that claim priority back to the provisional application. In other words, it is possible to get the provisional application related to a published nonprovisional application or granted patent, but it will not show up in the databases that inventors commonly search.

US008000000B2

(12) **United States Patent**
Greenberg et al.

(10) **Patent No.:**   **US 8,000,000 B2**
(45) **Date of Patent:**   *Aug. 16, 2011

(54) **VISUAL PROSTHESIS**

(75) Inventors: **Robert J. Greenberg**, Los Angeles, CA
(US); **Kelly H. McClure**, Simi Valley,
CA (US); **Arup Roy**, Valencia, CA (US)

(73) Assignee: **Second Sight Medical Products, Inc.,**
Sylmar, CA (US)

(*) Notice: Subject to any disclaimer, the term of this
patent is extended or adjusted under 35
U.S.C. 154(b) by 206 days.

This patent is subject to a terminal disclaimer.

(21) Appl. No.: **11/874,690**

(22) Filed: **Oct. 18, 2007**

(65)   **Prior Publication Data**
US 2008/0262568 A1   Oct. 23, 2008

Related U.S. Application Data

(60) Provisional application No. 60/852,875, filed on Oct.
19, 2006.

(51) **Int. Cl.**
A61N 1/372   (2006.01)
(52) **U.S. Cl.** 607/60; 607/53
(58) **Field of Classification Search** 623/6.63;
607/5, 17, 53–57, 62, 60
See application file for complete search history.

(56)   **References Cited**

U.S. PATENT DOCUMENTS

4,573,481 A	3/1986	Bullara
4,612,934 A *	9/1986	Borkan 607/62
4,628,933 A	12/1986	Michelson

4,837,049 A	6/1989	Byers et al.
5,109,844 A	5/1992	de Juan, Jr. et al.
5,215,088 A	6/1993	Normann et al.
5,569,307 A *	10/1996	Schulman et al. 607/56
5,935,155 A	8/1999	Humayun et al.
6,400,989 B1	6/2002	Eckmiller
6,458,157 B1 *	10/2002	Suaning 623/6.63
7,818,061 B1 *	10/2010	Palmer 607/32
2005/0078846 A1 *	4/2005	Single 381/326
2006/0247754 A1	11/2006	Greenberg et al.

FOREIGN PATENT DOCUMENTS

WO   WO 02/40095 A1   5/2002

OTHER PUBLICATIONS

Eugene De Juan, Retinal Tacks, American Journal of Ophthalmology
99: pp. 272-274, Mar. 1985.

* cited by examiner

Primary Examiner — Carl H Layno
Assistant Examiner — Luther Behringer
(74) *Attorney, Agent, or Firm* — Scott B. Dunbar;
Alessandro Steinfl

(57)   **ABSTRACT**

A visual prosthesis apparatus and a method for limiting power
consumption in a visual prosthesis apparatus. The visual
prosthesis apparatus comprises a camera for capturing a
video image, a video processing unit associated with the
camera, the video processing unit configured to convert the
video image to stimulation patterns, and a retinal stimulation
system configured to stop stimulating neural tissue in a subject's eye based on the stimulation patterns when an error is
detected in a forward telemetry received from the video processing unit.

12 Claims, 16 Drawing Sheets

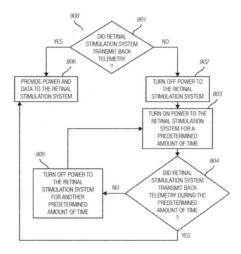

Figure 7.1   The front page of the patent US 8,000,000 B2, "Visual Prosthesis"

KEY PARTS OF INTEREST

Title and abstract. In theory, this should give you a good overview of what the invention is about. Many attorneys write these in very general terms, however, so be careful not to rely too heavily on them to understand the crux of the invention. Think of them more as a general description of the topic. Occasionally, the title is intentionally obscure ("Novel Composition" is one of my favorite less-than-informative titles).

Publication number. At the top right of the first page, you'll see US 8,000,000 B2. The "B" indicates that this is a granted patent, as does the seven-digit length of the number. If this were a publication of a patent application, it would say something like "Pub. No.: US 2011/0012345A1." The first four digits indicate the year in which the application was published, and the "A" indicates that it's an application. Keep in mind that this is the publication number for the application, *not* the application number (12/939,057 is the application number for US 2011/0012345A1; 11/874,690 is the application number for US 8,000,000). Most people rarely make this distinction, but it is important to remember when you are doing a patent search, since you'll need to have the right number in the right field in order to find the reference you're seeking.

Key dates. The "Date of Patent: Aug. 16, 2011" at the top right of the first page indicates when the patent was granted by the USPTO. "Filed: Oct. 18, 2007" indicates when the application was filed. The filing date is not the priority date, however. The priority date is October 19, 2006, based on the provisional application listed under "Related U.S. Application Data" and verbally claimed in the first paragraph of the written description (page 18, column 1). The earliest filing date listed in this section is usually the earliest priority date, and this can be used for a rough estimate of when the patent will expire. If it's important, never assume that this is correct without checking with an attorney—this is just a quick estimate. In this example, note that the term of the patent has been adjusted by 206 days. This is an important reminder that adding 20 years (21 when starting from a provisional) is only an estimate and is not to be relied upon. Continuations and divisionals, in particular, may have significantly earlier priority dates because they claim priority from the parent application, and this will shorten their useful life. Furthermore, many granted patents are allowed to expire early when the owner chooses not to pay maintenance fees.

Assignee: This is the entity that owned the patent at the time of filing. If this information is not listed, the owner may still be the inventors.

As previously mentioned, this information is not always current, since the PDF documents are not updated for later changes in ownership. In this example, the assignee is Second Sight Medical Products, Inc. Always check the USPTO's assignment database if you need more accurate information. But remember that recording assignments is optional, so even this database is not always correct.

Related applications. These are likely to include a provisional application, but they may also include other continuations and granted family members. This section will *not* include all international patent families (you'll need to go back to a patent database for that). Related applications are also described in the first paragraph of the text of the patent. In this example, the related applications include a provisional application filed on October 19, 2006.

Drawings. Patents are generally not required to include drawings, but most of them do. Drawings are usually black-and-white line drawings, with numbers used for reference in the text, although photographs are also allowed. The formats for drawings are relatively strict, and any numbers in the drawings will be used consistently throughout the entire text of the patent. There is also usually a brief description of the drawings somewhere in the specification (frequently before the "Detailed Description" section). In this example, on page 19, column 3, near the bottom of the page, you'll see a reference to figure 1 with accompanying descriptions—each of the bold numbers in the text corresponds to a number in the figures.

Background, summary, and detailed description. This is the bulk of the written part of the patent, sometimes referred to informally as the "specification." (The specification formally includes everything in the patent.) The largest part of the specification is usually the detailed description, but attorneys frequently write background sections (which may be used to illustrate differences from the related art) and a summary of the invention (which usually highlights the preferred embodiments). These sections aren't required to have any particular content, but the specification in its entirety must meet the enablement and best mode requirements. You will often find lots of alternative possibilities in the detailed description section because the specification is required to support the breadth of the claims. Attorneys usually like to call out all reasonable possibilities to illustrate other potential embodiments and to make sure that all reasonable alternatives are described.

Examples. The examples can be one of the best places to learn about the actual invention. The examples generally illustrate the invention in practice, and will also give you insight into how much supporting information has been generated. Examples aren't required (nor do they have to be labeled as a separate section), and there are no explicitly labeled examples in this patent.

Examples are usually a great place to look to find data, specific embodiments that are under development, and general competitive intelligence. Most attorneys prefer to include the best data possible to support the invention, particularly if the data are used to substantiate the unexpected results achieved by the invention. Often this is a great place to look to quickly understand the research that led to the invention.

It is also possible to write examples "prophetically," that is, without having conducted the experiment described. These examples will be written in the present tense, while examples that have actually been conducted will be written using the past tense. Why would anybody bother to write an example without having actually done what is described in the example? It's one way of addressing the enablement issue—if you include a step-by-step example that another researcher can follow, the invention should be enabled. However, this can cause problems later, especially if the example doesn't actually work.

Examples can also be useful for gleaning secondary information, such as what kind of lab equipment your competitor uses, who supplies a particular raw material, and whether or not its procedures use state-of-the-art technology. Remember that somewhere in the application, your competitor has to include a description of the best mode of practicing the invention. The best mode doesn't have to be in the examples, but they are still a good place to look.

Sequences. Biological sequences for proteins, DNA, or RNA are also included in an application when they are relevant. Sequences are referred to by a "sequence identification number," or SEQ ID (pronounced "seek ID") followed by a number. For an example of a short sequence listing, consider US 7,000,000. At the top of page 6, column 7, you'll see references to SEQ ID NO:1, among others. Additional information about the sequence is available in the "Sequence Listing," which is included in column 13, just above the claims. The sequence listing tells you more about the sequence (where it's from, what type of sequence it is, and so on), as well as the full sequence information. In this example, the sequences are fairly short and can be printed in the patent PDF file easily. However, genetic sequences can be extremely long and/or the number of sequences in a single patent can be enormous. Occasionally, applications will have hundreds of thousands of sequences. Not surprisingly, electronic formats are the only way to digest this information.

Claims. These will be at the end of the file and usually start with something like, "What is claimed is:" followed by a numbered list. For a quick review, check each independent claim to understand the scope, then skim the remaining claims to check for any key words of significance (specific technologies related to your project, for example). In US 8,000,000, Claims 1 and 8 are independent product claims; Claims 6 and 12 are independent method claims.

The claims describe the essence of the invention, as well as the distinct boundaries of legal rights. Anything can be written into the specification, but the claims are the parts that really matter. If it's a granted patent, that implies that the claims have been examined by the patent office and found to meet all of the criteria for patentability. If you're looking at a patent application, however, remember that you can apply for anything—even "Godly Powers" (see publication US 2007/0035812A1, for example). Claims in a patent application rarely make it into the granted patent without at least some modification, and sometimes they are rejected entirely.

Definitions. There isn't usually a "definitions" section in a patent. However, key words can be given specific definitions by the attorney when the patent application is being drafted. For example, the patent drafter may want to include specific numerical ranges associated with a commonly used term ("as used herein, the term yellow refers to an RGB value from 255, 255, 0 to 255, 215, 0"), create categorical lists ("the phrase commercial fish is used to describe fish with a common terminal size greater than 50 centimeters, including the following species"), or even make up an entirely new term ("as used herein, the 'nissing' is a unit measure of an author's propensity to include his own name within a written work, calculated by counting the number of occurrences of the author's name and dividing by the total number of words in said work").

Lists of alternatives. This isn't actually a section of most patents, but you will find them frequently. They may include something like, "and may be combined with the subject matter of any of the following patents:" with a list of dozens of other references. Or perhaps it will be something like, "preferably at least about 10, more preferably at least about 20, even more preferably at least about 30, and even more preferably at least about 40." While each attorney has her own style for dealing with incorporating alternatives, it is often easiest just to make a list of every reasonable possibility. There is no limit or cost for describing alternative embodiments, so attorneys often include as many potential alternatives as is practically possible.

PCT APPLICATIONS AND SEARCH REPORTS

Publications of applications filed under the Patent Cooperation Treaty (PCT) are filed with the World Intellectual Property Organization (WIPO). These are generally referred to as PCT applications. These applications are readily available in the databases, and they contain information similar to that just discussed. The formatting is usually different, but the content is much the same, as shown in Figure 7.2.

One important difference is the numbering system. Publication numbers will generally be of the form WO 2009/012345 A2; however, the year is sometimes abbreviated and the "/" is often left out. When searching for a particular document, it's important to know what form the database is using for the publication number. It may not be as it appears on the document. Furthermore, PCT applications are usually published several times, resulting in multiple documents (A1, A2, A3, and so on) for the same application. The following are the most common numbers:

- Documents ending in A1 are applications with an international search report.
- Documents ending in A2 are applications without a search report.
- Documents ending in A3 are separate publications of the search report.

The international search report is often a good resource for finding additional references related to a particular technology. If the underlying patent is of interest, the search report will highlight other art that the examiner believed to be relevant to the patent application. Reviewing the search report can be a relatively easy way to gain insight into related art in a technology area without doing the search yourself.

HELPFUL HINTS

1. *Don't read everything in order.* Go to the section of the patent that is most likely to answer the questions you have. My general approach is to go through the following list in roughly this order: I check the title, assignee, and abstract; if the patent still appears to be of interest, then I review the claims; after the claims, I move on to the examples. I will almost never read the entire specification unless I need a detailed understanding of the subject matter.
2. *OCR the PDF files.* All of the PDF files commonly used in patent databases are image files—in other words, they don't contain the text information, but only an image of the text. Why this is, I do not know. However, you will save enormous amounts of time by using

(19) World Intellectual Property Organization
International Bureau

(43) International Publication Date
22 January 2009 (22.01.2009)

PCT

|||||||||||||||||||||||||||||||||||||||||||||||||||||||||

(10) International Publication Number

WO 2009/012345 A2

(51) International Patent Classification:
H01L 31/18 (2006.01)

(21) International Application Number:
PCT/US2008/070239

(22) International Filing Date: 16 July 2008 (16.07.2008)

(25) Filing Language: English

(26) Publication Language: English

(30) Priority Data:
60/950,087   16 July 2007 (16.07.2007)   US
60/956,107   15 August 2007 (15.08.2007)   US
61/031,652   26 February 2008 (26.02.2008)   US

(71) Applicant *(for all designated States except US)*: ASCENT
SOLAR TECHNOLOGIES, INC. [US/US]; 8120 Shaffer Parkway, Littleton, CO 80127 (US).

(72) Inventors; and
(75) Inventors/Applicants *(for US only)*:   WOODS,
Lawrence, M. [US/US]; 29 Honey Locust, Littleton,
CO 80127 (US). RIBELIN, Rosine, M. [US/US]; 13807
West Pacific Avenue, Lakewood, CO 80228 (US). NATH,
Prem [US/US]; 1700 Bassett Street, #2216, Denver, CO
80202 (US).

(74) Agent: DIZEREGA, Philip; Lathrop & Gage LC, 4845
Pearl East Circle, Suite 300, Boulder, CO 80301 (US).

(81) Designated States *(unless otherwise indicated, for every kind of national protection available)*: AE, AG, AL, AM,
AO, AT, AU, AZ, BA, BB, BG, BH, BR, BW, BY, BZ, CA,
CH, CN, CO, CR, CU, CZ, DE, DK, DM, DO, DZ, EC, EE,
EG, ES, FI, GB, GD, GE, GH, GM, GT, HN, HR, HU, ID,
IL, IN, IS, JP, KE, KG, KM, KN, KP, KR, KZ, LA, LC, LK,
LR, LS, LT, LU, LY, MA, MD, ME, MG, MK, MN, MW,
MX, MY, MZ, NA, NG, NI, NO, NZ, OM, PG, PH, PL, PT,
RO, RS, RU, SC, SD, SE, SG, SK, SL, SM, ST, SV, SY, TJ,
TM, TN, TR, TT, TZ, UA, UG, US, UZ, VC, VN, ZA, ZM,
ZW.

(84) Designated States *(unless otherwise indicated, for every kind of regional protection available)*: ARIPO (BW, GH,
GM, KE, LS, MW, MZ, NA, SD, SL, SZ, TZ, UG, ZM,
ZW), Eurasian (AM, AZ, BY, KG, KZ, MD, RU, TJ, TM),
European (AT, BE, BG, CH, CY, CZ, DE, DK, EE, ES, FI,
FR, GB, GR, HR, HU, IE, IS, IT, LT, LU, LV, MC, MT, NL,
NO, PL, PT, RO, SE, SI, SK, TR), OAPI (BF, BJ, CF, CG,
CI, CM, GA, GN, GQ, GW, ML, MR, NE, SN, TD, TG).

Published:
— *without international search report and to be republished
upon receipt of that report*

A2

WO 2009/012345

(54) **Title:** HYBRID MULTI-JUNCTION PHOTOVOLTAIC CELLS AND ASSOCIATED METHODS

(57) **Abstract:** A multi-junction photovoltaic cell includes a substrate and a back contact layer formed on the substrate. A low bandgap Group IB-$IIIB$-VIB_2 material solar absorber layer is formed on the back contact layer. A heterojunction partner layer is formed on the low bandgap solar absorber layer, to help form the bottom cell junction, and the heterojunction partner layer includes at least one layer of a high resistivity material having a resistivity of at least 100 ohms-centimeter. The high resistivity material has the formula $(Zn$ and/or $Mg)(S,$ Se, O, and/or OH)$. A conductive interconnect layer is formed above the heterojunction partner layer, and at least one additional single-junction photovoltaic cell is formed on the conductive interconnect layer, as a top cell. The top cell may have an amorphous Silicon or p-type Cadmium Selenide solar absorber layer. Cadmium Selenide may be converted from n-type to p-type with a chloride doping process.

Figure 7.2   The front page of WO 2009/012345 A1, "Hybrid Multi-Junction
Photovoltaic Cells and Related Methods."

optical character recognition (OCR) software to create searchable text of these files. Using Adobe Acrobat Pro, this takes a few seconds per page. Once the text has been recognized, you can quickly search for key words or phrases so that you don't have to read the specification. You can also quickly search the text of patents using your browser's search function within a website (e.g., USPTO.gov or some other search provider). However, it's often easier and faster to do the search within the document that also contains all of the images.

3. *Pay attention to where the information is found.* The location of information within an application has a significant bearing on the relevance of that information. For example, you may find key terms in the claims that do not occur in the abstract. Since the claims describe the patented invention, the abstract may simply be misleading.

CHAPTER 8

The Impact of
the 2011 America
Invents Act

The legislation known as the Leahy-Smith America Invents Act (AIA) was signed into law on September 16, 2011 and has some key implications for corporate inventors. Patent reform of one kind or another has been in the legislative arena for several years, and it has been fiercely debated given the complex nature of the subject matter and the importance of patents to many industries. Some companies prefer stronger rights (usually those in long-product-cycle industries such as pharmaceuticals and biotechnology), while others prefer weaker rights (particularly those with fast product-cycle times, such as software and information technology). Furthermore, there is an interest in harmonizing U.S. law with that of other countries to minimize the differences and complexities of obtaining patent rights in multiple geographies.

This chapter will summarize some of the key changes, with an emphasis on the impact they are likely to have on the corporate inventor. Whether or not you are in favor of the changes, they do have some important practical implications for inventors.

FIRST INVENTOR TO FILE

One of the most significant changes to U.S. patent law in many decades is the switch from a "first-to-invent" system to a "first-inventor-to-file" system (effective March 16, 2013). The United States has historically been a holdout from most patent practice outside the United States in that the rights to a patent were possessed by the first person to invent the patented subject matter, even if that person was not the first person to file the patent application. If two similar patent applications were filed, and the claims covered the same subject matter, an "interference proceeding" was held to determine who rightfully owned the rights to the claimed subject matter. This would usually amount to the inventors providing documentation to show that they had invented the claimed subject matter at the earliest possible date. Documentation was preferably in the form of a signed and witnessed laboratory notebook, specifically kept for this purpose. Whoever could provide evidence to show the earliest date of invention was awarded rights to the patent.

The new approach under the AIA, sometimes referred to as "first inventor to file," changed the law to make the rightful owner of a newly invented technology the inventor who first files the application at the patent office. It is important to note that any application must still be filed by the actual inventor, not derived or copied from someone else. In other words, if a colleague sees your invention, quickly writes up a patent application based on your work, and beats you to the patent office, he would not be the rightful owner of the patent because he was not the inventor of the subject matter. On the other hand, if a competitor is working on a similar technology, and the same invention is developed in your lab and in your competitor's lab, rightful ownership will be determined by who files the application first, regardless of who developed the invention first.

Furthermore, there will potentially be "derivation proceedings" to determine whether or not the inventor who filed earlier derived (i.e., copied) the subject matter from the later-filing inventor. These will hopefully be less complicated than interference proceedings, but they do speak to the preference for an earlier filing date and a need for records of invention. Importantly, derivation proceedings must be filed within one year of the publication of a competitor's application—which means that you'll need to monitor your competitor's filings closely if you expect to make use of this provision.

Changing to the first-inventor-to-file system also comes with the change that inventors can no longer "swear behind" a prior art reference with an effective date within one year of the filing date of the inventor's application. Under previous law, an inventor was able to swear that the invention actually occurred before the prior art was published, for up to a year. In other words, there will be more prior art available to be used against your patent applications. This change further reinforces the need for an earlier filing date.

THE INVENTOR'S GRACE PERIOD VERSUS ABSOLUTE NOVELTY

This aspect of the law remains similar to the previous situation. However, it is worth pointing out there are some changes as well as distinct differences between the United States and most non-U.S. geographies in this area, which generally hold to a more strict "absolute novelty" rule. Inventors retain the one-year grace period for their own prior publication before the application date. If an inventor publishes the invention at a conference, for example, she has up to one year to file a patent application on the invention.

Under the old law, prior publication was never a good idea even with the grace period because it would jeopardize international rights based on absolute novelty. Interestingly, the new law creates a potential benefit for prior publication in that if someone else's application is filed between the first publication and the application date (within the one-year grace period), it is not considered prior art. In effect, the first publication of the invention could prevent someone else from obtaining a patent even when your application occurs later than theirs.

In general, the loss of potential international rights as a result of the prior publication is likely be a greater risk than the benefit of preventing another U.S. applicant from obtaining rights in the interim before your own filing. As a result, it seems unlikely that corporations would move to an intentional first-to-publish strategy unless there are no international interests. However, it is of potential concern from a competitive standpoint: your own application could be found to be invalid because of a prior publication by a competitor, even when you have an earlier application date.

These risks provide more good reasons not to delay the filing of an application.

BEST MODE DISCLOSURE REQUIREMENT

Interestingly, the new act removes the failure to disclose the "best mode" as a means for invalidating a patent, but does not remove the requirement for including best mode in a newly filed application. At face value, this seems somewhat contradictory, and it is likely to be refined further as the U.S. Patent and Trademark Office (USPTO) and the courts further interpret how this change will be applied.

In general, this should not change how the application is written, as the best mode still needs to be included at the time of filing. However, it will remove a potential avenue for invalidating a patent after it has been granted. From the perspective of an inventor, this should not have a significant impact, since the requirements for filing have not changed.

EXPANDED PRIOR USER RIGHTS

Under the pre-AIA system, if a company invented a new process, but decided to keep that process a trade secret, another inventor who arrived at the same process could file an application and rightfully be granted a patent. Furthermore, the original user that had kept the process a trade secret would now be infringing on a later-filed patent.

With the new law, greater protection has been given to prior users who can show that the patented invention had been in commercial use for at least a year before the applicant's filing date. For this purpose, "commercial use" includes regulatory review periods (such as FDA approval). This will significantly decrease the risk of holding trade secrets (particularly for processes that aren't easily reverse-engineered). It does not, however, eliminate the risk entirely, as there is still one year for a competitor to file an application if it independently invents the same process.

INVALIDITY CHALLENGES FOR FINANCIAL BUSINESS METHOD PATENTS

The new law institutes a special procedure for challenging a granted "business method" patent that claims data processing or other operations "used in the practice, administration, or management of a financial product or service." Essentially, this reduces some of the limitations established for postgrant review to make it easier to challenge finance-related business methods.

PRIORITIZED EXAMINATION

Another avenue for requesting a faster examination process, called a "prioritized examination," has been established; this is available for an additional $4,800 fee. The previous system allowed for "accelerated examination," which was also intended to reduce the time required for examination. Currently, both approaches are possible, although the filing requirements and timings are different. Either approach would require careful consideration and discussion with your attorney, as there are many important differences from the standard process. These issues are complex enough that we won't go into detail here. However, it's important to recognize that there are options available to accelerate the examination process if it would benefit your overall strategy.

PREISSUANCE SUBMISSIONS AND POSTGRANT REVIEW

If an application is published and a third party (e.g., a competitor) has identified relevant prior art against this invention, the third party can now submit those materials to the examiner before the application is granted.

There is also now a nine-month review period during which a third party can challenge the validity of a patent. The third party must be able to show that there is a high likelihood that at least one of the claims is unpatentable. After the nine-month window has passed, applications can still be challenged, but only on the basis of patents or printed publications.

Both of these changes will require significant attorney involvement to determine the best strategic uses of these opportunities. However, there will definitely be a greater need to watch your competitors' filings closely for relevant subject matter to make sure that the time periods for intervention are not exceeded. A portion of this responsibility is likely to fall to individual researchers and project teams—which is an important reason to understand patent searching and setting up search alerts.

IMPACTS ON CORPORATE INVENTORS

1. *Increasing emphasis on early filing dates.* There are potentially complex issues involving prior publication and derivation proceedings, but the net result in most instances will be a preference for earlier filing dates.
2. *Increased risk of delayed filings for life-cycle management.* We'll discuss life-cycle management in more detail in Chapter 16, but in general it refers to maximizing the useful life of a patent portfolio. One key aspect of life-cycle management is deciding when to file an application quickly and when to delay filing. The AIA changes have increased the risk of delayed filings as a result of the possibility of prior art or competitive filings in the interim.
3. *Inventors still need to keep good documentation.* The need for proving dates of invention as commonly argued in interference proceedings has diminished. However, the need for accurate inventorship determination and the need to argue against derivation mean that there is still a requirement for good documentation.
4. *Reduced risk of keeping trade secrets.* There is now a reasonable "prior-user" defense against later-filed applications, which will reduce the risk of being sued for something that has been in commercial use for at least a year. The risk is not eliminated entirely, but it is reduced.

5. *Increased emphasis on competitive intelligence.* The need to monitor competitive filings continuously has increased, particularly with regard to opportunities for postgrant review. It's likely that corporations will turn to inventors to help distribute the effort across the organization. There are plenty of good reasons to monitor your competitors' patent activities—if you aren't doing it already, now would be a good time to start.

CHAPTER 9

Working with Your Attorney: Nine Steps to a Better Utility Patent

Byron V. Olsen

Mr. Olsen is an assistant general counsel at Monsanto. His work is concentrated on global patent strategy development, including due diligence efforts in Monsanto acquisitions, complex licensing arrangements, and international technology transfer.

He is currently involved in the oversight of intellectual property efforts in China as well as enabling technologies. He has worked on intellectual property–related matters since 1985.

As a patent attorney, the one who hopes to aid you in the process of getting your patent drafted, defended, and allowed, I want to talk to you about what I need from you and what you need to do for me, perhaps even if I do not ask. Corporate attorneys often have a very full docket and too little time to spend with you on your newest creation. In these situations, the attorneys do not always thoughtfully consider and inform you of what they need from you. This is a shame because it cuts off an important avenue in the development of a better application and potentially a better, broader, and more defendable patent. How? To answer this, we need to walk through the ins and outs of the patent application drafting process and what can be done at each step to optimize the process.

FIRST: PICK THE RIGHT ATTORNEY

How do you quantify legal talent? The answer is: don't try. Look at objective things that you can actually confirm. If you have the ability to choose, how do you pick an attorney? What should you look for? Obviously this section matters little to those who have no choice in the selection of a patent attorney. For them, the organization may dictate that they get Attorney A, given their technical area or where they are located. If this is the case for you, then this section is of little value to you, even if the other items presented here become more important simply because of that.

After spending decades in this business as an attorney, I think the best answer is to find someone who has the right technical background and still retains an enthusiasm for the subject matter. Enthusiasm may be hard to measure, but technical expertise is relatively easy to verify. The easiest approach is to find the educational background and publication history for the individual involved. This can be done online via a number of websites, such as law firm websites and even corporate law websites that provide listings in Martinedale Hubbell, or by simply asking for a résumé and/or curriculum vitae.

You should also review one or more of the patents that your patent attorney has prosecuted before the U.S. Patent and Trademark Office (USPTO). If your choices include someone who has been educated in the area and has recently published in this space or even litigated there, you have a very good indicator that this person might be interested in your technology and be comfortable with it. Once your comparative list is done, pick the candidate who has a background as close to the technology as possible and who demonstrates an enthusiasm for the technology. This is not a perfect screen, but it will help.

SECOND: GROUND YOUR ATTORNEY IN THE TECHNOLOGY

Whether he tells you this or not, your attorney may not be as well versed in the technology of your invention as you are. His credentials may be older, his technical training may not be related to your invention, or he may simply be outclassed by the science involved. This is not always true, but providing him with an overview of the technology and how you have improved it is always helpful. Such an overview should walk through the technology, its foundations, and recent developments in the field. A solid review article is probably the best bet here, unless you are confident that your attorney knows the technical area completely. Once you have grounded your attorney in the technology, you then gain full access to his ability to draft a business-relevant patent application for you. I say "business-relevant" because this is, of course, the endgame for patent applications and patents: financial and/or strategic advantage. If you and your company intended to dedicate the invention to the public and the benefit of mankind, then you are at liberty to do so at any time.

This is also the reason why you need a professional who is trained in drafting patents and wresting the broadest claims possible from the patent office. Claims are the business end of any issued patent; they are what parties fight over in court and what businesses pay money to license. They are the verbal embodiment of the technical limits/defendable boundaries of your invention. Almost anyone can draft a simple patent with reference to a few self-help books and online guidance. The problem is that these sources will not, and are not designed to, be custom work that will examine and claim the full breadth of your invention. However, a fully engaged patent attorney who understands the technology and has a working relationship with you has a fighting chance to accomplish this. The courts, too, have recognized how hard it is to draft a patent properly.

The end of the story here is that you should be prepared to walk your attorney through the invention from start to finish and provide information that will allow her to do this walk on her own, up to and including citations in the art that will be particularly helpful or enlightening. Thereafter, you should make yourself available to your attorney to ask and answer questions as the drafting continues. In this process, do not be intimidated by the terminology. Patent lawyers have their own language, and you should learn some of it by reading the application as it is being drafted and by asking questions as you work through the process. If your attorney asks questions about the documents you have provided, mark that as a good sign. You may also need to negotiate how much time you are willing to invest to get her up to speed in the review material you have provided. The key is to find someone who is listening.

THIRD: KNOW WHO THE INVENTORS ARE

In the United States, you need to know all potential inventors and identify them to your attorney, even the disagreeable exchange student from Slovakia, the postdoc who is now in Beijing, and the lab tech who got lucky. Vanity aside, it is my experience that if the invention is particularly complex or took a significant amount of time to develop, then there are almost certainly multiple inventors. Even if it is uncomfortable, you need to make this list accurate and complete. You do not want your patent attorney spending time playing referee or chasing disgruntled former friends or colleagues who have been pushed out of the "inventive entity."

Why shouldn't you keep all the glory and potential money for yourself? Primarily because you may need your coinventors later.

You may need their testimony, their cooperation, their memory, and even their notebooks. You do not need them to sign separate deals with competitors or to leave your employ in a huff. This will be less true as the America Invents Act is implemented, since we are moving to a first-inventor-to-file system and not a first-to-invent process, but it still stands that being straightforward and honest with your inventors and your patent attorney from the beginning is by far the best policy. Note that this characteristic of inventorship by a real person is not shared with many other countries and could come as a bit of a surprise to those from other systems.

FOURTH: SUPERINVENT AND THINK STRATEGICALLY WITH YOUR ATTORNEY

You may be brilliant, capable of changing the world on a regular basis, but the full engagement of another set of trained eyes could broaden or strengthen the invention itself. Superinventing goes beyond claim drafting or modifying your draft patent application to be mindful of recent judicial precedent. This should be the primary benefit of having a good patent attorney involved, full stop.

Superinventing is a process in which your patent attorney adds new concepts or uses for the invention itself. He suggests how to modify the invention to make it more commercially valuable or provide alternative claim sets that encompass a new embodiment to broaden the scope of what is being pursued. This could go so far as to suggest the integration of the invention with other technologies that the attorney knows are in the public domain. This integration may constitute a different invention that may, in fact, need a separate filing but would tend to broaden the scope of your initial invention and may crimp the plans of the competition. Obviously the patent attorney must walk the line of protecting the confidentiality of other clients, but adding information here can greatly increase the impact of your original invention.

Often inventors see the world though the prism of their educational and work experience. A patent attorney is also bound by her educational experience, but she may have been involved in the development of several different technologies that may be interesting and useful additions to your invention. I actually enjoy this brainstorming with my clients, as it often results in a greatly improved commercial embodiment of the original idea.

When you engage in superinventing in this way, be mindful of the following rules that I employ: (1) remain focused on the specific invention that you want to improve, (2) be open to new technology that may be outside your area of expertise, and (3) think strategically when you prioritize ideas. Thinking strategically in this context means thinking in terms of those improvements of the technology that will allow your project and your invention to have a significant commercial impact. Finally, (4) before you file, look at your draft application and think like your competitor. When you have drafted your invention, ask yourself how your competitors could work around your claims. If you have a composition or a protein that you are claiming, then your competitors' options may be limited, but this is not always the case in biology, and it is certainly not the case in other fields. When you think like them, you may add claim sets to cover where they may be headed or embodiments to support additional continuation or divisional filings later in the process to make it harder for them to work around your invention.

FIFTH: KEEP RECORDS

Perhaps the most important part of this process is to keep, maintain, and regularly use a scientific notebook. An inventor's notebook is a place for you to log your progress from an experimental outline to a possible mental concept to a physical invention and a final reduction to practice.

Notebooks and record-keeping systems for corporate inventors do not have to be fancy. Basic requirements include the following:

1. The pages are permanently bound (meaning that you can't easily add loose pages) in a notebook with numbered pages.
2. The contents are understandable and are put in place permanently—including mounting included ancillary materials such as pictures of gels or other data with writing in ink.
3. All necessary steps in the protocols to create the invention or complete it are present.
4. Any corrections are made cleanly and dated.
5. The contents are periodically witnessed and signed by another person.

You should also keep what I call "ongoing notes" in it. These notes document when you come up with new processes, systems, or tools bringing your invention to life; make sure to write down everything. Not only will this potentially add to the invention, but it may also create new ones via the superinventing process when the material is reviewed by your attorney. This information may also be useful in any potential future litigation. It gives you powerful proof of the timeline of your idea. If you can show how your idea progressed before anyone else, you'll have a strong argument that you were the inventor.

As previously mentioned, under the America Invents Act (AIA), the United States is making the transition from a "first-to-invent" statutory position in mid–2013. Even after this transition, however, thorough records will bear fruit in prosecution and in litigation. Other examples of the continuing utility of notebooks after the implementation of the AIA include use in postgrant challenges or reviews, assistance in providing a basis for inventor affidavits, potential use in *inter partes* review procedures, and determining who the inventive entity is.

SIXTH: ASSIST IN DRAFTING AND QUIZ THE ATTORNEY

There are two parts to this section: first, you must deliver a document to the attorney that conveys the invention and its reduction to practice, and second, you need to be involved in the drafting process through active engagement with your attorney.

Initially at least, your disclosure to your patent attorney is best thought of as a draft for a peer-reviewed article. That is, you should prepare your invention disclosure along the lines of an article for a known peer-reviewed technical journal. You need this type of data, detail, and depth of information to help your patent attorney identify the appropriate embodiments and get a grasp of the needed claim set. Each portion of such an invention disclosure will be useful to the attorney, including related references and any prior art. Unfortunately, inventors often prefer to drop off their disclosure and be done with the process. This is simply insufficient and generally results in applications that are slow to be drafted, slow to be filed, and typically of inferior quality.

You also need to be involved in the drafting process even after you have provided your invention disclosure. If your attorney is reluctant to ask you to review the draft document, you should not take this as a good sign. At a minimum, you need to do a full review and edit prior to filing so that you can catch any scientific missteps that may be present and correct them. You should also provide a relevant list of prior art and new publications that have a bearing on or are in the same field as your invention, and you should insist that these be provided to the patent office. The patent attorney may add more citations, but those that you feel are closest to the invention must be added.

In addition to your duty of candor in disclosing art to the patent office, having all relevant art in front of the examiner makes for a stronger patent, even if it results in narrower claims. It is better to have a strong patent that may have limited claims than to have a patent with broader claims that may not be defendable in litigation. You get to a strong patent estate by providing the relevant art and persistently explaining to the patent office why your invention is different and/or better. In this, you should rely upon what Judge Learned Hand called the "ant-like persistence" of patent attorneys to aid you (Lyon v. Boh, 1 F.2d 48 [S.D.N.Y. 1924]). Remember that provisional applications need to be considered the real deal here as well. With this in place, you then have the opportunity to begin building a significant filing.

While you are reviewing your draft, you should keep a running list of questions and/or corrections for the draft. The corrections are usually relatively straightforward, but they should be provided and incorporated as needed. Remember that you are the expert on your invention and that your attorney probably isn't. Thus, your corrections may be ones that he would not be in a position to see easily. Your questions are also opportunities to engage the attorney in the science and technical aspects of your invention. Your attorney should be willing to answer your questions or to discuss with you the reasons why the draft is progressing the way it is. Often these questions help create a better draft, and they always help you understand where the draft application is going. Sample questions should be along the lines of: does the claim set include x step; do we need to add an embodiment for y usage of the invention; did you include a data table that demonstrates z results? In short, ask a lot of questions and push a bit on the answers.

SEVENTH: REVIEW CLAIMS, EXAMPLES, AND FIGURES

Most inventors skip this part of the job or do not pursue it with intent. This is a mistake. Reviewing the claims, examples, and figures in a patent application can be critical. In fact, there are many court cases in which patentability has rested on the content of figures. "In those instances where a visual representation can flesh out words, drawings may be used in the same manner and with the same limitations as the specification" (Autogiro Co. of America v. United States, 384 F.2d 391, 398 [Ct. Cl. 1967]). Also, see Lockwood v. American Airlines, Inc., 107 F.3d 1565, 1572 (Fed. Cir. 1997); If a gel does not look right or the drawings do not fully disclose your invention and alternative embodiments, then this should be addressed. The invention is embod-ied in the application and stretches to all its parts, and should be understood in this manner.

EIGHTH: DO NOT TALK ABOUT IT WITH ANYONE OUTSIDE THE COMPANY AND YOUR LEGAL STAFF

This is simple, but important. I have personally seen many inventions fail the novelty bar because people did not consider a thesis defense a publication, because a casual meeting with a colleague where a break-through is disclosed turns into a patent application that beats the inventor's application by a week, or because a "poster" defeats novelty in Europe. There should be no submissions to peer-reviewed journals until the patent attorney has reviewed your disclosure and given per-mission. Even then, you need to talk to her and determine how long your "confidential" submission has before it gets to a library near you. Academics are trained to publish from graduate school onward, but that drive to let the world know must be tempered until the appropri-ate patent application is on file.

NINTH: YOU HAVE ONE SHOT AT GETTING IT RIGHT

As a group, patent attorneys are very good at taking a filed application toward allowance of at least a limited subset of claims. The trick, then, is to get that initial filing correct. This must be done to ensure that the inven-tion is explained in the broadest way possible and claimed appropriately, as has been discussed. Failure to do this in the initial utility filing is very hard to correct. Simply put, you cannot capture subject matter that was not included and enabled at the time of filing. To this point, the Federal Circuit held in 2005 that the specification of a patent (for our purposes, the body of the application that explains the invention) is critically impor-tant when interpreting patent claims and the true parameters of the inven-tion. In fact, the court said, "The specification is always highly relevant to the claim construction analysis. Usually, it is dispositive; it is the single best guide to the meaning of a disputed term" (Phillips v. AWH Corp., 415 F.3d 1303, 1315 [Fed. Cir. 2005]).

Many patent attorneys pay more attention to the claims than to the body of the application (the specification) itself. This is a mistake. The specification and the claims are equally important. While the initial claims are designed carefully, they are allowed to be changed during prosecution. The same cannot be said of the specification. Only rarely can it be modified during prosecution, and not in ways that add new material or "new matter" to the disclosure. The specification is the explanation of the invention and how it works. If this explanation is not done well, a price will be paid for it in the claims that may eventually be issued. This is why the attorney needs to be grounded in the technology and the inventor needs to be involved in the process of patent drafting.

Moreover, I would argue that this joint effort is now more needed than ever, as the road to patent allowance is actually getting harder. As those who seek patents should be aware, inventions must be new, useful, and nonobvious in order to be patentable. But developments in relatively recent U.S. case law, most notably the 2007 case of KSR Intl. v. Teleflex Inc. (KSR), have made some of the hurdles to an issued patent with relevant claims even higher. What this means for us is that your patent application not only must be written clearly but must also include as much relevant data as can reasonably be put in place to overcome hurdles like obviousness objections (KSR Intl. v. Teleflex Inc., 550 U.S. 398 [2007]). As a practitioner, I can tell you that the USPTO now routinely rejects claims that would have been allowable pre-KSR.

This points to one conclusion: you get only one opportunity to draft the application, so make sure it's done well.

Carrying out each of these steps in a proactive manner will help you not only collaborate with your attorney, but do so in a timely and cost-efficient manner and help build trust for both parties. Your patent attorney will learn more about your invention, and you will learn more about your patent attorney. To get the best intellectual property protection for your inventions, you need to invest time in educating your attorney, and you need to be involved in the drafting process. Your attorney may not always thank you for your time, attention, and questions, but the resulting patent applications will be stronger and more valuable.

PART 2

PATENT STRATEGY

CHAPTER 10

KEY ELEMENTS OF A PATENT STRATEGY

The word *strategy* is used in many different ways and generally isn't precisely understood because of the subtle differences in usage. In its simplest form, strategy might be considered a plan for future resource allocation. The emphasis is on preparation for future situations, and the resources that are within your control are the tools for achieving the desired result. Resources are limited, of course, so a good strategy will also include an effort to optimize your resource allocation to the strategic opportunities and competitive landscape, including determining what you are not going to pursue.

More specifically, I use the term *patent strategy* to refer to the interaction of patents within the larger context of products, projects, business objectives, and other patents. A patent strategy related to a particular project will also be closely correlated with the product under development and how that product will establish a competitive advantage, where it will fit in the marketplace, distinctive features, and consumer benefits. A patent strategy at the corporate level will include aspects of in-licensing and out-licensing strategies, enforcement of patent rights against competitors, generating and acquiring intellectual property (IP), and efforts to reduce the risk of being entangled in lawsuits.

This broader perspective will dictate whether or not a patent application is ever filed, which countries it is filed in, when the application is filed, what technologies are kept as trade secrets, identification of future targets, avoiding competitors' strengths, and so on. While the overarching patent strategy certainly encompasses the claims written for each application, the key emphasis in our discussion will be on the interaction among multiple patents—sometimes a few and sometimes many, and including both your patents and your competitors' patents.

While the inventor should always be involved in developing the claims, the primary responsibility for writing the claims will always reside with your attorney. Your attorney will also be intimately involved in developing the overall patent strategy. However, many corporate attorneys don't have enough time to be as involved in discussions of the broader context as they would like. Your patent strategy may be affected by limited resources, business strategies, regulatory issues, and corporate policies that will require coordination of multiple objectives across functions in the corporation. As a result, a good understanding of these topics by researchers, managers, and executives can be a great benefit to the overall patent strategy.

The following questions should be considered in developing your strategy:

1. How will the patents be used in the context of the product (i.e., licensing, establishing competitive advantage, discouraging countersuits, or some other way)?
2. Who are your competitors for the purposes of this product and this strategy? What kinds of products and strategies do you expect from them?
3. What differentiates your product from those of your competitors? Are there ways to enhance your differentiation?
4. What alternative technologies already exist? Is your technology meaningfully different?
5. What claims are likely to be granted for this product?
6. Are there opportunities for keeping trade secrets, which might be better than filing patents?
7. Can patents related to this product be enforced? Are there methods of detection?
8. How will future technological innovations affect this strategy?
9. Can you predict future innovative cycles and leapfrog the competition?
10. Can you establish a meaningful competitive advantage for this product?
11. When do the key elements of the patent strategy need to be in place?
12. What geographies are likely to be relevant? Are there unique considerations for patentable subject matter or other differences in patent law that would have an impact on the effectiveness of your strategy?

In general, the strategies we will discuss involve multiple patents—and occasionally large numbers of filings. It is certainly true that a great invention can be protected with a single patent, but most corporations file in much larger numbers because of the difficulty in knowing, at the time of filing, which invention will be critical to marketplace success.

Furthermore, your competitors are likely to be creative in trying to design around your patent position. Multiple patents are usually used to protect against different features of the products, different places in the value chain, alternative materials, and alternative processing methods. Unfortunately, any single patent may not have much value.

Patents can also create value in different ways. Traditionally, patents are described as having two primary uses: offensive and defensive, the "sword" or the "shield." This is a great analogy for understanding some aspects of patent strategy, but it's really only a starting place.

OFFENSIVE, DEFENSIVE, OR WHAT?

Continuing with this sword-and-shield analogy, offensive objectives would be to limit your competitors' ability to imitate your product or business strategy and to maximize your own competitive advantage. Defensive objectives would be to protect against being excluded from an opportunity by one of your competitors, to establish freedom to operate, and to minimize your competitors' opportunity to establish a competitive advantage.

In general, the offensive purpose of patents is to create a competitive advantage by precluding competitors from making, using, selling, or importing the claimed invention for up 20 years from the priority date (21 years, if you are claiming priority based on a provisional). In other words, patents stop your competitors from doing something. They directly affect your competitors' business by prohibiting a competitive response based on imitation. As a side note, not all competitors are ethical; some may simply choose to ignore your patent and infringe on your claims. To be used effectively against the competition, your patent also needs to be of high enough quality to stand up to rigorous examination in the courts.

The defensive effect of patents primarily results from publishing the invention. Once the invention is in the public domain, it cannot be patented by anyone else. Generally, the defensive purpose will be given less emphasis in most of our discussions because there are alternative methods of publishing inventions that are cheaper and easier (e.g., publishing the information in a technical journal or other publicly available periodical, where any publication will do), and there tends to be less precision required in a defensive-focused strategy. I'm not suggesting that it will be easy to achieve these goals, but there are fewer obstacles to publishing (as patents or as literature) when there are fewer concerns about timing (sooner is always better) or about which claims will be granted (anything in the specification counts as a publication, no matter what is in the claims). However, it is important to keep this in mind because your prior publications (including patents) can also be used against *you* when you file future patent applications. Many inexperienced inventors are surprised to find out that their own publications can be the most significant obstacle to obtaining valid patents.

From an overall strategic perspective, patents primarily derive their value by stopping your competitors from imitating a valuable aspect of your product. If they don't hold up in court, they won't be effective and aren't worth much. Furthermore, if there are consumer-equivalent alternatives outside the scope of the claims, they aren't creating much of a competitive advantage and probably have little value. This is one reason that having a good patent strategy is necessary if you are to extract value from your intellectual property. Just having patents isn't enough. If they don't create a competitive advantage, they aren't helping your business. They aren't worth the time, effort, and money invested in getting them granted.

Unfortunately, describing the function of patents using just the terms *offensive* and *defensive* leaves out much of the critical information. These may be their most direct functions, but what about the bigger picture? Aren't there more options here?

Of course, there are many more elements of patent strategy—otherwise this would be a very short book. A better way to visualize the situation is by analogy to a chessboard. Each patent you get adds another piece to the board. But the value of that piece will depend on the strength of the patent—is it a knight or a pawn? The value of that piece will also depend on the strategic location of the technology. Is it in a strategic formation? Is it near your opponent's king? Or is it protecting your own valuable queen?

In the same way that a game of chess is usually won by the player who thinks the most moves ahead, the best patent strategy is developed by considering what "moves" you and your competitors will be making next. For patents, these moves can have effects that last for quite a long time.

Their value and purpose should be considered far beyond the immediate situation. This type of forward thinking can lend itself to strategies involving numerous patent applications, coordinated filings, submarine claims, life-cycle management, and other more advanced topics that we'll get into later.

HOW DO YOU KNOW IF YOU HAVE AN EFFECTIVE PATENT STRATEGY?

This can be a tough question to answer in the early stages of developing your strategy, although it will become easier to evaluate over time. A good strategy will help your company achieve its objective in establishing competitive advantage and/or licensing and transfer of technology. Often this will result in licenses being requested by the competition, citations of your patents by other applications and examiners, and, hopefully, an eventual reduction in imitative product competition. Conversely, how do you know that you don't have an effective patent strategy? One good indication is that your competitors are not affected by your strategy. You may be filing dozens or even hundreds of patents, but they have had minimal impact in the marketplace. Numbers of filings are a good measure of resource allocation and can be great sources of competitive intelligence, but they don't tell the full story about the effectiveness of the strategy. Perhaps you file more applications than your competitors, but they always seem to have the patents that matter—the patents that are licensed or that result in lawsuits.

Is it your patent strategy or a lack of innovation? If your products don't seem to be establishing a meaningful competitive advantage, either one could be the problem. If no one is imitating your products, it could be because your patent strategy is so comprehensive that there is no meaningful avenue for competition. Alternatively, it could be that your competitors believe that other technologies are as good or better. Some things to consider: Are competitors imitating your product strategy? Are your patents being granted? Are your patents being cited in your competitors' filings and examiners' search results? Are your patents showing up in international search results in the Patent Cooperation Treaty (PCT) process?

One question I like to ask when conducting training on these topics is, "Would you rather have patents on your own products or on the products your competitors are making?" Universally, the answer is that we prefer to protect our own products. However, this isn't as straightforward as it sounds. Patents are primarily a negative right—they preclude others from taking certain actions. Corporations generally pursue patents on their own products under the assumption that competitors would prefer to imitate those inventions. But patents don't create value unless the competition needs the patented technology. In other words, a large portfolio of patents on your products is not particularly valuable if your competitors have other ways to achieve the same or better results for the consumer.

As a quick reminder, patents on your own products provide value in at least two distinct additional ways: as a means for transferring rights (e.g., in-licensing or out-licensing), and as defensive novelty-destroying publications against competitors' filings. These sources of value are distinct from the value of competitive advantage described in the previous paragraph. These benefits will usually result in a balance of filings—some focused on your products and some focused on preventing competitive imitations. Each of these components of value should be considered when reviewing the effectiveness of your patent strategy.

In many cases, it's the transfer of these rights that presents the clearest picture of their value. If you work for a corporation with an emphasis on licensing, a start-up that is looking for a buyer, or a company that is trying to collaborate with other partners in a complex value chain, patents are one of the best ways for rights to be transferred between corporations. Licensing fees, M&A activity, and even the value of the entire corporation may be based heavily on the contents of the company's patent portfolio. One only has to look at the recent patent-driven transactions in the smartphone industry for billion-dollar examples. One might argue that Google's acquisition of Motorola Mobility for $12.5 billion was probably driven by Motorola's portfolio of 17,000 patents.

At the end of the day, evaluating the effectiveness of a strategy can be a very complicated process. Historical situations related to individual patents and associated products need to be evaluated and compared with competitive benchmarks. In general, however, it is worth doing a comparative analysis on occasion to understand whether or not your strategies are working and what improvements could be made.

KEY COMPONENTS OF A PATENT STRATEGY AT THE PROJECT LEVEL

It's always a good idea to have a written patent strategy document for your project. However, keep in mind that this information is highly sensitive and should be assembled under the guidance of an attorney.

In particular, it's best not to specifically address any freedom to operate (FTO) issues in writing.

As you create this document, here are a few things you should include:

- What's your objective? How will the patents be used? Options might include creating competitive advantage in the marketplace, out-licensing and royalty collection, ensuring freedom to operate through defensive publications, building a portfolio to discourage countersuits, and so on.
- How does the patent strategy support the overall project strategy? Is it tangential to the product (i.e., you'll go ahead even without patent coverage if necessary), or is it a core necessity (no patents means no project)?
- Who are the competitors for the purposes of this product and this strategy? What products do you expect them to bring forward in the future? How similar or different does your technology need to be from theirs?
- What's your time frame? When do the key elements of the patent strategy need to be in place? Are there any specific timing needs (e.g., coordination with any mandatory publication, life-cycle man-agement, or marketing disclosures), including when particular appli-cations need to be filed?
- What technologies are likely to be patentable? Which technologies are already in the prior art?
- What is the current competitive landscape in the field of interest? Does your company have an existing position that could be built upon? Can we define the "white space" and "red space"? See Step 9: White Space and Red Space in Chapter 11 for further discussion.
- What geographies are likely to be relevant? Are there unique con-siderations for patentable subject matter or other differences in patent law that would affect the effectiveness of your strategy?
- Is there opportunity for publication or trade secrets, which would provide greater strategic value than patenting?
- *If* things go as planned, what do you expect to have protected when your product is in the marketplace? Will you be able to detect and enforce against infringement?

A BRIEF WORD ON GEOGRAPHIC STRATEGY

Patent strategy is complicated enough when discussing the implications for a single geography. A thorough discussion of a geographic filing strategy is highly dependent on local patent laws (e.g., statutory subject matter), product value, costs for prosecution and maintenance fees, and other business objectives.

In most situations, multinational corporations will use the PCT system to get the process started, then make more specific elections of individual countries at 30 months (20 months for a small number of countries). For those countries that are not part of the PCT system, the filings will need to be done concurrently with the U.S. nonprovisional filing. The European Patent Office (EPO) system also allows for a similar filing and examination in one office, with subsequent granting by individual nations.

The process for determining the cost/benefit of filing in each country can be very complicated. In general, the following should be considered:

- Where are your competitors likely to launch infringing products?
- Where are your competitors' manufacturing facilities?
- Which countries are enforcing patent holders' rights in their court systems?
- Which countries grant patents for inventions of this type? (This is particularly relevant to biotech, software, and business methods.)

These topics are likely to be important for the overall effectiveness of a patent strategy at any multinational corporation. However, this aspect of the strategy is not usually the domain of the corporate inventor and therefore is outside the scope of this book. Nonetheless, it is worthwhile to be aware of the complexity and magnitude of the task, particularly for products that are sold on a global scale. At a cost of $10,000 to $20,000 per country, patent protection in 20 countries could easily cost a company $200,000 to $400,000. This is why the strategic relevance of each application is so important. Global patent strategy is a very expensive game.

AND DON'T FORGET . . .

Although we are focusing our discussion on patent strategy, this may be a good place to acknowledge that other forms of intellectual property should be considered along with the overall strategy for your project. The forms of IP that are relevant to your project are likely to extend beyond utility patents to include trademarks, trade dress, design patents, and/or copyrights. These topics are not central to the scope of our current discussion and are frequently outside the domain of the corporate inventor, but that doesn't mean that they aren't important. On the contrary, each form of intellectual property has a role to play in the overall IP strategy. It may not be your job to address these opportunities, but they should definitely be considered and coordinated with the patent strategy when possible.

CHAPTER 11

Patent Landscapes: Dividing Up the Pie

Now that we have a basic understanding of patent strategy, it's worthwhile to develop a more comprehensive view of the competitive situation, sometimes referred to as a "landscape." Looking at patent landscapes should always be one of the first steps in developing a good patent strategy. You need to know what the current competitive landscape looks like before you can adequately develop a strategy for the future. As with a game of chess, how the pieces are distributed on the board will determine your next move. You may be operating in a well-developed market where there are hundreds or even thousands of related patents, or perhaps this is a new technology and there is very little prior art.

There may be specialists at your corporation who will do this for you, and there are certainly consultants that specialize in this area. However, the basic process isn't as complicated as it sounds. Inventors are certainly capable of developing a patent landscape with minimal training. Learning the tools the first time through will take a bit of effort, however.

For projects where the number of references reaches into the 1,000+ range, it may be worthwhile to investigate some more advanced techniques or bring in a consulting firm. There is one important thing to watch out for, however: remember that a consultant's fancy graphics do not necessarily mean that the results are accurate or complete. It's extremely important that technology experts be closely involved in this process. While the external experts will have better tools for creating the landscape, they probably won't know your technology area much at all. Searches that are missing important key words or that include results from unrelated industries can be misleading—even if the graphics are brilliant.

Patent landscapes don't require this level of precision and can reasonably be conducted by a patent-savvy inventor. Importantly, we are not doing a formal freedom to operate (FTO) or patentability search. Those official searches need to be precise and will usually be conducted only with guidance from an attorney.

The steps that follow are presented in a general order. However, this sequence doesn't need to be adhered to rigorously, and you might even skip some steps. Also, the online database that you're using may have more or fewer tools for storing, refining, and analyzing search results. The available tools will probably dictate the most efficient approach. It's usually best to do as much as possible online, then export the results to another type of analysis software (generally a spreadsheet) to produce fancier charts and graphs. Thomson Innovation, Innography, and Orbit offer a variety of analysis tools online, and you may find that 90 percent of your needs can be met without your having to analyze your findings in more detail. However, I usually find that traditional spreadsheet-based analysis has added flexibility and usefulness for this task as well. Most scientists and engineers don't realize how many text-based analysis tools can be found within the desktop spreadsheet software they already have.

After going through this process, you should be able to answer the following questions:

- Who are the most active players in this field?
- What are the classifications that are most relevant to this technology area?
- Is this technology area heating up or cooling down?
- Is there significant interest from universities, government agencies, small players, or other technology providers?
- Who are the key inventors? And, whom do they work for?
- How is your company positioned in this field? Are you ahead of or behind your competition in patenting activity?

STEP 1: WHAT IS THE SCOPE OF THE LANDSCAPE?

Which technologies are you considering developing, or have you already developed? What alternatives exist? What technologies do your competitors employ? What bleeding-edge technologies are believed to be in development? Ideally, this will be an early step in your project, not something that is postponed until after the product design is finished (we'll talk more about timing in Part 3 when we discuss strategic inventing). You may not have answers to all of these questions, but thinking about all of the possible options will help you formulate your search strategy as well as the output required.

Also, keep in mind that you may have to refine your scope as the process develops. For example, you may find that your initial area of interest is so broad that it returns thousands of hits for all of your searches. This may be appropriate, but analyzing the data adequately will require an enormous amount of effort (and may require assistance from specialists). However, it's more likely that the scope is too broad and that many of these references can be removed from the data set by optimizing the search strategy. On the other hand, if you uncover very little prior art, perhaps you're defining your technology too narrowly.

You definitely don't want to start with too small a scope, particularly if this is a new area of development. You probably don't know every technology that is out there, and narrowly defining your scope may cause you to miss some cutting-edge new inventions. There is clearly a balance to be defined: a broader scope is usually better, but will require more effort to analyze; a narrower scope will be easier to analyze, but also will be more likely to miss emerging or adjacent technologies.

STEP 2: WHAT DO YOU ALREADY OWN?

Answering this question will require collecting information about existing technology that your company has already filed, including applications and granted patents. This will probably include filings that are not directly related to the current project, but that may indirectly affect your future strategy. If you work at a large corporation, there is a good chance that similar technologies and projects have existed before within your company. Be sure to investigate thoroughly to understand key areas where you may already have an established competitive advantage.

This step is often referred to as an "intellectual property (IP) audit" and may be an entirely separate endeavor as a means to understand the corporation's current assets. For patent strategy, however, any particular patent needs to be viewed in the context of the competitive landscape. Therefore, it is important that your competitive landscape also include information about your own company's assets. For example, if you have 10 patents related to XYZ technology, is that a lot? It's hard to say. What if I tell you that your competitor has 100 patents on the same technology? Now the perspective is more meaningful, and the contrast between each of the assignees in your analysis will be put in context. In this example, you may have some catching up to do. Numbers of filings are only an indicator, however. The true situation will only be illuminated by identification of key technologies and a closer examination of the claimed subject matter in each portfolio.

STEP 3: DETERMINE YOUR HISTORICAL AND GEOGRAPHICAL RANGE

Doing a global search may seem like a great idea when you start, but it usually isn't practical because of the number of hits that will be returned and the number of family members you'll find. For example, if one of your competitors has a filing strategy that leads it to file only in the United States, and another competitor files in 12 foreign geographies, the second competitor will appear to have a much stronger IP position. If these other geographies are relevant, that may be an accurate conclusion. However, if your company competes only in the United States, it may be misleading.

In general, I like to include U.S., European Patent Office (EPO), and Patent Cooperation Treaty (PCT) sources and will let the technology and the objective dictate the time frame. For most corporations in the United States, it makes a lot of sense to file key technologies in either the United States or the PCT, while foreign entities may file locally and then in the PCT. The net result is that most important technologies will end up being filed in at least one of the United States and the PCT, so neglecting other individual countries is often an acceptable approach for landscape-building purposes. However, it is always worthwhile to investigate the filing strategy of key competitors before you rely on this assumption. Create a simple search for assignees in your technology of interest and limit the results to the United States, then to the PCT, then to other potential geographies. Are the results similar? Do their PCT and U.S. applications claim priority to an earlier-filed local application?

Similar trade-offs can be made for the historical range of your analysis. For example, if you're looking for technologies on a fast development cycle or cutting-edge new developments, you might consider shortening the time frame to the last five years. Much less than five years can be misleading, however, so be careful not to draw too many conclusions from limited data sets. For example, if filing trends over time are of interest, these tend to be noisy data and definitely shouldn't be evaluated based on less than about five years' worth of data.

On the other hand, you may need to make sure that you capture all of the art that may be in force, which would mean going back at least 20 years from the time your product is likely to be launched. This would be a much more thorough approach, but it is likely to result in substantially more art in your analysis.

STEP 4: DEVELOP A SEARCH STRATEGY

This will probably mean combining a number of individual searches—key words, assignees, classes, maybe even key inventors. However, since you are building a technology landscape, you should generally avoid using too many entity-based terms (i.e., inventors and assignees).

For example, you may already know that your primary competitor is Company XYZ, Inc. However, XYZ may not be assigning all of its patent applications when they are filed. In fact, XYZ may choose never to register its assigned patents until after they are granted, so you could miss a large chunk of its holdings. Likewise, it may have acquired IP from another company or licensed-in technology from a university. None of these will show up with an assignee-based search.

It is certainly worthwhile to check the veracity of your results by adding assignees to your technology search, however. For example, once you have developed your key word– or class-based search, add the assignee = [your company] to the search. Does it return all of the technologies you uncovered in Step 2? Likewise, try the same search with your primary competitor—does it return known technologies? If the answer is no, you need to refine your search strategy.

It is not necessary to have 100 percent of the patents for a technology area in order to create a landscape. In fact, many insights can be uncovered with a much lower percentage—even 80 percent. The less thorough the search, however, the lower your confidence in the results should be. If your primary objective is to find out who the players in this technology area are, 80 percent is probably fine. For a more detailed threat analysis and forward-looking strategy development, a more complete search will be required.

STEP 5: COMPILE AND REFINE THE RESULTS

No matter how good your search strategy is, you will almost always end up with a percentage of "false positive" results. In other words, there are results that show up in the search, but that are not really relevant to your industry. For example, perhaps you're searching for insulin pumps, but some industrial pumps continually show up in your search results. You may be able to remove these within the search results by including a NOT term (e.g., NOT "concrete pump"). However, negative terms can be dangerous when constructing searches, so I prefer to avoid them unless they are necessary.

A more accurate way to refine the results is to compile all the results into one electronic file (if you're using multiple search strategies) and manually remove anything that doesn't look like it fits. Your patent database provider probably has tools to help you do this online, and this is one of the significant benefits of using a paid search engine. Manually refining these results can be time-consuming if you have a long list of patents, but it's definitely worth it in the long run.

At the end of this step, you should be reasonably comfortable that the results you have are of interest to you, and that you haven't missed too many relevant documents. I like to target at least 90 percent being relevant (i.e., upon closer examination, about 10 percent of the references are false positives and aren't really of interest), as well as making sure that I've captured at least 90 percent of the art that is relevant (in other words, up to 10 percent may have been missed by the search). Either of these numbers can be adjusted up or down depending on the objective of your landscape, as mentioned earlier. However, *don't* expect to be 100 percent accurate; it's not worth the effort, and you probably won't ever get there. It becomes exponentially more difficult to improve beyond the 90 percent threshold, and doing so is rarely a benefit to the overall strategy.

STEP 6: REMOVE DUPLICATES FROM THE RESULTS

As mentioned earlier, including multiple geographies can create some double-counting issues. In addition, PCT applications are frequently published multiple times (i.e., the same publication numbers ending in A1, A2, and A3 are the same application). Also, remember that a single application can result in multiple divisionals or continuations. Should you count these separately or only once? I prefer to count them separately, because pursuing multiple applications is usually an indication that significant resources are being devoted to this area (and therefore, that it is important to your competitor). This is clearly a subjective assessment, however, and arguments can be made that family members should be ignored.

You'll need to decide which of these are relevant enough to be counted if you are to best achieve your objective. If you do want to remove all duplicates in a family, this can usually be done within the database software or by exporting the INPADOC family number into your desktop spreadsheet software along with the other relevant fields and then removing duplicates based on that column. The most important consideration is to make sure that comparisons are made on an apples-to-apples basis; make sure the same process is used for all entities in the landscape. Double counting family members is fine as long as you're double counting for everyone.

STEP 7: PERFORM BASIC TREND ANALYSIS

Depending on the patent database you're using, you probably have access to tools for creating simple charts and graphs based on the search results from Step 5 or 6. If you don't, you should be able to export the search results into a spreadsheet and continue the analysis there. When exporting information, you'll want to include all the relevant fields, but probably not all the fields that are available. A good place to start would be to export the publication number, title, assignee, inventor, abstract, priority date, publication date, abstract, first claim and/or all claims, family members, and family number.

That sounds like a long list, but there are many other fields that you might consider. It would be worth a brief review of all the options provided by your search database, just in case one of the fields will help you answer a specific question—directly or indirectly. For example, you might be interested in how many times a particular publication has been referenced by other patents (the number of "forward citations"). This number is often used to indicate the perceived importance of a particular patent. If you do use this metric, remember that the longer a patent has been around, the more citations it is likely to have.

When evaluating trends over time, I usually use the publication date as the primary axis. Many people use the application date instead. However, even when the filing rate is constant, the application date will always show a negative trend over the last two years. This is due to the gradual publication of applications (i.e., some are published at less than three months as a result of earlier priority claims, whereas some go all the way up to the full 18 months or more). Data from the most recent two years are incomplete because not everything that was applied for in a given year will be published in that year. So, if you're presenting the data using the application year to an audience with less experience with patents, be careful to explain this limitation.

Another trend that can be interesting is viewing the results by priority date. This provides a view of when the inventing was actually being done. Related family members may show up as new applications and publish at much later dates—particularly for important technologies. By viewing trends based on priority date, we get a bit closer to when the original invention actually occurred. This can be particularly relevant when trying to understand if a competitor has stopped research in a particular area.

STEP 8: CATEGORIZE THE REFERENCES

This step will undoubtedly take some time, but it will also highlight the important issues for this technology area much more accurately. The key to this step is understanding which technologies can be grouped together into categories in a way that will be informative for your strategy. Generally, I would aim for less than 12 categories, but the important thing is to make sure that your categories adequately reflect the key segments of the technology or industry that you are analyzing. Five might be sufficient, but for some projects you may need more like 35.

In defining these categories, consider how technologies can be grouped along the value chain and/or as complementary or competing groups. Also, which technologies will be required to enable the next generation of products? Keep any of these separate from more traditional technologies.

This process usually requires at least some manual input and can be done either online or offline, depending on the software you have available. I usually like to do this in a spreadsheet, since it allows more freedom for analysis. One way to do this is to create a column for each category adjacent to the exported information, then type a number into each category column that is relevant for that application. Then, you can sort, filter, chart, pivot chart, pivot table, ad nauseam.

If the data set is large, text-analysis tools can be used to automate the categorization. It's always preferable to do the categorization manually, one reference at a time. Unfortunately, this usually isn't practical. Not many inventors have the time to review all of the patents manually. Some form of text analysis will probably be required, either through your database provider or using other tools. Microsoft Excel can be used to pull out key terms using the text functions. For example, the following formula will look to see if the term in cell A1 is found in cell B3, returning 1 if it's present and 0 if it isn't.

$$=ISNUMBER(SEARCH(\$A\$1,B3))*1$$

This formula can be pointed toward the abstract for each reference, then copied down the entire list of patents. In a few seconds, you have created a categorization based on key words in the abstract, as shown in the example in Table 11.1. While the presence of a key word indicates something about the subject matter, some amount of manual review will greatly enhance the categorization of these references. Manual annotations and adjustments to the categories can always be used to improve the overall results.

At this point, trend analysis similar to that in Step 7 can be performed, but much more resolution will be obtained. One of your goals should be to identify emerging technologies that are being developed by your competitors, or perhaps even by other industry players that aren't currently competing in your product categories.

Another way to look at this would be to create a chart of technology areas by assignee and include the number of references related to those key words in the appropriate cell. This will help create an easy-to-understand landscape that can be used for communication with management and your attorneys, with an emphasis on illustrating the differences in resource allocation between each of the assignees.

In Table 11.2, for example, Your Company appears to be leading the field in Category 1, but it is significantly lagging in Categories 4 and 5. Perhaps an alliance with Company 8 or Company 9 would be worth evaluating. Company 5 appears to be your most similar competitor, but Company 6 has a more balanced portfolio.

STEP 9: WHITE SPACE AND RED SPACE

After creating the technology trends and heat maps mentioned previously, you should start to get a feel for which areas of the prior art are already heavily patented by others. We can call these "red space." Future inventions in these areas may be more difficult to patent. Conversely,

Table 11.1   Identifying Key Words in a Spreadsheet

Number	Title	Assignee	Pub Date	Title Terms				Abstract Terms				Abstract
				Method	Cotton	Chocolate	Candy	Method	Cotton	Chocolate	Candy	
D635,621	Candy container	Sabritas, s. De R. L. De C. V.	4/5/11				1					—
7,811,621	Candy having a syrup composition dispersed with chocolate	Nestec S.A.	10/12/10			1	1			1	1	A candy product of chocolate and of a syrup confectionery composition which are interspersed so that the syrup confectionery composition defines a plurality of veins dispersed in the product.
7,641,460	Cotton candy handling device	C. Cretors & Company	1/5/10		1		1	1	1			A device and method for continuous production of cotton candy and automated handling of the cotton candy in a way that collects and condenses the cotton candy into a continuous strand.
8,092,847	Candy product and method of making same	N/A	1/10/12	1			1					A body (60) of hard candy is formed on a tubular stem (32) that extends from a reservoir/handle (12) in which an edible fluid (72) is contained. The outer end (36) of the tubular passageway (32) is open.
7,931,835	Heater control for cotton candy spinner head	Gold Medal Products Company Inc.	4/26/11		1		1		1		1	Within a cotton candy machine a delay-on-break delay timer is used to delay the de-energization of the spinner-head motor for a predetermined period of time after the heater elements are turned off.

Table 11.2   A Company-Technology Landscape

	Category 1	Category 2	Category 3	Category 4	Category 5	Category 6
Your Company	31	15	12	0	0	16
Company 2	3	2	10	22	28	2
Company 3	4	5	8	19	29	3
Company 4	0	1	3	16	17	15
Company 5	26	15	3	2	1	4
Company 6	15	11	10	12	15	19
Company 7	0	0	18	2	1	1
Company 8	0	2	3	31	1	0
Company 9	0	0	0	2	28	2

there may be technology areas with very little prior art, and these are "white space." When doing a competitive landscape, it's always a good idea to have a subjective analysis of the white and red space in mind to help guide product development strategy as well as target future inventions (i.e., engage in strategic inventing). White space will be much more friendly toward establishing a competitive advantage because of the likelihood of having broad claims granted that can be more readily used to protect against competitive imitation. Red space is more likely to have FTO risk as well as allowing only relatively narrow claims, which may be of lesser value.

While it is important to know which technologies fall into the white and red space, don't assume that red space must be avoided. Just because a field has been highly patented doesn't mean that there are no opportunities left. It might just mean that it is an extremely valuable market for whoever can best address the consumer's needs in this area.

VISUALIZATION

Don't overlook the importance of visualizing the output of your efforts. If you do this work yourself, you may learn a great deal about your competition. However, you'll need to be able to communicate this information to others. If your corporation has patent analysts or consultants who do the analysis for you, make sure that you understand their conclusions and can present this information in a concise, yet meaningful way. Usually, this requires a visual output of some kind.

Some options might include:

- A company-technology landscape
- Filing trend analysis to identify which categories are heating up or cooling down

- Overall filing rates categorized by classification codes or competitors
- A network map of assignees to identify collaborations where formal collaborations haven't been announced
- An inventor analysis to identify key inventors and their networks of co-inventors

IMPORTANT CAVEATS

Some attorneys are hesitant about relying on landscape analysis because it is inherently imprecise. The geographic scope, search strategies, duplicates, divisionals, assignee changes, M&A, and differences in filing strategies can all lead to results that don't accurately reflect reality. They do have a point—this kind of analysis is not an exact science. Any conclusions drawn from this exercise should be considered *indications* of the competitive landscape, but not absolute truth. Creating a landscape is an exploratory process, and is used to identify good questions as much as it is used to find answers. I like to think of it this way: would you prefer to play chess blindfolded or with blurry glasses? A patent landscape will never be better than blurry glasses, but it's much better than the alternative.

SO HOW LONG SHOULD THIS TAKE?

The effort required for this process will vary greatly. It depends on the size of the data set, the uniqueness of your industry's key words, and the degree of accuracy required to meet your objectives. Developing a good search strategy can be done quickly if your industry has unusual terminology that makes it easy to identify references of interest, but it might take much longer.

As a first step, familiarize yourself with the tools that are available (e.g., the basics of how to search, online analysis, and exporting). Once you're comfortable with the tools, I would generally set aside about one day for developing the search strategy and two days for a basic analysis. If it takes much less than that, you're probably missing something important.

In a field with relatively little art, I would definitely suggest that the inventor be directly involved in creating the landscape. If there are thousands of references, don't attempt to do this yourself. Work with an internal or external specialist to make sure that you get the results you need in order to develop a strategy for your project.

KEY POINTS TO REMEMBER

The outline provided in this chapter is a starting point to give you perspective on the basic steps and the issues to consider. There are many different ways to evaluate a patent landscape, and you'll probably find some of these techniques more helpful than others. In some technology areas, you may need the help of patent analysis specialists or consultants. However you choose to pursue this analysis, you cannot develop a good patent strategy without first understanding the competitive landscape.

CHAPTER 12

VISUALIZING
PATENT SPACE

One difficulty in comparing and contrasting patent strategies is that comprehending the implications of particular patents relative to competitors' positions or even your own portfolio can be very difficult. Visualizing the impact of patents in a spatial diagram can support both comprehension and communication. In my experience, the best way to do this is with two-dimensional "blob" diagrams. These diagrams are not intended to capture all relevant information, but rather to highlight key positions relative to one another based on relationships among the technologies of the different inventions.

These diagrams are best done on a whiteboard while brainstorming for potential patent strategies and/or identifying white space, which represents opportunity for new inventions. The goal of these diagrams is to be simple enough to be readily understood and easily communicated so that the primary objectives can be addressed without getting stuck in the minutiae.

A SIMPLE EXAMPLE: BUILDING FENCES

One of the most straightforward diagrams, which also serves as a description of a common patent strategy, is building "fences" or "thickets" around a key technology. In Figure 12.1, you see the primary invention (P1) surrounded by a number of potential alternative technologies (A2 to A8). The primary invention is most likely where your company is planning to practice, and is believed to be the most valuable space to protect. However, there are always potential alternatives that might be left to your competitors, even if your claims protecting P1 are strong. In filing these closely related patents around your core technology, you are hoping to protect against imitation by a competitor using similar technology that is outside

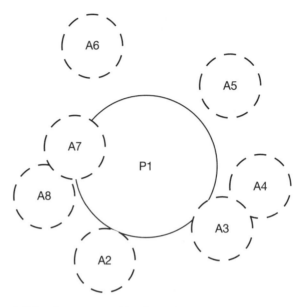

Figure 12.1   Building fences around key inventions

the claims scope of P1 and against alternative methods of achieving the same consumer benefit using different technology.

In Figure 12.1, proximity is used to illustrate similarities in the technology, and overlaps of the circles indicate some overlap in the claim space. For example, A6 is more distinct from P1 than A7 is. In fact, A7 shares some but not all of the claim space of P1. Overlapping claims might exist when P1 includes product-focused claims and A7 includes process-focused claims. The process is useful for making the product in question, but it could also be used to make similar products that are outside the claims of the primary invention.

PROGRESS OVER TIME

One variation of this diagram would be to illustrate key technologies as they progress over time. In Figure 12.2, for example, your internal technology is currently distinct from a competitor's technology. However, as time progresses and performance improves, the next generation's technology may be the same for both. As the technologies converge, establishing a strong patent position will be key to maintaining your market position. If you can identify this technology before your competitor does, you will have a distinct advantage in constructing a patent position while much of the technology area is still white space.

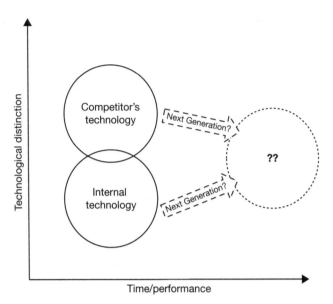

Figure 12.2 Visualizing key patent positions of today and into the future

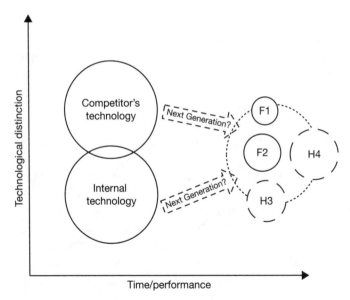

Figure 12.3 Insight into the future creates filing opportunities

As shown in Figure 12.3, you might consider filing inventions related to this evolving technology (labeled F1 and F2) even if the technology needed to fully realize the final product isn't completely developed. These could be key enabling technologies, for example.

In some situations, it may be worthwhile to consider filing "prophetic" applications even if you haven't fully developed the core technology yet. I personally prefer to call these "hypothetical" rather than prophetic filings simply because it doesn't require a prophet to do the inventing. Rather, any scientist who can enable the claims without actually having experimental results can describe the invention as a hypothesis, and the patent application can be filed. Furthermore, these applications may prove to be valuable for freedom-to-operate (FTO) reasons even if they are not granted. The amount of data required to file does vary by industry, however, so it may be worthwhile to discuss with your attorney the amount of data he requires before he will file the application. Attorneys will almost always prefer to have more data, so make sure you press him on what is "needed" as opposed to what is "nice to have."

Consider illustrating your current and future patent positions using diagrams similar to those in Figures 12.2 and 12.3.

THE BRIDGE DIAGRAM

Another diagram that I find helpful is a "bridge" of technologies across the value chain, from starting materials to delivering the end consumer benefit. These diagrams can be complicated, but they will help you identify opportunities for strong patent positions that may be outside the scope of your current filings. It's also important to recognize that alternative ways to deliver a benefit significantly decrease the value of a patent position, even if the claims are very strong.

For example, in Figure 12.4, a series of steps defined by key technologies, from the starting material to the consumer benefit, is created using a series of shapes. Each shape represents a key technology but does not necessarily represent a patent. For example, some of these alternative methods may not be patented at all. However, knowing the alternatives exist will help to illustrate the strategic importance of that technology. If there are equivalent alternatives in the public domain, creating a valuable patent position will be nearly impossible.

Some technologies, like R2, are required for any method of creating the product. This would be an extremely valuable patent position. On the other hand, technologies A1, A2, and A3 are alternative methods for delivering the same functional step in the value chain—these are likely to be of less value unless a proprietary position can be established for each alternative. Likewise, the single-step technology S will require fewer patents to establish a position than will the multistep alternative S1 to S4.

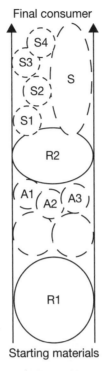

Figure 12.4   The bridge model for visualizing the value chain

This type of illustration can be useful in visualizing the relative value of patent positions across the value chain. In particular, if the scope of your company is limited to R1 through R2, it may still be worthwhile to establish a position in the S and S1 to S4 technologies, if possible. This approach may serve primarily defensive purposes, to ensure that your customers have FTO.

VISUALIZING WHITE SPACE

As mentioned in the previous chapter, identifying white space and red space is an important step in understanding the competitive situation. When you've finished your patent landscape, it may be helpful to create simple diagrams using the approaches discussed in this chapter to illustrate which technologies are primarily being pursued by which competitors, and which technologies appear to be white space. The quantitative numbers resulting from the categorization we previously discussed may need to be turned into conceptual representations that help to visualize the strategic situation in more simple terms.

It is often as important to illustrate the white space—that is, the areas where there is currently no prior art—as it is to illustrate the existing patent landscape. In other words, most of these illustrations focus on the patents and applications that already exist in the prior art—the red space. It is extremely important to know this information for your competitors' filings, emerging competitors, and technology providers (i.e., potential collaborators). However, it's the space where there *isn't* yet a publication that provides the greatest opportunity for future filings. In other words, we need to identify the *absence* of filings as much as the presence of filings.

What if there is no white space? In general, jumping to the conclusion that there is no opportunity for invention is usually the result of an incomplete analysis. Or perhaps it's the result of a less creative analysis. In my experience, average attorneys will tell you what cannot be filed because of existing prior art. Great attorneys, however, will help you develop alternatives that fit within nearby spaces and allow for some level of protection. Perhaps the product needs to be changed slightly. Perhaps a slightly more complicated approach would allow for more significant protection. Perhaps some of the assumptions need to be changed. Perhaps a nascent technology can be combined with your current embodiment. We'll address these questions, and the role of white space in defining invention strategy, in more detail in Part 3 of this book, when we discuss techniques for strategic inventing.

CHAPTER 13

NOT ALL CLAIMS ARE CREATED EQUAL

The competitive landscape and related visualizations will give you great information about the relative magnitude of filings from competitors, technology providers, and even your own corporation. However, to make key decisions, you need to look closely at each patent and application that may affect your project. The information provided by the landscape primarily describes resource allocation, but it usually can't provide much detailed information about specific claims because there are too many individual references to evaluate simultaneously. However, the landscape will help you identify key areas for detailed analysis, with an emphasis on deciding which patents actually matter and which can be ignored.

In fact, many of the patents in your competitive landscape may have little impact on your patent strategy. Having a patent on a product doesn't necessarily create any useful competitive advantage, because the value of a patent can be dramatically affected by the content of the claims that are granted. This misunderstanding can be seen in the common late-night TV advertisements for invention-submission services, which often manipulate this misconception to promote their products. It can be relatively easy to get a patent granted if the scope of the claims is extremely narrow. For some invention-promotion scams, for example, the inventor would be supplied with design patents to protect what should have been filed as a utility application (or simply not filed at all).

As we discussed in Chapter 3, there are two common types of claims: product and method (also referred to as "process"). In general, your invention is described as either a thing or a series of steps; it's either a noun or a verb. The same product, however, may involve both product and method claims—product claims related to the thing itself, and method claims related to making and using the product.

How the claims are written will have a great impact on the likelihood of their being granted as well as on their strategic value. Different claims strategies will yield significantly different results.

The first concept that we'll address is the overall scope of the claims—how much space do these claims protect?

BROAD OR NARROW

Claims covering more or less technological space are generally referred to as being either relatively broad or relatively narrow with respect to a certain parameter. A claim with a wider numerical range of coverage would be said to have broader protection. In the following example, Claim 1 is significantly broader than Claim 2.

Claim 1. The mixture of Compounds A, B, C, and D, wherein D is between 25 and 75 percent of the mixture.

Claim 2. The mixture of compounds A, B, C, and D, wherein D is between 25 and 30 percent of the mixture.

Claim 3. The mixture of compounds A, B, and D, wherein D is between 25 and 75 percent of the mixture.

With regard to Claim 3, note that this claim lacks Component C. Claim 3 is broader than Claim 1 or Claim 2 because it lacks one of the elements entirely. Remember, to infringe a claim, the infringer must practice *each* element of the claim. Therefore, the more elements the claim requires, the less likely it is to be infringed.

In general, shorter claims tend to be broader and longer claims tend to be narrower. Keep in mind, however, that the relative breadth of claims usually can't be established without knowing the significance of the individual components, such as how important they are to the final product and whether or not alternatives are readily available.

In fact, it is almost always possible to get some kind of claim granted for a product by writing the claim extremely narrowly. The narrower a claim is, the more likely it is to be granted. However, narrow claims may not prevent your competitors from imitating your product, especially if there are readily available opportunities to design around your claims. As a result, these claims are likely to be much less valuable.

There is one key exception to this rule: in a situation in which the product is narrowly defined and alternatives are not available, even very narrow claims can be valuable. For example, regulatory costs and delays for developing alternatives may discourage imitators with *similar* products. Since it is the exact compound that has been approved by the regulatory bodies, even minor variations cannot be sold as the same thing. Furthermore, even narrow claims will satisfy the need for establishing ownership and transferable rights, which may be required for contracts and technology licenses.

Depending on your industry, there will be specific structures of claims that are written more often than others. The basic framework will always be the same, but there are unique practices that go beyond product/method and independent/dependent. In fact, some technology areas (e.g., biotechnology) have unique methods of claiming that are rarely used elsewhere. The best way to investigate the types of claims that are relevant to your technology is by doing a quick patent search using assignees (your company and key competitors) along with a few technology key words. Read the claims in recent applications related to your technology, as well as some granted claims.

Finally, keep in mind that most new developments can usually be claimed in many different ways, including both product and process claims. Creative claim construction is a great opportunity for collaboration between attorneys and inventors.

THE VALUE OF PRODUCT VERSUS METHOD CLAIMS

While the specifics of your invention and the related art will probably influence the type of claims filed for your invention, it's important to recognize that the type of claims often has significant strategic implications. Furthermore, product and method claims are usually both possible, even if the core invention is of the opposite category. For example, if the invention is a highly valuable product, numerous related patent applications are likely to be filed in an attempt to claim the final product, intermediates, processes for making, methods of using, and so on. Each of these patents will create a different form of protection and hopefully preclude the competition from imitating your product.

However, product and method claims have some significant strategic differences. In particular, claims related to the final product are usually easily analyzed for infringement and easily enforced because the invention is exchanged in commerce. Process claims often suffer from the opposite problem: there may not be an easy way to know if they are being infringed. In general, it is often assumed that product claims offer greater value than process claims because of the ease of enforcement. This is not always true, but it is something that should be considered in your overall filing strategy.

With respect to method claims, a key question to consider is whether or not there is an avenue for enforcement. Is there some kind of unique property left in the article of commerce that can be tied to the patented process—that is, a "fingerprint"? A process with no detectable fingerprint will be relatively difficult to enforce.

Does this mean that it isn't worth filing method claims if there isn't an associated fingerprint? Not necessarily. Remember that filing a product claim will require enablement of the invention, as well as disclosure of the best mode. You may be required to describe the process in the application. If so, there is no benefit to not claiming the process. This is also an important argument for strategically defining the scope and timing of each application, as the disclosure in one application is likely to affect the scope of patentability of all later applications.

Furthermore, many companies are ethical when it comes to respecting well-defined patent rights, particularly in technology areas that would present significant investment risk. For example, if large equipment is involved and the process requires significant investment in steel in the ground, this would be considered a significant risk if that process were found to be infringing. Even if you cannot identify a process infringer based on a publicly available fingerprint, ethical competitors will avoid infringing on your valid patent claims.

Claim Scope—An Example

The following is a favorite example, in part because it's entertaining to read, but also because it describes a patent that was granted for something that most people might think was unpatentable: playing with your cat using a laser pointer. In fact, the claims are much narrower than they appear at first glance, given that they require specific apparatus to be involved.

Take a look at US 6,701,872 for additional detail. For our purposes, I've extracted the first seven claims here.

1. An apparatus for exercising a curious animal comprising: a pedestal; a motor having a shaft, said motor being mounted to the pedestal; and a laser pointer producing a spot beam and mounted on said shaft to project the spot beam from the pedestal, said motor causing said shaft to oscillate so that said spot beam tracks about said pedestal with a vector of motion to attract the curious animal into interaction with the spot beam.

2. The apparatus according to claim 1 wherein said shaft is generally vertically disposed.

3. The apparatus according to claim 2 wherein motion of said shaft invokes complete rotation of said spot beam.

4. The apparatus according to claim 1 wherein motion of said shaft invokes complete rotation of said spot beam.

5. The apparatus according to claim 1 wherein the rotatable shaft is preferably generally vertically disposed and the disposition of the laser pointer is preferably obliquely downward so that activation of the motor causes the spot beam to track around the pedestal.

6. An apparatus for exercising a curious animal comprising: a pedestal; a motor having a shaft, said motor being mounted to the pedestal; a laser pointer producing a spot beam and mounted on said shaft to project the spot beam from the pedestal, said motor causing said shaft to oscillate so that said spot beam tracks about said pedestal with a vector of motion to attract the curious animal into interaction with the spot beam; and an oscillatory air circulation fan on a head, wherein said motor is mounted to provide oscillatory motion of said head, and wherein said laser pointer is mounted to said head such that said motor induces oscillation of the spot beam about said pedestal, together with the air movement of the oscillatory fan to stimulate activity in a cat while conveniently inducing convective cooling.

7. A method for automatically exercising a curious animal comprising: providing a laser spot beam from a fixed location to an exercise area; causing said spot beam to move under automatic action of a motor with a vector of motion to induce interaction of the curious animal with the spot beam.

Recall from our earlier discussion that claims can be separated into independent and dependent claims. Figure 13.1 illustrates an approximation of the claims just given. The size of each circle shows the scope of each claim, and each circle's position shows its dependence (or lack thereof) on other claims. The relative sizes are subjective assessments, although dependent claims will always be smaller than any claims on which they are based.

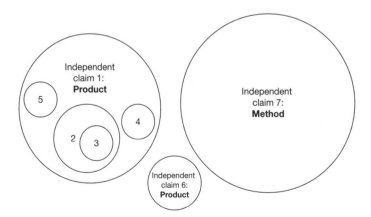

Figure 13.1   A rough diagram of the first seven claims of US 6,701,872

Claims 2, 3, 4, and 5 are dependent on Claim 1 and therefore must be smaller in scope—each has added at least one element to Claim 1, thereby making it narrower in scope. Claim 6 is an independent claim, but it includes more limitations than Claim 1, so it is represented with smaller scope. Claim 7 is a method claim, entirely distinct from the product claims, and therefore it is more difficult to estimate its scope (given that I'm not an expert in this technology category, of course). However, I would suggest that Claim 7 is of at least the same order of magnitude as Claim 1, if not greater. Claim 7 requires none of the apparatus-specific limitations found in Claim 1, which makes Claim 1 potentially easier for a competitor to design around.

While we're on the subject, how would you get outside the scope of Claim 1? The primary requirement to avoid infringement is to eliminate at least one element of the claim from your product. For example, if you made a device exactly as described in Claim 1, but lacking the pedestal (e.g., hanging from the ceiling), it would not infringe. Likewise, a similar apparatus lacking a motor would also not infringe. If we continue with our ceiling-mounted product, perhaps it could be made to oscillate using the earth's rotation as a traditional pendulum, avoiding the need for a motor.

TO FILE OR NOT TO FILE?

The primary goal of drafting and filing patent applications is to obtain granted patents with well-constructed, strategically relevant claims. However, a good patent strategy should always include an evaluation of alternatives—including *not* filing patents. The key options to consider include keeping the invention a trade secret and publishing the invention.

In many companies, patenting (or not patenting) is ingrained enough in the corporate culture that the standard practice usually carries the day. However, a specific strategy should be developed for each product, and the result may be significantly different strategies for similar products. A few examples include the following:

- Different competitive situations may create a unique cost-benefit relationship. For example, your competition may be focused on countries with minimal enforcement of intellectual property (IP) rights.
- The relevant patent law may have changed. Perhaps the statutory subject matter has expanded or contracted (something that is particularly likely if the invention involves biotechnology, software, or business methods).
- The overall value of the product may not justify the cost of obtaining and enforcing protection.

- Your strategy may be affected by recent changes in patent law that have provided more protection for processes that are already in use (i.e., "prior user rights").

Patent or Trade Secret?

Another important consideration is whether the invention should be kept as a trade secret. Trade secrets have some distinct strategic advantages and disadvantages. Most important, a trade secret is valid only as long as the technology is kept secret, which potentially could be forever.

In general, process innovations are more likely to be kept as trade secrets, particularly if there are no clues left in the product that would aid in reverse-engineering it (e.g., commodity chemical manufacturing). As we discussed earlier, products are much less likely to be kept as a trade secret, since nearly all products can be reverse-engineered once competitors gain access to the product.

However, the disclosure required for filing a patent application and enabling the best mode may be more detrimental to the overall strategy than simply keeping the information secret. For example, in industries with very fast-moving product cycles, the patent may not even be granted within the useful life of the product. In this situation, the value of a trade secret may outweigh the value of a patent.

It is possible to keep a trade secret and file an application at the same time by filing a request for "nonpublication" of the application. This is possible only if no related applications will be filed in foreign countries and is a relatively rare approach, particularly for multinational companies. However, it will postpone publication of the application (and keep the technology secret longer) while still preserving the right to obtain a patent.

Key questions to consider in the decision concerning whether to file a patent application or keep the invention a secret include the following:

- Is it patentable subject matter?
- What kinds of claims are likely to be granted?
- Would a patent help to establish a competitive advantage?
- Is the timing required for publication, granting, and expiration appropriate for the product in question?
- Would it be possible to keep the technology a secret for a long period—more than 20 years?
- Are there intangible benefits or concerns, such as public acceptance of a new technology?
- Are patents needed to define transferable rights for licensing or sale of the technology?

Patent *or* Publish?

Another consideration is whether the technology would be better off with nonpatented publication. In most situations, publication in nonpatent literature, such as a scientific journal, will not hinder the filing of related patents as long as the patent filing precedes the publication. In other words, if a research scientist is determined to have his results recognized by the academic community, this is still possible in parallel with the filing of a patent application.

The primary benefit from publishing information about a technology when you are not filing a patent application would be to destroy the patentability of this technology—both for you and for your competitors. In other words, this is solely a defensive strategy. Perhaps you don't think the invention is valuable enough to file at present, but you want to make sure you aren't blocked from potentially using it in the future. Publication would be more cost-effective than filing a patent application, and will still preserve your ability to practice this invention. So, when should you publish?

- If you are unlikely to be granted a patent, but you are afraid that others might be more likely to be successful.
- If your objectives are solely defensive (i.e., freedom to operate [FTO]).
- If the cost to obtain patent protection outweighs the potential benefit created by the patent.
- If the timeline for the patent is not appropriate for the project.
- For greater intangible benefits, such as transparency and public acceptance.
- After *all* related patents are filed. (For a U.S.-only business, there is the one-year grace period; however, it's rarely a good idea to rely on the grace period unless this is necessary.)

Patent *and* Publish

As mentioned in our earlier discussion on the 2011 America Invents Act (AIA) law changes, there is also a potential benefit to publishing an invention because of the initiation of the one-year grace period for filing an application and associated priority over a competitor's application that is filed during that year. While the implications of this approach are still being worked out, it would never be advisable to rely on this approach when you are seeking protection in non-U.S. geographies that have absolute novelty rules.

However, there may be some situations in which a U.S.-only strategy would benefit from this approach. For example, immediate publication might preempt a competitor's publication (for example, if a competitor with a similar invention was planning to publish something next week, you could preempt that competitor by publishing tomorrow). In this instance, you may be able to establish a publication date sooner than you could establish a patent application date.

Situations of this type are likely to be rare, so this would seem to be an unlikely strategy for most corporations. However, it is still early in the development of practice in this area, so you may see some creative strategies come to light in the future. If there is ever a situation of intense time pressure, it would certainly be worth a discussion with your attorney to determine how best to handle the situation—whether by preemptive publication or by filing an application. However, keep in mind that this approach is limited to U.S.-only strategies and will have negative implications for absolute novelty countries.

CHAPTER 14

EIGHT PORTFOLIO STRATEGY MODELS

One objective of defining a patent strategy for your project is to make sure that the individual applications work together to achieve your overall strategic goals. In most industries, a single application is unlikely to provide all the protection needed to establish a significant competitive advantage in the marketplace. Alternatives may exist that make claiming every reasonable variation almost impossible within a single application, not to mention the challenge of predicting future developments that might alter the landscape.

Furthermore, the timing of each filing is likely to create consequences for later-filed applications. In some situations, these may be deliberate, but they may also be the result of external factors that are beyond the corporation's control (e.g., requirements for regulatory disclosure). A strategy for coordinating your inventions across multiple applications will help meet your overall objectives.

THE MODELS

The models described in this chapter are intended to illustrate potential differences among strategies for multiple patents and applications at the project level or above. For example, the "incremental features" model (lots of patents, each with modest value) is at the opposite end of the spectrum from the "silver strand" model (a small number of patents with extremely high value). Most corporations will fall somewhere between these two extremes and are likely to find that different patent strategies are appropriate for different projects within the same company. Your corporation's overall strategy will probably determine the level of resources available for filing patents and the way in which patents are used, but the appropriate strategy for any given project is always a function of the project's intellectual property (IP) needs, the competitive landscape, business needs related to licensing and/or value capture, and the patentability of the product itself.

These models are not mutually exclusive. Rather, you will probably find that a blend of approaches works best for your project. The question to consider is which model best fits each aspect of your project. Perhaps one part of the project would be most efficiently introduced using an open-source model, whereas another part needs strong protection requiring multiple filings, and another aspect lends itself to competitively focused and prophetic applications. Perhaps the core technology can be protected by one single patent (e.g., a new compound), but the overall project has many different features that fit the incremental model better.

Furthermore, your industry will probably have patent strategy models that are unique to the needs of your technologies and your competition. Ask your attorney to describe the models typically used in your field of interest. Perhaps even consider creating new models to meet your strategic objectives more effectively.

The Picket Fence

With the classic "fence" strategy, the primary objective is to create enough obstacles around a fundamental invention to make imitative products difficult to create without infringing, and design-around inventions more challenging. This strategy was mentioned in Chapter 12 during our discussion of visualizing patent strategies and illustrated in Figure 12.1.

Frequently, the same product can be created using several different technologies. The inventor may not even know which process competitors use to make their product (although this would be a good topic for a competitive-intelligence effort). Remember that the objective of a patent strategy is to create a competitive advantage—that is, something that your competitors cannot imitate. While your fundamental invention is most likely aimed at your internal business and product strategies along with your established processes and manufacturing capabilities, your competitors' situations may be different. If you protect only the invention that you will practice, you may miss the product that is most economical for one of your competitors to produce.

In order to define each of the individual inventions that will make up this fence, consider which technologies your competitors are most likely to use. What are they good at? Do they have platform technologies or processes that are likely to be employed? Do they have "steel in the ground" that differs from yours? Would they make combinations with other products in their portfolio? Are there enabling technologies that will be required in order to make the invention faster, better, cheaper, with greater stability, or with longer shelf life?

As you consider these questions, you may be thinking: yes, but I can't invent using my competitors' equipment or technology. This may be a valid concern. Most companies have limited equipment and expertise in their competitors' areas of strength. Don't forget that you can file on hypothetical ("prophetic") inventions without actually reducing them to practice. Some attorneys are reluctant to file on prophetic inventions because there are fewer data and less support for the invention, which may make it more difficult to obtain a patent. But, even if the proposed invention may not work as described, and even if the validity of your patent may be questioned, negative consequences are usually modest, since you aren't expecting to practice this invention anyway.

The Silver Strand

Another strategy that is frequently employed is what can be called the "silver strand." Unfortunately, this often describes something that is not so much an intentional strategy as an acknowledgment of the situation. A silver strand means that a company's competitive advantage relies largely on a single key invention or a small group of inventions, such as a pharmaceutical composition. While the patent is in force, protection is very strong. It is nearly impossible to design around the invention because of the regulatory requirements for marketing the product, and because of the ease of testing and enforcement for any potential infringer. This single strand supports a highly profitable business, hence its silver hue.

However, that strand will break suddenly and completely, leaving little or no protection. Consider a pharmaceutical company that relies heavily on one or two patented blockbuster products. When one of its star products goes off-patent, generic manufacturers are likely to swoop in with their own versions of the formula. This generally means that the original innovative company must drop its prices and will probably lose market share very quickly.

While the strong initial protection creates an enviable position, the rapid loss of protection can have catastrophic consequences. Where possible, some form of strategic inventing may be considered to minimize this effect through deliberate methods of life-cycle management.

Incremental Features

Unlike the companies in the previous example, companies in many industries are unable to produce a regular flow of breakthrough inventions that can be protected with such certainty. In these industries (consumer products, for example), incremental change is the name of the game. Each minor invention brings additional value to the product, but at the end of the day, it is only a small piece of a much larger strategic position. This portfolio will build gradually and decay gradually. The gradual growth and loss may result from progress in the development of a single feature (i.e., each invention builds on the previous), or they may be based on multiple different inventions that are incorporated into a single product.

One potential feature of this model is that the pace of innovation may require that the product also change along with the life span of patent protection. In other words, both the patent strategy and the product will be changing over time. A constant stream of innovations is required to keep the product competitive in the marketplace, and a constant stream of inventions is required to keep a meaningful patent strategy in place.

Many complex products with multiple features fit this model—for example, automobiles, electronics, and computers. The device performs many individual functions, so few features can be captured by each individual invention. Likewise, each feature has an independent development cycle that may not correspond to the development cycle of the other features, leading to the gradual development and decay of the value associated with each protected feature.

The Teddy Roosevelt

As we slide up the scale from individual patents to macro strategies, one important strategy has been attracting a lot of attention in recent years. This strategy focuses on the collection of an enormous portfolio of patent applications (usually in the hundreds or even thousands) that serves as a deterrent to competitors. The sheer scope and magnitude of any potential lawsuit is daunting. This approach is analogous to the nuclear strategy called "mutual assured destruction" (MAD). No one will attack this entity because the potential legal backlash has immeasurable implications.

To play off Teddy Roosevelt's famous words, "Speak softly and carry a big patent portfolio."

This approach is probably not as relevant to the average corporate inventor as it is to the C-level executives who may or may not decide to invest enormous amounts of resources in building and/or acquiring a gigantic "big stick" patent portfolio.

On a smaller scale, it is still worth considering a similar strategy for specific technologies. It may be worth intentionally developing a large portfolio around a key technology, particularly if this technology area is likely to result in lawsuits. As the portfolio grows, the hope is that the incentive to avoid litigation will encourage licensing and other amicable transactions.

Of course, the *number* of patents and applications filed does not necessarily dictate the *value* of a patent position. It's the granted claims that really matter. But, given the inherently complex nature of patent claims, the intricate—and ever-changing—rules, courts' occasionally inconsistent approaches to claim interpretation, and thus uncertain enforcement prospects, more usually is better.

The Nonpracticing Entity

Another common strategy involves companies that are not actually competing in a given technology arena—nonpracticing entities (NPEs) that hold a large portfolio of patents but produce no actual products. These corporations are sometimes derisively called "trolls"—particularly by those who find themselves on the receiving end of an infringement suit. However, it's important to recognize that the granted patents in question are still related to inventions that required resources to develop.

Why then, are NPEs so often derided by others that do compete in the marketplace? One reason is that an NPE cannot be countersued. In most patent lawsuits, the recipient of the infringement claim will quickly evaluate the competitor's products and its own patent portfolio to find any patents that can be used to create a plausible countersuit. This procedure is likely to dilute the effect of the initial lawsuit, with the result, it is hoped, being minimal impact on the corporation's business. With an NPE, there is nothing on which to file a countersuit. The MAD rationale mentioned earlier no longer applies—one party risks very little in filing a lawsuit.

At this point, you're probably thinking that these must be horrible entities indeed, and why should they be allowed to exist? In fact, there are probably many more NPEs out there than you currently have in mind. Universities are a great example. While many of them support research, patenting, and licensing, most universities don't make any actual products. So, when a university comes knocking on your door insisting that you obtain a license, there are usually no grounds for a countersuit.

Patents are intended to help encourage innovation by providing inventors with a reasonable reward for the resources used in making those inventions. If the inventions are indeed valid, these entities also deserve a reasonable reward. In many of the disputes that make the news, the inventions in question are of dubious validity, which makes the discussion slanted at best. As a matter of principle, however, NPEs are well within the intent of the patent system.

How might this be relevant to your company (assuming that you don't already work at an NPE)? Any company, no matter what its focus, practices in a limited range of technologies and services. For those fields in which you do not compete, you are essentially an NPE. In other words, if you consider the strategy from the technology level and not the corporate level, there may be an opportunity to monetize inventions in indirectly related fields. Perhaps your invention in medical electronics could be used in Walmart's inventory tracking system. Perhaps your patent portfolio for the analysis of satellite imagery could be relevant to real estate valuation.

Much has previously been written on this topic, and readers might want to consult books such as *Edison in the Boardroom Revisited* by Harrison and Sullivan (2011) for a more thorough discussion of monetizing noncore intellectual property.

Bundling and Patent Pools

In this model, several entities bundle patents together to enable a particular product or standard, using shared technology. This approach is common in electronics because of the problems in getting products by different manufacturers to work with each other.

If each manufacturer held to its own plug style for data transfer, consumers would need dozens of cables, possibly one for each possible combination of products. So manufacturers have worked together to create some standard interfaces, such as the IEEE 1394 ("Firewire") standard, which is protected by dozens of patents held by 10 different companies.

This kind of bundling supports broader market penetration and minimizes complexity for consumers. It is also useful in areas where independent development is not profitable, but the technology is still required in order to implement the product. For example, perhaps new regulatory requirements are causing significant changes to key aspects of producing your product, but these changes offer no direct benefit to the consumer. The consumer probably won't want to pay for them, and your company most likely won't have a competitive advantage, since the entire industry is required to move to the new standard. Pooling resources might allow for lower individual investment while still maximizing value for your company.

Open Source and Crowdsourcing

Another valid strategy is to deliberately avoid patented technology altogether. This has recently become much more popular with the development of large open-source collaborative projects such as Wikipedia and Linux. Crowdsourcing and innovations in business models that emphasize microcollaborations have also reduced the focus on patent protection. In some instances, such as Wikipedia, these new approaches are nonprofit efforts. The range of possibilities also includes partial openness, as can be seen in the developer-driven "app" community for mobile phones and tablets.

At the extreme, all patent rights could be given over to the community or even formally abandoned. This may be a reasonable strategic decision if the benefit of including others in the development of the product outweighs the potential benefit of exclusive differentiated features. Perhaps the development costs outweigh the value to the corporation unless they are shared between multiple entities. Or perhaps the development has many applications outside your industry, and competing against the broad spectrum of alternatives is infeasible (for example, the development of a technological "tool" with applications in many industries).

As of this writing, HP has recently decided to convert webOS to open-source. By the time you read this, you'll probably be able to evaluate whether or not this was a good strategic decision.

The Predictive Portfolio

Patent strategy is inherently a forward-looking endeavor. Patents take years to be granted, and may be in force for up to 21 years from the date when you first filed the application. That's a long time horizon for strategic planning. Nonetheless, it is often possible to predict which products and technologies will affect your category in the future. For example, consider weather forecasting. It is sometimes easier to predict what will happen six months from now than it is to predict what will happen six days from now—I don't know whether it will rain next week, but I do know that it will be cold in January. The same may be true of your industry—you cannot predict exactly what your competitors will do next, but large-scale technological changes are often reasonably predictable.

As a quick example, I predict that flat-screen panels will continue to get larger and thinner and lighter. Although I've never worked in the electronics industry, I'm guessing that this is a safe prediction, since the trend has been going on for years. Assuming that I'm right, consider the potential implications if it continues. A provisional patent application filed today will expire in 21 years. What will TVs look like then? Can we predict that they will have become huge, as well as extraordinarily cheap? Will there be walls covered with electronic screens in the way that we use wallpaper today? How about clear glass and windows being used as electronic screens? Can we predict that disposable products like milk cartons will have built-in screens? If screens are everywhere, can we predict that the user will interface directly with each local screen, instead of bringing the screen with her as people do today? Perhaps one's phone (or even one's watch) will be the laptop of the future, commandeering any screen within view to display relevant content. A quick look at the patent literature suggests that most of these possibilities have already been envisioned in the portfolios of companies competing in this space.

In some situations, it may be worthwhile to consider filing prophetic applications even if you haven't developed the core technology yet. In other words, you can file applications on inventions that have not yet been reduced to practice. Or perhaps they have been reduced to practice in a way that would never be marketable because of impractical complications such as manufacturing or cost. As previously mentioned, many attorneys are reluctant to file prophetic applications. A filing of this type may, for example, create prior art against future inventions that have actually been proven to work, as the prophetic application may still count against the patentability of the working invention.

However, it's important to realize that you can file an application based solely on your belief that the invention in the application can be enabled. One situation in which this can be useful is when the technology has been committed to a test, but the workability of the test will take a long time to verify. If the test doesn't yield the expected results, you can just abandon the application.

As with all strategies, it's important to keep in mind that these future-oriented applications also have the potential to make your competitors aware of the opportunity. As a result, these applications should be carefully written to make sure they don't reveal any more information than necessary. Furthermore, remember that these applications will also create prior art against your own future inventions. It is usually worthwhile to evaluate your strategy through several forward-looking steps to project when key inventions are likely to be ready for filing, and how each invention will affect the patentability of future inventions. You may, for example, hold back the filing of some inventions until they can be filed concurrently with another invention to avoid creating your own prior art.

We'll discuss some additional considerations when we look more closely at strategic inventing in Part 3. For now, consider that at least a portion of your portfolio should probably be intentionally focused on future developments—new consumer needs, emerging technologies, disruptive innovation, and competitive developments.

WHICH STRATEGY MODEL IS RIGHT FOR YOU?

Deciding how to use the patents that you create is truly a strategic decision, and one that is likely to depend heavily on factors such as the type of industry in which you compete, the competitive landscape, the need for the transfer of rights to others, and regulatory requirements. Each of the models described in this chapter has distinct positive and negative consequences, and some will align better with your project than others. Alignment of the strategy with your situation is the primary goal. Consider how each strategy might be implemented, and compare the opportunities and consequences. Also, keep in mind that there are no mutually exclusive models. You will probably find that you need to combine several models to meet your objectives. Or perhaps you'll create new models that are more suited to your situation. As with other examples in this book, consider these as tools in your strategic toolbox, helping you build more diverse strategic options as your product and your project develop.

CHAPTER 15

PORTFOLIO BUILDING: A BUSINESS PERSPECTIVE

Dr. Elvir Causevic

Dr. Causevic heads the intellectual property (IP) strategy practice of Ocean Tomo, advising the world's largest companies and brightest start-ups. Starting as a faculty member at Yale University, he has been involved with innovation and intellectual property for 20 years, including technology transfer with leading universities, NASA, NIST, the OECD, and the European Union. He has been named an inventor on more than 20 U.S. and international patents and patent applications, and he has founded and run several high-technology businesses, two of which were acquired by Fortune 500 companies.

The process of creating a powerful intellectual property portfolio is complex. It goes well beyond the core task of generating and capturing new knowledge and discoveries. It also involves legal (patent prosecution and litigation) and business (patent valuation and transactions) concerns. This chapter explores these other aspects, with a focus on practical observations and tasks that a savvy inventor can incorporate into his normal workday. If the inventor does so, she will dramatically increase the value of the resulting intellectual property.

CORPORATE INVENTOR VERSUS CORPORATE MANAGER

The corporate inventor lives in the world of knowledge and discovery. In contrast, the corporate manager lives in the world of markets, budgets, and profits. They speak different languages, and they usually have different personal drives and professional priorities. However, they have to work together to create value. As with other areas of corporate life, the "golden rule" often applies to innovation and intellectual property as well: "the guy with the gold makes the rules." In most companies, the "gold" is the resources needed to convert the inventor's knowledge and invention into market value. The corporate manager holds the purse strings to make that happen. Paradoxically, however, it is the corporate inventor who is best placed to understand where the real innovative value lies and how to create it, not the manager. The new intellectual property value could be inside the inventor's lab, elsewhere in the company, or quite possibly in the outside world, where the inventor has connections and relationships. Learning the language of the corporate manager will provide many benefits to the corporate inventor, leveraging the purse strings with an understanding of the source of IP value.

The following several sections lay some foundation to help the corporate inventor understand how her corporate manager views innovation and intellectual property, in general. The hope is to establish a broader understanding of key issues and to teach the corporate inventor how to communicate most effectively across various boundaries. Armed with new insights and new language, the corporate inventor will be able to chart an intellectual property strategy, to the handsome benefit of both the corporation and herself, over the long term.

BACK TO THE BASICS—IT'S ABOUT THE VALUE

It is important to remember the main (if uninteresting) goal of investing time, money, and energy in intellectual property protection: it is to create new value as soon as possible and as cost-effectively as possible. At its core, the purpose of any corporation is to generate value for its stakeholders, and that usually means to generate a financial return on investment for its shareholders. Corporate social responsibility and being a good corporate citizen notwithstanding, management teams and boards of directors of profitable companies are given incentives to create just that financial return. Every part of return on investment (ROI) is measured very precisely—usually as new profit added to the bottom line or as an increase in the market value of the company's stock. The corporate inventor should accept the need for ROI as an axiom, and never forget it.

Traditionally, intellectual property creates value primarily by keeping others out of the market. This is the "sword" strategy mentioned earlier. The owner can charge the buyers of products whatever price the market will bear, without fear that competition will lower the price, because the competition is not there, at least for a while. Alternatively, intellectual property can be converted into value by licensing others (one or many) to practice the inventions as described in the patents, for example. Furthermore, the patents can be sold outright. Intangibly, but still measurably, the patents that a company owns can provide a defense against competitors asserting their own patents in court by creating a fear of retribution. This is the "shield" strategy discussed earlier. This will allow a company at least the freedom to operate, without the fear of being attacked. However, there are many other ways to turn intellectual property into value.

Innovation versus Intellectual Property

Innovation is a process that generates and aggregates ideas and transforms them into measurable value. The link between innovation and a healthy corporate bottom line over the long term has been well documented and researched in the academic business community.

Intellectual property protection, on the other hand, is deployed as a separate set of activities to capture the full value from innovation. It is largely an independent and additive activity that usually complicates the innovation process itself. It is also an expensive investment, with benefits accruing only in the long term. It is usually driven by the corporate manager, strategies, and policies, but enabled by the corporate inventor—with the added benefit of inserting patent attorneys somewhere in the equation.

Separately, corporate managers also know that innovation by itself can generate a return on investment even without intellectual property, depending on the industry. This complicates matters of intellectual property protection even further.

The corporate manager must ask himself why she should bother with intellectual property if it seems only to:

- Make innovation harder.
- Make everything more expensive.
- Promise a return only after a long time (by which time she may be gone).
- Annoy the inventors.

After all, the manager will ask: "Can't I get by without too much IP, and still be successful in the market?"

For many industries, the answer is: probably not. Intellectual property is one of our core social contracts, embedded in our constitution and part of the core laws in most developed and developing countries in the world. It's a tried-and-true system, albeit with some annoying abusers, to ensure that the full benefits of the innovation investment accrue to the rightful owner. In this decade especially, IP has transformed how businesses operate, and hundreds of billions of dollars of value have been generated through IP-related activities by the world's most respected and innovative companies, such as IBM, Hewlett-Packard, Pfizer, Disney, and General Motors, among others. All this value was generated by the savvy corporate inventors at its point of origin, then turned into billions by their partners, the corporate managers.

Intellectual Property Is an Asset Class

From a business perspective, intellectual property is simply an asset class, just like the buildings, equipment, and trucks that a company owns. However, it is a dramatically more complex asset, existing in a completely different environment from physical assets. It is governed by a different set of rules, and it has its own set of risks.

On the positive side, intellectual property protection offers a set of ways to better monetize the innovation that the company produces by keeping competitors out. Additional monetization beyond the bounds of the company's operations is sometimes possible—by selling or licensing unused portions to others. Sometimes, others are licensed to compete with the IP owner in the same marketplace, with similar products. Proper intellectual property management can also offer an opportunity to legally leverage the innovation produced by others to create value for the corporation, a good example being Procter & Gamble and its famous "360-degree-innovation" process.

But above all else, intellectual property has one key value that no other asset class has: it is *divisible* in a way that does not diminish its worth. As a matter of fact, a strong case can be made that multiplying the use of intellectual property actually increases its value. The more we use it, the more we get.

If we want to double the production capacity of a physical plant that is producing a drug, we have to buy new machines, build new buildings to house them, and hire new people to run them. We have to make a significant incremental investment to generate meaningful incremental profit. But if we live in the IP land, things are very different. Imagine that we have one licensee who is producing a drug off our patents in a particular country. We can license the same patents to another licensee without any investment of our own. All of the new profit is going directly to the bottom line. And we can repeat the process again and again and again. "It's turtles all the way down."[1]

A cleverly assembled portfolio can be licensed to different companies within the same industry, to companies in different industries, in different countries, for distinct features, and so on. It can be carved up in a dizzying number of combinations and permutations. Rights can be given to one market player on an exclusive basis, or to many on a nonexclusive basis. To be profitable, a comprehensive intellectual property solution probably has to cut across innovation, markets, business, law, litigation, and entire other fields of endeavor. It pushes and blurs the company's boundaries. It affects how a company interacts with its ecosystem: its own inventors, customers, suppliers, partners, competitors, and previously unrelated entities.

Portfolio implies that several different kinds of things are put together in the same package. It could be a series of patents within one company, in-licensed patents from another company, acquired patents and know-how from a third company, open-source information from the public domain, know-how and trade secrets, and several other kinds of rights, all bundled together. When these packaged IP rights happen to cover proven transformative new technologies, processes, or products that expand their usable reach to other industries, other fields, and new types of products, then multiple and extraordinary monetization opportunities exist. Relatively small companies with no assets other than R&D staff and patents have been valued by the markets at hundreds of millions or even billions of dollars and are viewed as being among the most profitable types of companies, with profit margins greater than 40 percent.[2]

VALUING INTELLECTUAL PROPERTY

The first question that a corporate manager will ask is, what is the value of this new asset class? An entire boutique industry has grown up around intangible asset valuation, and the topic of proper valuation is a subject of continued debate in business and academic circles. Several key books[3] set out the basics of the field, and professional organizations such as the Licensing Executives Society organize committees and propose best practices and educational courses.

There are three general methods used for the valuation of intangible assets, including intellectual property:

- Cost approach: what did it cost to invent and protect?
- Market approach: how much did similar IP sell/license/litigate for?
- Income approach: how much money could IP alone generate if licensed?

Of these, the income approach is most often used for new IP. However, the corporate inventor should be familiar with what others in a particular field are doing and what areas are important for future licensing.

Valuation, at the End of the Day

One key question to ask about royalty rates, patent sale prices, and the value of intellectual property in general is, why did the market set those values? There are a number of different explanations, but at the end of the day, the chain of value is most credibly established through enforcement. This usually means litigation in U.S. federal district courts (where all patent cases get tried) and the subsequent appellate courts. There are only two higher instances: the U.S. Court of Appeals for the Federal Circuit (CAFC), set up exclusively for intellectual property litigation, and, if you can get on the docket, the U.S. Supreme Court. (There is also the International Trade Commission [ITC] in the United States and there are international courts, but we'll stay focused on the U.S. system.)

Why would a company enter into a license agreement if it can just infringe the patents? Because the courts will find that it infringed, and they will award damages to the injured party and make the infringer pay. One of the old rules of thumb for economic damages used to be that 25 percent of the profits generated by the infringer were awarded to the holder of the patents, if those patents were found to be valid and infringed. That rule of thumb recently got thrown out of the CAFC[4] in a Uniloc v. Microsoft case that went to appeal in front of it. The court stated:

> The 25 percent rule of thumb is a tool that has been used to approximate the reasonable royalty rate that the manufacturer of a patented product would be willing to offer to pay to the patentee during a hypothetical negotiation. The Rule suggests that the licensee pay a royalty rate equivalent to 25 percent of its expected profits for the product that incorporates the IP at issue. . . . [The underlying] "assumption is that the licensee should retain a majority (i.e. 75 percent) of the profits, because it has undertaken substantial development, operational and commercialization risks, contributed other technology/IP and/or brought to bear its own development, operational and commercialization contributions. . . . This court now holds as a matter of Federal Circuit law that the 25 percent rule of thumb is a fundamentally flawed tool for determining a baseline royalty rate in a hypothetical negotiation. Evidence relying on the 25 percent rule of thumb is thus inadmissible under Daubert and the Federal Rules of Evidence, because it fails to tie a reasonable royalty base to the facts of the case at issue.

What this court didn't do, and none of the others has done thus far, is establish a new, simple rule. What is clear is that every case is very fact-specific, and the standard themes that have been around for the past 20 years may still be used in some fashion.

Royalty rates vary widely—some are under a penny or $0.10 or $2 per chip, in the semiconductor industry; others are in the area of 3 to 5 percent of net sales for some earlier-stage technologies; and I've gotten as high as 30 percent on licensing IP and products in the medical device industry, for a fully developed product. Whatever the royalty rate is in a particular market, for a particular stage of technology development, it is critically important that the creator of the initial patents understands that there is a chance that her work may end up in litigation as the final opportunity to determine value, and hence should understand what that means.

PATENT LITIGATION AND THE CORPORATE INVENTOR

Intellectual property litigation is one of the most complex fields of litigation, staffed by some of the most brilliant and highly paid attorneys. Experts—all leaders in their fields, with advanced degrees and years of experience—help the attorneys and the courts, and testify on law, technical issues, and economic damages. Fact patterns vary widely among cases, and even trying to understand, let alone influence, the outcome is not for the faint of heart.

Why should the corporate inventor care at all about these things? Because the value of the patents may essentially be set by the courts—or at least an estimation of what the courts may do. The corporate inventor can have a material impact on the factors surrounding a company's intellectual property portfolio years before there is any mention of litigation. If this is done properly, the corporate inventor can significantly increase the value of the portfolio as it is being created.

The economic value of any particular patent being considered in litigation will be ascertained in detail by a sea of CPAs, technical experts, patent attorneys, and litigators, who will prepare for their clients detailed analyses of what the likely outcome of patent litigation would be if either party won or lost. They will painstakingly calculate what the financial damages might be. They will then advise their clients to either acquire those patents, sign a license for an amount comparable to the amount of damages that a court would be likely to determine, or continue the dispute in court.

Why do they do so much analysis? Because the average cost of intellectual property litigation is in the millions of dollars, and the damages awards can range from millions to hundreds of millions of dollars. A lot is at stake. The corporate inventor should know what happens in litigation, what the key factors are, and how decisions are made, and should adapt his normal daily behavior, starting today, to support what might be coming down the road.

The facts of most patent litigation cases, especially on the economic damages calculation side, revolve mainly around matters that concern primarily the corporate inventor and his area of expertise in the field. Some of the key elements include:

- What is patented in the final product and what is not
- What the comparable license payments might be in the industry
- What were prior licenses with the company
- How the patented features provide an advantage over older models
- What noninfringing alternatives exist, and so on

The corporate inventor may be considered the expert on some of these topics. She knows who does what in the field, what value technologies deliver, what her contributions to the new product features were, how important they were to its commercial success, and so on. Given that these factors affect litigation, they also affect the value of the portfolio, either directly or indirectly. The corporate inventor should be familiar with them, and should think, daily, what actions she can take consistent with these rules of the IP game to increase the value of her own portfolio. Your patent counsel can provide specific advice on how best to be prepared for litigation, in terms of record keeping regarding inventions, reduction to practice, and other such areas.

One issue that is often overlooked is that the discovery process, ordered by the courts, often produces very damaging internal e-mails from inexperienced inventors guessing at the value of their or others' patents. It is best not to discuss infringement, applicability, or the value of your patents or others' patents with anyone (especially not in writing) unless you are specifically asked to do so by patent counsel. Every senior patent litigator has dozens of stories of old, casual internal e-mails sinking a case or costing a client hundreds of millions of dollars.

BUILDING THE PORTFOLIO

The first element of building a great intellectual property portfolio is adequately capturing the corporate inventor's own inventions. Another key element of building an intellectual property portfolio is knowledge of the market—who else is doing what relative to the technology being developed by the company. Is there a university doing a development project, a government grant in the area, or a start-up being funded by a venture capital organization? If so, is there an opportunity to license or acquire rights from them?

If there are larger companies that own patents in the area, what information can we glean about them? Do they have an active licensing program? Do they partner in development? Does the inventor's company have patents that may be related to other businesses of the competitor, so that we can effectuate a trade or a cross-license?

Separately, it is important to know who is publishing what and where. Who are the key people, what organizations do they belong to, and what is the policy of their organizations regarding publishing and intellectual property rights? There may be particularly interesting opportunities with international competitors. How broadly are they patenting their work, and which parts of their own portfolios are they patenting only locally, regionally, or broadly?

If rights can't be acquired, can people? Who are the key up-and-coming inventors, and what deal can be negotiated with the corporate manager to attempt to recruit this promising new inventor?

Analyzing a patent landscape for opportunities and threats can be a significant task. One might hope that an in-house patent attorney would keep track of all this information. In a corporate setting, this is often not possible, given the sheer volume of work facing these individuals and their departments. This job is again best executed by the corporate inventor himself, at least the "market research" phase. The corporate inventor is best placed to keep track of what is happening in his area of interest, not just from a scientific viewpoint, but also from an intellectual property value viewpoint.

How Value Is Realized from the Intellectual Property Portfolio

The savvy corporate inventor will be building an armamentarium of all these types of crucial facts about her invention, the competition, the markets, and the implementation of her inventions in the company's products. She will then ascertain the "true" value of the intellectual property that she has created, and will advise the corporate manager how to best make money from the cleverly assembled portfolio. The corporate manager will enter any negotiation speaking softly and carrying a big stick—the impeccable and deep knowledge of the innovation and market data surrounding the intellectual property being transacted.

The corporate inventor will be on the lookout for opportunities to strengthen the portfolio by her own inventive process, acquisition of rights, or acquisition of people. She will also be continuously exploring options for monetizing the portfolio—both the active parts of it that are aimed at a specific product and the inactive parts that have been either abandoned or postponed. She will keep her corporate manager engaged when new opportunities show up; when new entrants appear; when meaningful publications, patent applications, or transactions happen; or when she feels that joint development or licensing possibilities exist. She will not endanger the enforcement process by creating e-mails and other documents that may be used against the company in unforeseen future litigation.

The corporate inventor, who has now become a savvy producer, consumer, and monetizer of intellectual property, will herself become an invaluable asset to the company. The corporate manager, who is also IP savvy, will make sure to recognize, appreciate, and reward such unique skills and talents, to make sure that the extraordinary value generated by the corporate inventor accrues to the benefit of the company in the long run.

CHAPTER 16

ENHANCING PRODUCT VALUE THROUGH LIFE-CYCLE MANAGEMENT

Once a great product has been developed, one of the key questions related to the patent strategy is how long you can protect the product against imitators. Patents are primarily focused on creating a sustainable competitive advantage in the marketplace, and how long this advantage can be sustained is a key metric for the success of a patent strategy. Most projects will require multiple patent applications to be filed in order to create a portfolio of protection. One potential benefit of multiple filings is the opportunity to extend the life span of effective protection.

In an industry with very short product life cycles, the life span of a patent may be far longer than the useful life span of the product. Or new technologies may be created so quickly that the previous generation of technology is discarded rapidly. However, a more common situation is that development times, regulatory approval, scale-up, building manufacturing facilities and infrastructure, and geographic dispersion create long product life cycles. In particular, the pharmaceutical and biotech industries rely heavily on the patent term to create a sustainable competitive advantage, but they are also handicapped by lengthy regulatory processes. The development time plus the time required for regulatory approval often results in only a few years of useful patent protection.

As we begin our discussion, recall the general timeline of the patenting process that we discussed in Chapter 4. Key steps in the process usually occur as follows:

- A provisional U.S. application is filed ($t = 0$).
- A nonprovisional U.S. application is filed, claiming priority from the provisional application ($t < 12$ months).
- A Patent Cooperation Treaty (PCT) application is filed within the first 12 months of the first U.S. application filing ($t < 12$ months).

- The application is published at 18 months from the earliest claimed priority date ($t \sim 18$ months).
- Substantive examination starts in the 1- to 2-year range after filing the nonprovisional application ($t \sim 24 - 36$ months).
- Prosecution for most PCT countries must be requested at 30 months, although some start as early as 20 months.
- The U.S. application is granted about 3 to 4 years after filing of the nonprovisional application ($t = 4 - 5$ years when starting from a provisional).
- This granted U.S. patent (and most granted foreign patents resulting from the PCT application) will remain in force until about 20 years from the nonprovisional filing date, assuming that maintenance fees are paid.

GO FASTER

There may be a benefit to getting a patent granted faster, even at the expense of reducing the length of the patent term. In this situation, it may be better to skip the provisional filing process entirely. Remember, filing the provisional is primarily intended to delay additional prosecution and costs, while establishing an early priority date. If your strategy dictates moving quickly, it will probably be best to skip provisional filing.

Requesting an accelerated examination or prioritized examination by the U.S. Patent and Trademark Office (USPTO) can also speed your application. This approach requires higher fees, additional paperwork, and other formalities, and also limits the number of claims. In practice, these additional requirements mean that in most industries, these procedures are not used on a regular basis.

However, if a product will be reaching the market quickly and it's important to have substantial claims granted to establish a competitive advantage, accelerating prosecution may be an option that is worth considering. This is a complicated decision because of the additional risks, and you may need a long discussion with your attorney to understand the full implications.

GO SLOWER

As mentioned earlier, filing a provisional is primarily a delaying tactic—while it may seem to lengthen the patent's life, it really just postpones the patent term. You cannot extend the term of a single invention beyond the 21-year end point established by the provisional filing route. As a result, if the product life cycle is likely to be substantially longer than the expected patent term, it may be strategically sound to delay the start of the process. In other words, wait to file the provisional. The last possible date on which you can file the provisional will depend on any required public disclosures. It may be right before the product goes on sale, for example. However, in most situations, it is likely to be much sooner—prior to regulatory disclosure, publication in the literature, sales and marketing presentations, and other such events. It is possible to invoke the one-year grace period for U.S.-only strategies, of course, though this is generally not advisable.

Recall our earlier discussion about the 2011 America Invents Act (AIA) patent law changes. Given the change to the first-inventor-to-file system, there will be additional risk in waiting to file. Critical applications should be filed quickly to avoid the possibility of competitive filings on similar subject matter. Intentional delaying tactics will probably be most appropriate for inventions that are of secondary importance, and/or inventions that are designed to strengthen the overall portfolio. However, these are complex decisions, and they should be made only after consulting with your attorney.

The Droplet Model: A Strategy for a Gradually Decaying Frontier

If the simple "go slower" approach is not enough to meet the needs of your strategy, another approach would be to create a gradually decaying frontier of multiple inventions, the way a droplet landing in a smooth pool of water creates expanding waves that gradually dissipate. This may sound complicated, but the strategy is actually relatively simple. In order to create most products, a number of inventions will have to be made. The staggered invention dates will provide an opportunity for protection that exceeds the life span of a single patent.

For example, as shown in Figure 16.1, a new compound may be invented in the lab (Invention 1). This compound will require changes to the existing process (Invention 2). The compound may benefit from being formed into or incorporated into a secondary structure (Invention 3). Then, there may be stability issues to address or perhaps methods of quality control or interaction with other elements of the process will be developed (Invention 4). The unique properties of the compound will create new methods of use by the consumer (Invention 5). And, these new methods of use may be coordinated on a larger scale for distribution and other efficiencies, a "business methods" invention of sorts (Invention 6).

This series of inventions provides potential new filing dates for each new invention, assuming that the inventions don't all happen at the

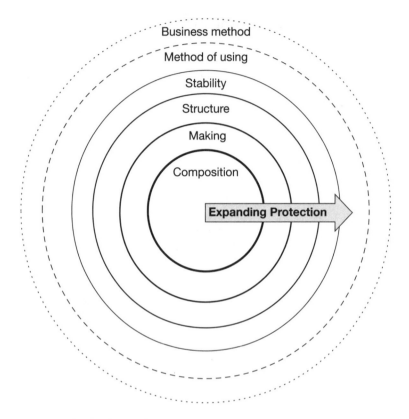

Figure 16.1   The droplet model: initiating the patent position

same time. It is unlikely that your product will have a nicely defined sequence of inventions as just described, but I encourage you to look for the opportunity, as even a small number of distinct inventions related to a single product can be used to create this decaying frontier and thereby extend the useful competitive advantage for your product.

Because of the best mode and enablement requirements, each application may need to include information related to these later inventions if that information exists at the time of filing. Consider the following example. Assume that a compound is invented in the lab, and it takes six months to get the patent application filed. During those six months, additional process improvements are made that would constitute another distinct invention. Unfortunately, this later process invention is now the best mode to the first invention, and must be disclosed when filing that application. This can be a complicated issue, so it is definitely something that should be discussed with your attorney.

Assuming that our idealized sequence of inventions comes to fruition and that patents are granted roughly in sequence according to their filing dates, the portfolio will be gradually expanding in protection, as described in Figure 16.1. First the patent on the composition will be granted, then that on the process for making it, then that on secondary structures, and so on.

As drawn, the circles indicate that each subsequent invention is required for practicing the previous invention (i.e., subsequent inventions are essential for creating the final product). This is an idealized example, as most subsequent inventions will protect only part of the fundamental invention. The key strategy is to use as many later filings as possible to create multiple layers of protection.

Following through with our droplet model, the gradually increasing competitive advantage will eventually give way to a gradually decreasing competitive advantage, as shown in Figure 16.2. If the later inventions are truly required to create a competing product, they will effectively increase the useful life of the competitive advantage. If not, they will hopefully at least require your competitor to invest additional resources to invent around your less fundamental patents.

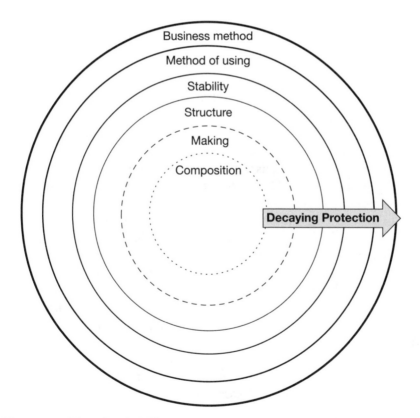

Figure 16.2   The tail end of the droplet model: gradual decay over time

FILING CONTINUATIONS AND SUBMARINE CLAIMS

Recall that continuations are applications that claim priority based on a previously filed application but that have different claims. Frequently, continuations are a consequence of the normal prosecution that develops between your attorney and the patent office and don't require much attention from the inventor. However, continuations can also provide some additional strategic options.

For example, the patent office may find that you have filed more than one invention in the same application—a product and its related process, perhaps. As a result, the examiner may send back a *restriction requirement* that requires you to pick one specific invention to prosecute. All is not lost, however; you can still file the other inventions as continuations during the time that the initial application is pending. In this example, the continuation might also be called a *divisional*, since the new application will be a division of the original. There is a fuzzy line determining how much "inventiveness" can go into one application, but a general rule of thumb is that the examiner will not want to search two distinctly different fields of prior art for one application. If the examiner feels that the claims would require searching multiple fields, he is likely to issue a restriction requirement.

Why bring this up in a discussion on life-cycle management? It is also possible to file continuations with new claims for any subject matter that exists within a previously filed application, as long as that application is still pending at the patent office. In other words, if you realize that there is an invention hidden in the specification that you forgot to claim, you can file a continuation application—as long as you do so before the day your parent application is issued as a patent. The primary downside is that the priority date will be established by the parent application, which will result in a shorter patent term.

As such, it's possible to modify the *claims* at any time during the period in which an application is pending by filing a new continuing application. You may, for example, find that your competitor is pursuing a specific embodiment of your invention that is mentioned in one of your examples, but is not explicitly claimed. As long as the invention exists in the original specification (including best mode, enablement, and so on) and the application is still pending, you can file a continuing application that more specifically claims your competitor's product. As shown in Figure 16.3, each successive application is filed with a new set of claims during the pendency of a preceding application, and all continuations will expire on the date defined by the parent application.

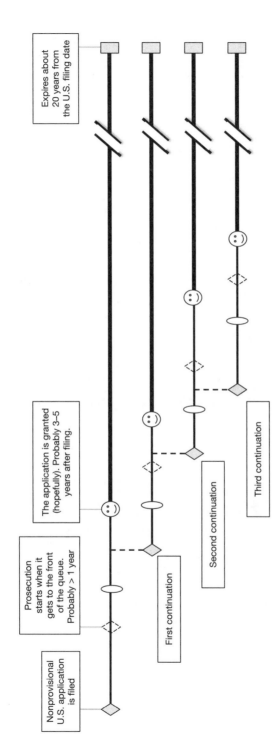

Figure 16.3 An example of multiple continuations filed sequentially

Wait, that doesn't sound right . . . aren't you claiming an invention after the fact? Remember, this works only in situations where the invention is supported by the original application. In other words, you already made the invention, but you didn't realize its significance at the time.

This approach is sometimes called a "submarine claim" because of the claim's being out of sight until long after filing. Under previous U.S. patent law, the patent term was not defined until the patent was granted (i.e., the term was 17 years after granting), which made this a much more powerful and controversial strategy. Jerome Lemelson is often considered the progenitor of this approach and was quite successful using it. With the current patent law, any later-filed claims will result in a significantly shorter patent term (ending at the same time as the parent), which has greatly reduced the impact of this approach.

The ability to make changes to the claims at a later time can be a distinct advantage over the life span of your product. For a critical invention, it is often a good idea to keep at least one continuation pending at all times. This will require significant resources (money and attorney's time), so it should be considered only for extremely important inventions.

CHAPTER 17

Intellectual Property as a Currency of Collaboration

Mark B. Mondry

Mr. Mondry is the managing partner and a registered patent attorney in the Colorado office of Phase M, an intellectual property law and strategy firm (www.phaseM.com). He has served as in-house counsel for Fortune 500 medical technology companies, as a CEO in the electronics industry, and as managing director for a global innovation consulting firm. His career focus has been the identification, prioritization, and optimization of strategic innovation.

The preceding chapters in this book offer a compendium of valuable ideas, considerations, and processes that corporate inventors can employ to help them generate patent portfolios that are strategic and valuable in the business context. Those chapters, while revealing the intricacies of patent strategy and strategic inventing, suggest a valuable discipline: equipping each corporate citizen with a working knowledge of topics such as patentability, claim interpretation, prior art, and the nuances of white space and red space to help them identify intellectual property opportunities that will advance the strategic intent of the business. This suggestion, and the results it would accomplish, is valuable indeed. In practice, however, such education is most difficult to achieve.

As in most business endeavors, the first step is to put into place a shared language that everyone understands. Product developers must share a common language (agile, Lean, or some other approach); designers and software developers also have their own. For strategic inventing, the shared language is the lexicon of patents. But what about those who do not have either patent knowledge or the inclination, interest, or resources to attain it? Are these people outside the potential circle of strategic inventors? I believe the answer is no. But to attract them into the circle and make them productive contributors to your strategic patenting efforts, we must include a more common, less patent-specific language that is easier to understand and communicate with. Basically, we need a language that invites valuable contributions from those who do not speak patents.

A REALITY CHECK ON PATENTS

Let's first acknowledge a bit of reality. Inside most corporations of significant size, roles are fairly specialized. In addition, the domain of patents uses a fairly specialized language that can be intimidating when you are not familiar with it. The community of people who are involved with the patenting process and who know the required specialized language can be fairly small compared to the overall population of the company. Typically, the patent-savvy community is made up of patent attorneys, patent agents, engineers, and perhaps other technologists who are subject to performance metrics that include patent submissions. These people find the mechanics of patenting a fascinating topic. For most others, however, the topic is about as interesting as the tax code. From their perspective, the topic is best handled by someone else.

Fortunately, if you are reading this book, either you have already embraced an interest in patents or, alternatively, you have been provided with this book as an instruction manual on a preferred way to think and communicate. You now have the burden of carrying the torch in an effort to get others in the organization to participate in the strategic inventing journey. This effort will probably involve language lessons.

One-on-one conversations among colleagues, particularly from patent expert to non-patent expert, is a terribly inefficient way to raise the intellectual property expertise across an organization. As a result, in-house patent counsel, typically in conjunction with R&D leadership, is often charged with the mandate of raising intellectual property sophistication throughout the organization via training seminars or brown-bag lunches, online, or through other forms of educational communication. In my experience, however, patent experts tend to focus on educating others the same way they were educated: through eye-watering explanations of the layers of complex rules and considerations in patent law and of patent prosecution. After all, if you understand this stuff, why not flaunt it?

To compound the challenge of raising enthusiasm for such potentially dry subject matter, many patent experts come from a technology background, and sometimes their intense technical focus combines with a lack of broad nontechnical business experience that would facilitate the translation of patent complexities into more universal business propositions and opportunities. It is the business opportunity, not the technology that enables it, that typically provides the most value.

Technologies themselves are constantly being replaced. Over the course of many years jumping back and forth between the business and legal domains, I have embraced a valuable method of communicating how patents play a role in the larger commercial system: *visualizing patents as a currency among interested parties.* This recasting of patents provides a powerful way to engage members of the organization outside the typically technically oriented audience that is already comfortable with patent language. In fact, the "currency" analogy can be applied to intellectual property (IP) in general. Explaining IP opportunity in the currency context, at least initially, helps to liberate colleagues who are unfamiliar with patents to think more creatively, and ultimately engage more strategically, in the inventing process. Here is how it works.

The Currency Analogy

Currencies are used in and across societies to exchange value and facilitate the flow of commerce. More specifically, currencies provide a generally accepted medium of trade in the form of coins and paper banknotes that can be exchanged by one party to acquire or gain access to goods, services, promises, or other interactions. Currency is money. Everyone in your organization, technical or not, is comfortable with the concept and value proposition of money.

Now, think about how broadly we all use money. We use money to pursue objects, services, and interactions across the wide spectrum of our personal human needs, wants, or desires. The vast amount of commercial interaction in society demands currency systems to facilitate the flow of value among individuals and organizations. This interaction is a necessary part of commerce in society. Of course, there are many forms of currency internationally, and all forms of currency facilitate commercial collaboration and interaction in various forms. The foundation of the IP-as-currency analogy is that intellectual property rights are increasingly being used to induce interaction and collaboration. Thus, intellectual property is being used as a form of currency. Just as a central bank controls financial currency strategy, your company controls its strategy of using IP as a currency in your commercial environment.

Until somewhat recently, the primary corporate economic justification for creating and acquiring patents has been the offensive and defensive "sword" and "shield" strategies centered upon current or future product offerings and the technology domains used to enable them. An excellent example is the enormous amounts of resources that web-based product companies like Google, Yahoo!, and Facebook are spending to acquire large mobile communications patent portfolios. In the corporate boardroom, these acquisitions are justified from the sword and shield philoshophy.

These strategies, including building portfolios around the freedom to operate and the stockpiling of patents to be used as leverage in potential patent litigation, generally focus narrowly on the corporation's competitive market in a "game of chess" analogy further described in Chapter 10.

The emergence of nonpracticing entities (NPEs) expanded this traditional commercial product technology focus by perpetuating the business model of acquiring and asserting patents as investment assets in order to derive rents from others who are commercializing the applicable technology, thereby generating profits for the NPE without the necessity of actually competing by using the technology. In early 2012, there were an estimated 350 operating NPEs that collectively owned more than 40,000 patents.

The next level of expansion is now beginning. This expansion is directed toward using patents and other forms of IP not just offensively or defensively, or to create lucrative royalty streams. Rather, the concept looks at IP as a medium of exchange to facilitate commercial transactions—positive collaborations involving cross-industry interaction, collaboration, and other relationships across economic or business ecosystems and across industries and global markets. This expanded way of thinking is very different from the narrower offensive and defensive focus explained in earlier chapters, and it clearly presents a different strategic intent. In fact, the concept anticipates the growing trend of increased commercial collaboration among entities globally, where companies must find new ways of exchanging value in order to succeed commercially. The value of using patents as a sword and shield is not going away, but it is being supplemented.

Communicating a shared thinking about intellectual property as a collection of different currencies allows anyone in the organization to visualize related value propositions more easily and to contribute ideas on how to strategically "invest" in or "spend" those resources. The focus shifts from patent technicalities to defining the needs, wants, and desires of other businesses in your commercial ecosystem, whether upstream, downstream, or all around. The key here is identifying opportunities generally. The patent experts still need to engage to help translate the resulting ideas into actual intellectual property strategies and tactics where they are available. Thus, the currency approach becomes yet another tool for the strategic inventor.

Designing IP Currency to Invite Interactions

Our global economy incorporates numerous independent currencies that have become increasingly interrelated and codependent. Even the smallest businesses now operate globally. International supply chains, the outsourcing of specialized research and development expertise, and the increasing importance of emerging marketshare made the processes of innovation, new product development, and business itself globally dispersed undertakings. Consider the impact of the "reverse innovation" trend, where significant innovation is moving from developing economies to mature economies rather than the other way around.

The same is true of intellectual property systems. Decades of patent harmonization efforts have yielded stronger patent enforcement systems in emerging economies as well as global unification around the first-to-file standard of inventorship in patents (see Chapter 8 on the impact of the 2011 America Invents Act). The market for intellectual property also continues to mature as the development of more standardized valuation metrics amplifies patent and brand liquidity globally. These trends are multiplying the number of transactions involving IP.

To be most effective, our currency concept should be applied to all forms of IP, not just patents. These forms include trademarks, copyrights, trade dress, trade secrets, and design rights and the bundle of rights that each represents, all on a country-by-country basis. The national intellectual property rights recognized by each country, along with the corresponding practical enforceability of those rights (a jurisdictional issue), form a varying range of values across the different currencies. Just like professional currency traders, companies using this approach must carefully study and monitor the global landscape for intellectual property–related trends and events (legislative changes, treaty negotiations, court decisions, and, of course, politics) that would affect intellectual property values and investment strategies in order to place informed bets on the markets, technologies, and IP that look most promising. As a currency, intellectual property is also subject to fluctuations caused by macroeconomic and microeconomic issues over time as industries in each country expand or shrink and supply chains react to labor cost and infrastructure changes.

These variables may make the intellectual property strategist's role far more complex than has been traditionally expected. The corporate inventor becomes an IP strategist, monitoring and collecting global inputs with the same mindset required of other complex global asset investors.

IP INVESTMENT STRATEGIES

In the financial world, professional investors deploy numerous quantitative and qualitative models to help them determine what kind of assets to invest in and how to deploy those investments. Over time, it is likely that intellectual property investing will become equally sophisticated. Many organizations are already using models to help them determine which technologies to invest in and how to prioritize those investments. For simplicity in this discussion, however, let's focus on how to engage members of the corporate community in participation in identifying how and where value can be created internally and externally to the organization, using the IP-as-currency analogy.

The methodologies already presented in previous chapters of this book still apply. The currency approach should be viewed as a supplement. When soliciting coworkers for strategic inventing ideas using this approach, general value-identifying questions are presented early in the process, exploring topics such as:

1. What companies participate in our business value chain, how do they add value to the value chain, and how much value do they add?
2. What business collaborations, transactions, or relationships do we currently have in this value chain, and which do we need to make stronger for strategic or competitive purposes?
3. Is there IP that either exists or can be created that would be of value to those strategic partners and why?
4. Looking at companies with which we do not currently have relationships, and looking out at our larger commercial ecosystem, are there other parties that could be valuable as collaborators, suppliers, sellers, or other partners, and if so, is there IP that either exists or can be created that would be of value to those parties and why?
5. What would the rights, relationships, or value propositions around any of these new potential collaborations need to look like to be valuable to specific parties?
6. How could we create, acquire, or otherwise secure those rights and be able to offer to share them for this purpose?

These inquiries focus on collaborations, not just patents. Using this approach, the scope of opportunities considered is likely to increase, and the potential community of strategic innovators is likely to expand significantly. Once these opportunities are identified and prioritized, methodologies such as patent landscaping (Chapter 11) and spatial diagramming (Chapter 12) can be applied to map these opportunities onto existing IP arenas. These visual methods almost always provoke additional strategic discussion.

Example: Upstream Suppliers

Let's use an example to illustrate the IP-as-currency approach. In this simple example, we'll look at one aspect of the value chain: suppliers. In the markets and technologies your company participates in, there may be a wide range of current and potential suppliers available globally that offer the various components or services needed in order to provide your product or service offerings to customers. Some of these suppliers may be key strategic suppliers that are instrumental to your business. For those key strategic suppliers, it would be valuable to first analyze intellectual property opportunities from their perspective in the value chain. Clearly, if you can create or acquire intellectual property that is valuable to those suppliers, you can offer licenses or other contractual terms (including outright sale) of the rights associated with that intellectual property in order to strengthen your relationship, gain pricing leverage, or obtain other preferred terms from those key suppliers. There may also be joint development opportunities and other prospects to create new business with them.

The next step might be to look at *the suppliers supporting* your key strategic suppliers. If there are intellectual property opportunities that could bring value to those one-step-removed suppliers (let's focus on one of them and call it Supplier B), creative transactions can be fashioned to both strengthen your ties to that company and strengthen the ties between that company and your strategic supplier (Supplier A). For example, is there process-related or packaging-related IP that can be obtained? If you can indirectly help the business of your strategic supplier (Supplier A), this can directly and indirectly help your business. There are many creative approaches here.

When analyzing the opportunities involving actual and potential supplier relationships, there are broad resources within your organization that can provide valuable input into the analysis. In addition to

engineers or members of the technical staff who would have knowledge of the actual technologies and tangible products available through
these suppliers, there are salespeople, marketing or business development professionals, and financial staff members who may be able to
offer insights concerning other external relationships or market
dynamics that can be brought into the discussion. Going back to our
supplier example, suppose someone in your finance department knows
that Supplier B is in a potential commercial dispute with a competitor
(Supplier C) concerning technology that is not related to your products. There is an opportunity here. Strategically, you might ask: is there
any kind of intellectual property or business relationship that we
can leverage to help Supplier B? This would require looking more
deeply into the nature of the dispute and the business of Supplier C.
However, using our currency concept, if your company can offer something of value to Supplier B that could help it resolve the dispute with
Supplier C, say an alternative supply relationship or access to IP that
is of value to Supplier C (perhaps that you acquire for this purpose),
you have used IP currency to strengthen your business relationship
with Supplier A (your key strategic supplier) indirectly by reducing the
risk to Supplier A (potential disruption of supply from Supplier B
because of financial exposure resulting from the dispute between
Suppliers B and C, for example). It is a bit like thinking as a strategic
investor, correct? This potentially brings a three-dimensional aspect
to patent strategy (see Figure 17.1).

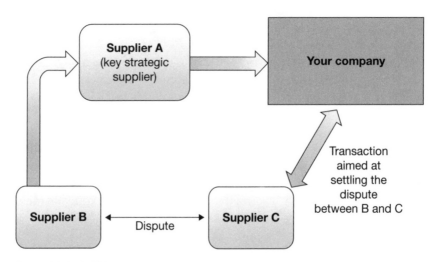

Figure 17.1 Collaborative leverage

THINKING GLOBALLY

Like other investments, the currency of intellectual property requires careful and coordinated asset management. Global enterprises have long engaged in currency hedging and other financial efforts to minimize risk and expand their investment opportunities. Likewise, strategic global corporations must invest in global intellectual property across their business ecosystem in order to hedge risks and leverage interactions. Traditionally, foreign patent filing decisions are based on where the company does business and perhaps the largest commercial markets. Under our currency approach, an expanded range of variables is considered: supply chain locations, competitor locations, collaborator locations, and other economic and legal considerations. These considerations are dynamic, and successful asset management may require increased divestiture and acquisition activities. Additionally, investments in intellectual property that is unrelated to your own technologies or product portfolio are likely to increase. Careful attention should be given to budget implications and assigning costs and benefits from a financial perspective.

The strategy behind such investments is to provide transaction "money" for multiparty collaboration, which is essential in cross-border business. These investments need to be made in advance; the glacial pace of the patent process will not speed up just because you need something *now*. Forecasting collaboration needs and developing an IP portfolio for such a purpose involve much more strategic input than creating patents that are intended to exclude or to extract royalties; it is making the difficult analysis related to seeking out intellectual property and other commercial opportunities that can *benefit your existing and potential business partners* in the geographies *that are important to them*. These are the currencies that you are trying to identify and invest in.

FOCUS ON DIVERSIFICATION

Successful investors diversify their investments. In your business ecosystem, you must also diversify by looking well beyond the scope of your own product road map for intellectual property investment opportunities that can be a hedge if your plans change, or that can be of value to potential business partners in the event of such a change. Suppose your product plans include a specific communications protocol. What if an alternative protocol emerges as a viable threat? Have you hedged your IP investments? Such a hedge can take the form of alternative embodiments in patent filings or entire separate portfolios. A strategic bet must be placed. This is a sophisticated approach to intellectual property strategy, requiring close coordination between your intellectual property strategy and other strategies within the business. It involves truly integrated strategic thinking.

Integrated strategic IP thinking requires the organization to engage nontechnical employees and contractors as resources for insight into value propositions in your ecosystem. Again, the key differentiation from the other strategic inventing concepts in this book is a focus on building value not from the context of what intellectual property already exists (red space) or doesn't (white space) in your product path, but what is important to potential business partners and collaborators. Apple has patent filings on technologies that are likely to be commercialized only by accessory makers and not by Apple itself. Yet these investments are being made.

LINKING STRATEGIES

Our currency approach also requires closer integration of strategies within the business and frequent communication and coordination within the organizational leadership. For example, patent counsel may have overall responsibility for formulating and executing the intellectual property strategy for the organization. The head of product development may have the corresponding responsibility for the product development pipeline and managing current and future product portfolios. Of necessity, these two strategies must be tightly integrated to yield currency opportunities that are important to the business. Organizationally, how is this coordination being encouraged by the leadership?

Most large companies also have a research and development (R&D) strategy. The R&D resources, whether internal or external, are a wonderful source of knowledge concerning technology trends and significant external discoveries outside of your core business that could be candidates for IP investment. Of course, the R&D, product, and IP strategies must all be aligned and connected to the overall business strategy itself (Figure 17.2). Again, are the organization's incentive systems supporting such coordination or working against it? The late Steve Jobs of Apple insisted on a single profit and loss (P&L) statement for the entire company and a weekly meeting of the top management team to prioritize resources and projects. Every leader was marching to the same priorities and constantly tuning strategy to align with the company's top goals and product priorities. The result was the elegantly interconnected hardware and software offerings that have made Apple

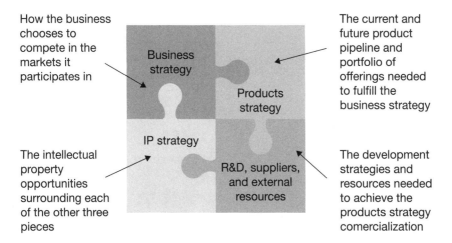

How the business chooses to compete in the markets it participates in

The current and future product pipeline and portfolio of offerings needed to fulfill the business strategy

The intellectual property opportunities surrounding each of the other three pieces

The development strategies and resources needed to achieve the products strategy comercialization

Figure 17.2   The strategy puzzle

so successful. The IP strategy was so connected that industry watchers would monitor the weekly publication of Apple patent applications to determine where *the entire industry* was likely to go!

FROM CURRENCY TO COLLABORATION

No corporation, no matter how large or how integrated, believes that it can succeed without the help, support, and resources of other entities. Even the traditional core competencies of product and service innovation have become a coordinated effort among diverse global partners. Companies such as Procter & Gamble, Apple, and Boeing have embraced open innovation as a catalyst to get to market sooner and with less risk.

This does not mean that corporations have discounted investment in internally created intellectual property; rather, it means that intellectual property investments have become more diverse and globally strategic. Protecting the corporation's core technologies is still essential for securing the freedom to operate globally, for example. But increasingly, patent strategies need to focus more broadly and analyze where IP value can be created in the larger industry ecosystem rather than just on how the IP enhances the company's narrow product pipeline. Once identified, the resulting intellectual property opportunities can be leveraged into a form of currency to be deployed in the pursuit of the overall business strategy.

Intellectual property has become a currency, a currency that can facilitate collaborative innovation between organizations by providing a transfer of value. Invest wisely because you and your colleages must now think like currency traders.

PART 3

STRATEGIC INVENTING

CHAPTER 18

The Cart or the Horse? An Introduction to Strategic Inventing

So far we've been discussing patent strategies involving multiple inventions and the implications of these patent portfolios. The significance of the competitive advantage you create will depend on the competitive landscapes, your project's patent filings, your company's intellectual property (IP) strategy, and needs for life-cycle management. However, building up these portfolios and developing the individual inventions that make up your strategic position can be difficult—particularly if you're limited to the inventions that just happen to occur within your research program. Another approach is to focus on the needs of the strategy, and then deliberately create inventions to fit that strategy.

Many great inventions result from fundamental discoveries that improve scientific understanding, manufacturing processes, materials, or methods. Some new inventions are the result of identifying and addressing an important consumer need. From the vast array of books on creativity and innovation, we can surmise that many inventions result from sheer creative insight. Is it possible to create inventions on an "as-needed" basis?

This approach is what might be called *strategic inventing*—creating inventions as a result of a deliberate strategy. In general, this refers to intentionally targeting a patent application or new product to improve the strength of the related patent strategy. Specifically, the strategic objective is identified before the invention is made, unlike a more traditional "discovery-driven" approach, in which the product is created before the IP strategy is developed. Strategic inventing could be as simple as designing-around a competitor's patents to ensure freedom to operate (FTO) early in a project's life. Another use might be developing products by emphasizing or deliberately enhancing patentable features that are likely to achieve consumer-relevant differentiation.

The strategy might also entail creating multiple new inventions to build elements of a larger overall strategy, such as life-cycle management or a patent thicket.

In some industries with a heavy emphasis on patent protection, such as pharmaceuticals, this approach has existed for some time. Compositional claims are extremely strong, particularly when regulatory approval creates an additional hurdle for potential design-around inventions. Patents are so important to this industry that expirations of key patents often make newspaper headlines.

In other industries, the new product development (NPD) process is heavily discovery-driven: a new product or process is created, and then the patent attorneys are called in to develop a filing strategy. While this approach does work, some situations call for an emphasis on creating a sustainable competitive advantage that can be achieved only through a more integrated patent strategy.

One element of maximizing the value of the patent portfolio is focusing on the development of products and inventions that fit a predetermined strategy. In short, the patent strategy drives the creation of the product or invention. I use the phrase "product or invention" because the strategy may affect the actual product you sell, but it may also require you to patent inventions that are never sold as products. Most successful products require multiple patents to adequately protect against imitators. Recall our earlier discussions about portfolios of multiple patents—the strategies often involve numerous patents and applications, many of which do not directly correspond to a product in the marketplace. Some may be intended to protect against a competitor's potential alternatives, projecting to the next generation of future products, or combinations with functions that aren't yet in the current product. Even though the inventions described in these patents are not in the marketplace, they create value by strengthening the overall portfolio.

If it seems as if this approach might result in the filing of a large number of patent applications—well, it might. Even relatively simple products are frequently protected by what seems like a large number of patent filings, particularly if the product is expected to be valuable. Gillette's Mach 3 razor is a famous example, often cited as being protected by more than 50 patents.

Furthermore, now would be a good time to investigate the typical patent strategy that is applied at your corporation, if you haven't done so already. How many patents are typically filed in a given year? Are patents required and/or expected for every project, or are patents usually a secondary consideration? Is the patent strategy for each project aggressively managed, or is it a concern only after a significant advancement has been made in the lab? Are the resources available to file on every reasonable invention, or are there guidelines and procedures in place to select only the most strategically relevant applications to file? These questions will give you a better picture of the norm at your corporation. You may find that strategic inventing techniques are already employed, or perhaps they are considered too exotic for your corporation's patent strategy needs.

STRATEGIC INVENTING VERSUS A DISCOVERY-DRIVEN STRATEGY

Which comes first, the product or the strategy for protecting the product? On some projects, the patent strategy is defined only after the invention has been made. Strategic inventing is the other way around: creating inventions to fit a predetermined strategy. As mentioned before, this isn't a new approach, but it is much more concentrated in industries with a heavy emphasis on establishing competitive advantage through patents. Many other industries use a more traditional sequential approach in which the discovery or product definition occurs first, and the patent strategy is developed later in the process.

In the sequential patent strategy approach, the product is defined first, and then the patent strategy for protecting the product is created. In a simplified model, consumer insight, business strategy, and research results are inputs into the concept-development stage, as can be seen in the example in Figure 18.1. This approach is sometimes referred to as the *discovery-driven* patent strategy model, since the research discovery

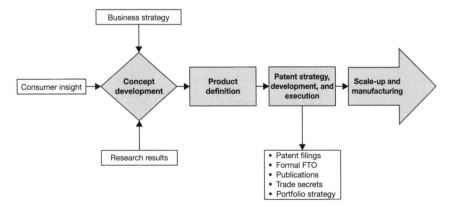

Figure 18.1   A sequential, discovery-driven approach to new product development

often drives the patent strategy: first the research, then the strategy. This diagram is highly simplified, of course, but the basic stages should be sufficient for our purposes.

This process can be appropriate in industries where the intellectual property is generally not valuable enough to justify a more sophisticated approach. It can be quite effective, particularly if you're lucky enough to have really good attorneys. The more proactive and strategically oriented your attorneys are, the more reasonable this approach becomes.

Ideally, however, the NPD process should have at least some input from IP strategy in the earliest phases of concept development. In the most basic form, attorneys will be contacted for freedom-to-operate opinions at a very early stage. More sophisticated projects may be almost entirely directed by the patent strategy (when designing around a competitor's patent portfolio, for example).

With a strategic inventing model, the patent strategy may even be used to focus the front end of concept development. Information from the published patent art and nonpatent literature is used to identify the most valuable intellectual property space. White space and red space are clearly defined. The types of claims likely to be granted, potential uses of the patents, and important geographies are discussed with the attorney. The product is then developed based on this information. As shown in Figure 18.2, this information will be used to develop the patent strategy and aid the concept-development process. It may come from patent attorneys, IP audits, and patent strategy objectives, as well as researchers who understand the patent system (a.k.a., you).

Note that in Figure 18.2, the development of the patent strategy precedes the product definition. It isn't necessary that there be less traditional

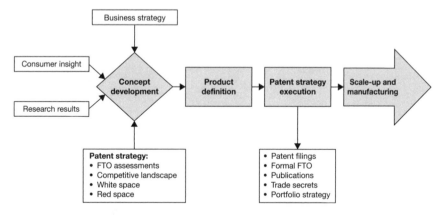

Figure 18.2   Strategic inventing in new product development (short cycle time)

research, but this illustration is intended to highlight a key point about strategic inventing: the focus is on adding value to the patent strategy, even if that doesn't fit within the traditional research plan.

If it's possible to create a dramatically new product with better features and functional benefits, there may be less need for a sophisticated patent strategy approach. Broad claims should be more readily granted for such an invention. Obviously, this is the preferred solution every time. Such breakthrough products can usually be protected quite well. More difficult situations arise when there are less dramatic functional benefits and only minor technical differences from the prior art.

In other words, if you discover a process to turn lead into gold, you should be able to get some very strong patents (assuming that you can enable the invention), and the patent strategy is likely to be straightforward. On the other hand, if your product is a bath soap that is only slightly sudsier than that of the competition and has minimal compositional changes, the patent protection (if any) is likely to be of little value unless a more sophisticated strategy is employed. For example, you could consider modifying or improving the product specifically for the sake of an improved patent position, even though there may be no other reason to make these changes.

Furthermore, there is likely to be an iterative nature to the patent strategy, particularly in industries with long product development cycles, such as biotechnology or pharmaceuticals (see Figure 18.3). The patent strategy will likely evolve through many iterations, as the product is being developed and commercialized. For example, it may be five or ten years before scale-up and manufacturing, because of the time needed to verify the results and surmount regulatory hurdles. For each

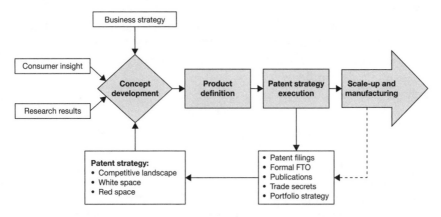

Figure 18.3   Strategic investing in new product development (long-cycle-time projects)

product concept, numerous potential technical solutions may be developed in parallel for years. As time goes on, the landscape will change. Your patents will be granted or rejected. Your competitors' patents will be granted or rejected. Business strategies and consumer needs will change. Each of these changes may require adjustments to your patent strategy along the way.

Creating Inventions to Fit the Strategy

It may seem that creating an invention or product to fit the patent strategy is an exotic approach to inventing. However, one of the most basic examples of strategic inventing is the design-around invention. This phrase describes creating a new product that is similar to a competitor's, but that specifically does *not* infringe on the competitor's patents. This is common practice primarily because everyone would prefer to avoid infringement if possible. While the intentional design of products with enhanced patentability may be controversial at times, design-around inventing is a well-accepted practice that is commonly attempted whenever the need arises.

Let's imagine that a patent search early in the development process for a new product has identified one or more patents that your product is likely to infringe. Your company has the option of contacting the patent holder to obtain a license, consulting with attorneys to evaluate the validity of the claims, and/or attempting to come up with an alternative technical solution. Assuming that the third strategy is chosen, different products are created. The claims of the nearest patents are evaluated, and great care is taken to ensure that the newly developed process or product delivers benefits that are as close as possible to your objective without falling within the claim scope of the competitor's patents.

In this example, the intended product—although it would generate significant value for the consumer in its original form—must be revised based on an element of patent strategy (avoiding infringement). That is, the product design flows from the patent strategy. Another important example of strategic inventing occurs when attempting to build a multi-patent portfolio according to a larger strategy.

For example, if your focus is life-cycle management and you decide to develop a "droplet" strategy to extend the meaningful life of your patent portfolio by layering different types of inventions, you should consider what potential opportunities exist between the current technology and the future final product (i.e., you should identify the white space). A good patent landscape will be invaluable, as will an understanding of other points in the value chain—even segments in which you don't normally compete. Some of these inventions will require extrapolating to future scenarios and perhaps even prophetic inventions. Insights from the patent landscape may help to direct a focused effort to identify potential new inventions. This will probably include inventor-focused brainstorming, some actual research, and at least a few hours of attorney time—if not much more. Ideally, you'll have identified a handful of opportunities for new inventions, each of which will reinforce your patent portfolio and extend its usefulness over time.

So, is it really possible to decide on a patent strategy and then invent to fit the strategy? Absolutely. Most significant advancements create opportunities for multiple inventions through combinations with related technologies, applications to different markets, changes to intermediate processes, ways in which the consumer interacts with the product, combinations with your competitors' technologies, or other unexpected impacts along the value chain. If your primary invention is successful, what else will change? How will your competitors respond? Will the consumer use the product differently? Are there indirect benefits? Are there likely substitutions that aren't within the scope of the primary filing? Answers to these questions may point toward opportunities for new inventions.

Creating Products to Fit the Patents

Fortunately or unfortunately, we live in a time in which low-cost manufacturers and rapid NPD cycle times mean that many new products have imitators on the market soon after they are launched. While innovation remains one of the greatest competitive advantages possible, these imitators may dilute the value of new ideas.

Competitive advantage may also come from other areas: lower costs, higher quality, more efficient manufacturing, more sophisticated business models, and so on. However, innovation can and should be an important source of competitive advantage for any company with an emphasis on new product development and a differentiating consumer experience. Patents are the way to turn this potentially short-lived competitive advantage into a sustainable long-term advantage.

A well-protected product should be fortified against imitators for the life of the patent portfolio. Therefore, patent portfolios can help to create tremendous value—directly, through limiting the competition's new product features, or indirectly, through licensing, cross-licensing, discouraging new entrants into the market, or even enforcing the patents against infringing imitators.

For example, if your research leads to an improved product using techniques and compounds that are known in the art, your product may initially be successful. However, if your new product does not have any protectable benefits, competitors will probably act quickly to adopt these improvements in their own products. Even though your new product is initially successful, its life span is likely to be short.

Alternatively, an approach focused on strategic inventing would evaluate the potential improvements early in the development cycle and avoid the nonpatentable solutions if at all possible. A search of the prior art would be done to identify potential areas of white space and key aspects of novelty that might be incorporated. Novel materials with unique functions might be evaluated to identify an unexpected benefit and increase the level of differentiation.

The strategy-focused approach may result in a significantly different product from what would come from a purely discovery-driven approach. However, the benefit will be a higher level of protection for any successful new developments.

Consider a rather famous, though controversial, example of two pharmaceuticals. Prilosec (omeprazole magnesium) and Nexium (esomeprazole magnesium) have similar chemical compositions, but different stereochemistry. Prilosec is an older drug whose patent protection was running out. Nexium was developed with relatively minor technical distinctions from Prilosec, but enough to obtain a new patent and a new period of exclusivity. As might be expected, the minor technical distinction results in what some people consider a minor functional distinction. The new patent position afforded by the minor technical distinction and a substantial marketing effort has created a significant competitive advantage—and billions of dollars in revenue. It has also created some significant public controversy. (Please note: I'm not a doctor, and I have no medical training. My comments are based on a purely superficial analysis of this information—contact your physician for any medical questions related to these drugs.)

Importantly, the patent system is about inventiveness and unexpected results, not efficacy. While one could reasonably argue that the patentability test could be more stringent in some instances, the claimed invention does not need to produce a qualitatively "better" result than the prior art does. For example, commercials for nutraceuticals that include a tagline like "so effective it's been patented" obscure a salient point: the U.S. Patent and Trademark Office (USPTO) doesn't investigate efficacy, marketing, or other trade practices. Those are the responsibility of other organizations like the Food and Drug Administration (FDA) and the Federal Trade Commission (FTC).

Of course, misleading consumers to get them to buy your product is *not* the purpose of developing a product with a strong patent position. Rather, the purpose is to protect a market position through a proprietary benefit or feature: something your product can do that your competition can't imitate. Occasionally, there may even be some overlap with another form of intellectual property: trademarks.

Consumers pay more for branded products all the time—that's the purpose of creating a brand and investing in brand equity. Trademarks (e.g., brand names, product names, and identifying logos) convey value to the consumer, even if there are no overt functional advantages. A strong patent portfolio based on consumer-relevant differentiating features can be used in a similar way. Consumers will seek out the differentiating feature just as they would a traditional trademark, whether they are unique designs or differentiating functions.

FIRST THE CART. . .

There are many differences between strategic inventing and traditional methods of discovery-driven patent strategy. The methods used to develop the strategy are different, and the resulting products and inventions may also be different. Strategic inventing emphasizes putting intellectual property at the forefront of the innovation process. As Stephen Covey would say, "Begin with the end in mind." If the objective is a great patent position, these issues need to be evaluated from the very beginning.

Generally, this means that the beginning stages of the R&D or NPD process should include steps such as patent landscapes, predictive invention, life-cycle management, and IP-based competitive intelligence. Scientists, engineers, managers, and executives should be conversant in the basic elements of patent strategy. Involving patent attorneys only after a new product or discovery is well on its way to implementation and scale-up is not the ideal approach.

There are important opportunities for improving competitive advantage by involving patent strategy at the front end of the product development process. Key inventions and related products will be more valuable if competitors are precluded from imitation and minor variations through an intentional and deliberate strategy of invention.

CHAPTER 19

COMPETITIVE ADVANTAGE AND THE MAGIC OF DIFFERENTIATION

The goal of new product development is to deliver ever-greater value to the consumer so that your product is preferred over those of the competition. The differences between your product and your competitors' products—differentiation—are the driving forces that influence a consumer's choice. If there is no differentiation between your product and those of your competitors, there won't be a compelling reason for the consumer to pick your product over your competitors' products. This need for differentiation provides parallel benefits in the realm of strategic inventing—deliberately seeking differentiating products is one approach to ensuring competitive advantage and a significant patent position.

In some industries, such as commodity chemicals, product specifications are tightly defined—differentiation at a product level is nearly impossible. However, the source of differentiation need not be in the product, but it must still be relevant to the consumer. For example, if your research were on improved processes, the improvement should be significant enough to improve the economics, quality, or some other tangible element of the product. Otherwise, your differentiation—no matter how well it's protected—will be of little value.

Now, let's turn to the issue of competition and imitation. Once you have created your differentiated product, your competitors are likely to try to deliver the same benefits to the consumer. If your product or feature is easily copied, the value created will be short-lived. This is where patents come into the picture. They can provide a form of sustainable competitive advantage that can protect your product's differentiating features from imitation.

DIFFERENTIATION IN PATENT LAW AND IN THE MARKETPLACE

Interestingly, there is a strong parallel between the need for differentiation in the marketplace and the need for differentiation in patent law. In patent terms, we're looking for novelty and nonobviousness to define protectable inventions. Therefore, inventions must be distinct from things that have gone before. For many of the patents that are granted, the level of distinctiveness may not seem significant. However, if a product is highly differentiated in the marketplace, there is a good chance that the differentiation is based on patentable features.

Recall our probability curve from Figure 2.1. The more distinctive and unexpected the invention is, the more likely it is that the patent application will be granted. Furthermore, significant differentiation will usually allow for a more meaningful granted claim scope. The more different your invention is from the prior art, the broader your claims should be.

Likewise, differentiation in the marketplace is a hallmark of a successful product and business strategy. The degree of competitive advantage that your corporation enjoys will be proportional to the degree of differentiation offered to consumers. However, differentiating features are not always patentable, and they frequently don't involve the product. For example, a successful gas station may be selling exactly the same product as every other gas station but have a more convenient location. The location differentiates it from its competitors. Or perhaps a soft drink has a unique brand with longstanding trademarks and substantial cultural ties. Even a competitor with a nearly identical product will struggle to compete because of the differentiation offered by the trademarks and associated goodwill. A reputation for quality, as established by a corporation across its product lines, can also be a differentiating feature that is difficult to imitate.

Some of these sources of differentiation would be difficult or impossible to protect using patents. However, it's the differentiation that provides the competitive advantage. Our goal is to seek out and protect patentable differentiated features wherever possible.

DIFFERENTIATION AND THE INNOVATION S CURVE

You're probably familiar with the concept of the "innovation S curve," which suggests that most innovations proceed through a period of slow adoption followed by rapid expansion and finally a saturated, low-growth period. This is a theoretical framework that has some shortcomings, but that is often useful in illustrating categories of issues related to a technology or product.

For example, one might divide the S curve into three general stages, as shown in Figures 19.1 and 19.2. These stages can be described as follows:

Stage 1. This is the *technology-driven* portion of the curve; a new technology has been developed, but it lacks broad adoption, and there may be secondary considerations that prevent its widespread use. Early adopters are willing to take a risk and try something new, but the general market has yet to see the value of this technology.

Stage 2. This is the *consumer-driven* segment; the technology is clearly providing incremental value above the competitive offerings and is being widely adopted by consumers. Its value in the marketplace is rapidly expanding. As competitors become aware of the success of the product, imitators begin to emerge. There may be competitive products with similar features.

Stage 3. This is the *price-driven* or commoditization stage; the technology has reached saturation, and the level of competition has increased to

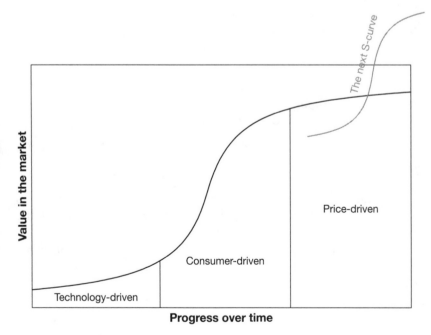

Figure 19.1   The innovation S curve

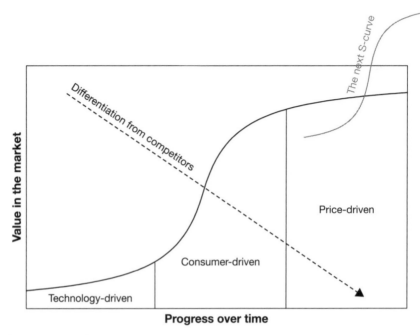

Figure 19.2   Differentiation relative to the innovation S curve

such an extent that further improvements return only small incremental benefit to the consumer. There is now minimal differentiation between your product and competitive products. Given the lack of differentiation, the total value in the marketplace is being split among more and more competitors. Competition without differentiation should lead to significant price pressures and the eventual commoditization of the product or technology.

So, if this is a model for the long-term prospects of a significantly differentiated product, what do we do next? We invent something new. Ideally, innovative companies create new avenues for differentiation as the cycle for a product begins to reach the later stages. As competitors begin to reduce the level of differentiation among existing products, the need for the next innovation S curve steadily increases.

This cycle of differentiation is also a key motivator for establishing a sustainable competitive advantage through differentiation that is protected by a patent portfolio. If you are able to patent the key differentiating features that are driving this innovation S curve, you can delay the onset of imitation and related price pressures. Your competitors are free to create their own innovations, and they surely will. However, they won't be able to practice your technology during the life of your patent portfolio.

Understanding this cycle can open up great opportunities for strategic inventing. As the cycle progresses, the patent strategy for your product must also change. At the beginning of the cycle, you should seek significant new inventions with broad claim scope. Toward the middle of the cycle, a strategy more like the value-added model, with small incremental improvements to the original inventions, may be best. Toward the end of the cycle, as cost pressures become relevant, process improvements or raw material changes may be opportunities for invention.

As each cycle draws closer to the commoditization phase, opportunities lie in disruptive innovations that may initiate the next S curve. Being aware of the S-curve principle can help the patent-savvy inventor predict when the next cycle is about to occur, anticipate potential disruptive inventions, and begin development of the patent strategy for the next product cycle.

DIFFERENTIATION MUST BE RELEVANT TO THE CONSUMER

The differentiation that we're discussing must be relevant to both the consumer and the marketplace. Ideally, this differentiation will include a feature that is significant enough to influence the consumer's purchasing decision. Consumers should know immediately when they have purchased a product with your invention, as opposed to a product without your invention.

In the field of negotiating, practitioners use the acronym *BATNA* to refer to the "best alternative to a negotiated agreement." This is the best-case scenario that will result when negotiations fall apart. Any logical negotiated solution should have a value greater than one's BATNA. When assessing the value of inventions, a similar principle applies. The "best alternative to the new invention" (BATNI) is the worst-case scenario that competitors will be forced to apply if they are kept from using your new invention entirely. What's the difference between your invention and your competitors' BATNI? Will your competitors continue with the technology that they have been using, or will they create something new? Is the differentiation significant enough that consumers will recognize this difference? Will they actively seek products containing your invention in place of your competitor's BATNI?

The difference between your offering and your competitors' BATNI is the maximum value of your competitive advantage. The value created and the closely related degree of consumer-relevant differentiation are two key criteria.

Differentiation in the product is also associated with a certain level of "activation energy" for the consumer. For example, I've seen countless commercials telling me that one brand of gasoline is better than another. I can intellectually agree that there are probably differentiating features in gasoline brands. Yet I can't recall ever having decided on where to stop for gas because of the brand name of the gasoline. Car aficionados may be surprised, but my decision process is based primarily on convenience— I'm not going to drive too far out of my way to fill my car's gas tank. If two gas stations are reasonably close, my next logical motivation is price. My perception of the differences in quality does not surpass my activation energy for changing my purchasing habits. As you consider what differentiating features you may be able to incorporate into your next product, keep in mind that these features must be significant enough to drive a change in consumer response.

Furthermore, this level of differentiation will also be more likely to lead to greater claim scope and more meaningful patents.

Hopefully, the examples given here have provided a brief introduction to the various aspects of product development and patent strategy, which are tied together through this unique property of differentiation. In short, different is better for both. So, think different. You might recognize that phrase as an Apple trademark—it's definitely worked well for that company.

CHAPTER 20

INTELLECTUAL PROPERTY AND DISRUPTIVE INNOVATION: STRATEGIES, TACTICS, AND LESSONS FROM CHINA

Jeffrey D. Lindsay, PhD

Jeffrey D. Lindsay is Head of Intellectual Property at Asia Pulp & Paper in Shanghai, China. Jeff is the lead author of Conquering Innovation Fatigue *(John Wiley & Sons, 2009), with C. Perkins and M. Karanjikar. Previously he was a Director at Innovationedge, Corporate Patent Strategist and Senior Research Fellow at Kimberly-Clark Corp., and Associate Professor at IPST on the Georgia Tech campus. Jeff is a registered U.S. patent agent with a PhD in chemical engineering from Brigham Young University.*

Disruptive innovation has become an entrenched concept in modern business parlance. However, in spite of significant advances in scholarship, many companies and innovators seem no more capable of dealing with disruptive threats than they were before. Visionaries who recognize disruptive threats or opportunities often lack the power to change the course of a company to enable it to respond in time. One tool that has been largely neglected in the literature can be used to advantage: intellectual property (IP). An approach to disruptive innovation is not complete until the power of intellectual property as a strategic tool is fully considered.

While there are many loose definitions of "disruptive innovation," the framework defined by Clayton Christensen offers rigor that can guide thinking and decision making. The theory of disruptive innovation provides insights that can help to explain why large companies often fail to recognize and respond to the emerging innovations that may destroy their business. The theory can also guide innovators in selecting business models and approaches in the market for disruptive success. Knowledge of the theory can also, as we shall see, guide those who are developing intellectual property to help them solve the biggest conundrum of disruptive innovation: overcoming the corporate filters and systems that are essential for business success, yet leave the company vulnerable to disruption.

Professor Clayton Christensen of Harvard Business School has sought to explain common aspects of business success and failure in terms of "disruption innovation." His popular theories are elaborated in three books, *The Innovator's Dilemma* (1997),[1] *The Innovator's Solution* (2003),[2] and, most recently, *Seeing What's Next* (2004).[3] According to Christensen, disruptive innovations are generally those that allow a new product or service to get a foothold in a market by appealing to nonusers or low-end users of previously available products or services. Disruptive innovations are often "worse" in terms of the established metrics and customer expectations in the existing market, but offer new benefits such as reduced cost, increased convenience or ease of use, or other features that may appeal to current nonusers. The new offering is provided in a way that motivates the incumbents in the area to avoid direct competition with the entrants. Rather than fighting a head-on battle with the market entrant, the incumbents are motivated to focus their efforts on mainstream or high-end customers.

On the other hand, "sustaining" innovations are the ones that large companies are most adept at providing. These are innovations based on listening to current customers and making existing products better. The filters and decision-making processes used to select and market innovations are well adapted for sustaining innovations, and they inherently tend to reject disruptive innovations.

Figure 20.1 illustrates the march of products over time to illustrate some of the principles of disruptive innovation. Both incumbents and new entrants naturally apply sustaining innovation to improve their products over time. But the disruptive newcomers have the advantage of being largely ignored initially because their products are "worse" and don't siphon off the most profitable mainstream customers. They do, however, provide new benefits that appeal to nonusers and perhaps low-end users of existing products. They may also rely on skills, networks, and technologies that are not readily available to the incumbent. In response to losing some of the low-end, low-margin customers, the incumbents may move upstream and offer further sustaining innovations, but these can exceed what the market really requires, further increasing the risk of disruption from below.

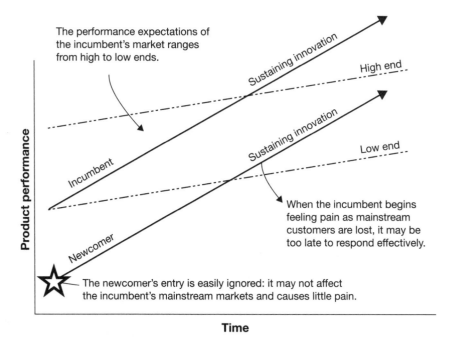

Figure 20.1   The path of disruptive innovation (adapted from Clayton Christensen)

Examples of disruptive innovations include the emergence of disposable facial tissue, disrupting the handkerchief market; do-it-yourself dental whitening systems relative to clinical treatments; Netflix relative to brick-and-mortar video rentals; and Bekaert's Dramix® metal fibers that can be conveniently blended into cement to replace rebar. These new products required skills and infrastructure that would be difficult for the incumbents to develop.

In the models provided by Christensen and expanded upon in subsequent literature, several characteristics are found in disruptive innovations:[4]

1. The innovation underperforms according to the metrics valued by the mainstream customer base.
2. New features offered by the innovation are not highly valued by mainstream customers.
3. The innovation is often simpler and more convenient than existing solutions and may be less expensive.
4. The innovation is further developed over time until it can compete in the mainstream market space and draw away high-end customers.

FACING THE BARRIERS

In hindsight, the ultimate killer of innovation always seems to be myopia.[5] However, corporate failure to deal with disruptive innovation typically does not happen because the managers are blind or stupid. The fate of disruptive innovations follows naturally from managers making sound decisions to achieve exactly what they have been trained to do. The very filters and systems that are essential for sustaining innovation can blind the corporation to disruptive innovation.

To cope with disruptive threats and opportunities, Christensen and others have called for visionary leaders to create special units with different systems and cultures. Christensen also calls for organizational change to overcome the natural mechanisms that kill disruptive innovations. Such changes, though, require buy-in at multiple levels and often flounder because of a corporate culture that is geared to sustaining innovation.

Intellectual property, on the other hand, offers a practical avenue through which visionaries can help the company be ready when the need for change becomes more apparent years later. Even if the corporation is able to implement the strategies outlined by Christensen and others, if it also pays attention to intellectual property as a tool for dealing with disruption, it will be much further ahead.

A Proposed Solution: Disruptive Intellectual Asset Strategy

While organizational change to support disruption is difficult to bring about, a small group can proactively pursue intellectual assets that can protect a company from some disruptive threats and lay a foundation for future disruptive offerings. Visionary intellectual property can weaken competitors' impact and give the corporation room to adapt and succeed. In *Conquering Innovation Fatigue*,[6] we proposed that intellectual assets, particularly patents and, to a lesser degree, publications, be used in a two-pronged approach to deal with disruptive innovation proactively at early stages.

This two-pronged strategy involves (1) defensive actions, such as filed patents and publications, aimed at reducing the harm that potential disruptive innovation could do to the business, and (2) offensive steps, particularly patent filings, but also publications, aimed at opening future doors for new products in potentially disruptive areas. The defensive actions are easily justified, especially if low-cost IP-creation tools are used, but even the defensive IP can be crafted with the second objective in mind.

Executing this strategy requires a group that is empowered to pursue IP and tap creative individuals with disruptive innovation in mind. Low-cost IP-creation exercises can be carried out that move past brainstorming to enabled invention concepts that can be quickly documented for conversion to IP.[7] In my experience with exercises of this sort,[8] one of the keys is having a facilitator or some other team member who is thoroughly prepared with an understanding of the prior art and basic technologies to guide efforts toward concepts with higher patentability potential.

Creating IP in emerging areas is related to what Marshall Phelps and John Cronin called "forward inventing."[9] In light of disruptive innovation theory, with properly trained team members, doing this can help a company cope with disruptive innovation. Surprisingly, the role of IP is almost uniformly neglected in the literature on disruptive innovation and is probably receiving inadequate attention in practice. It's time for proactive inventors, innovators, and IP leaders to change that.

In one sense, the approach of using "disruptive intellectual asset strategy" involves considering both disruptive risks and disruptive opportunities, with an initial emphasis on averting risk—in part to mobilize the needed resources to respond swiftly, but generally at low cost. The risk aversion efforts, however, are informed by a longer-term agenda of creating territory for protected growth. Maintaining flexible options for future growth is the key. Following the two-pronged approach to disruption, territory that is in the path of a potential competitive disruption and that could be valuable to competitors is secured with intellectual barbed wire and other fortifications to keep them from using it, but the longer-term vision is to retain the option to eventually harvest growth from that territory. In other words, the defensive act of limiting competitive threats may also involve securing territory for one's own growth in the future, even though the business may not see that territory as currently valuable for its own activities. Naturally, this requires a disruptive intellectual asset (IA) strategy team with the vision to understand how external technologies and potentially disruptive trends may affect the business and may *eventually* be desirable to the business. The goal is to lay a foundation early and at low cost before the business acknowledges the desirability of the opportunity, because by the time a large corporation sees the business opportunity in a potentially disruptive area and reaches enough consensus to move forward, it is very likely that competitors, especially smaller competitors, will have already seen that opportunity and created intellectual property that could prove to be a costly barrier to the larger corporation's entry. The goal, then, is early defense, with a possible later transition to protected growth.

DISRUPTION AT THE MACROSCOPIC SCALE: LESSONS FROM CHINA'S RENAISSANCE

Listed below are the lessons from the China's renaissance, which include the background, the classic pattern, and how to prepare for the disruption.

Background: Western Attitudes Toward Asian Innovation

The West sometimes struggles when it comes to recognizing innovation from the East. An important step in Western appreciation of the Chinese origins of many important inventions came in 1954, when the illustrious British scholar Joseph Needham published the first volume of *Science and Civilisation in China*, a masterpiece of scholarship that would grow to 27 volumes. That project began by seeking to list every invention that had been made in China. Needham's work clarified the Chinese origins of numerous technologies, including many that were long held to be Western inventions. These inventions include cast iron, the ploughshare, the stirrup, gunpowder, the magnetic compass, clockwork escapements, and printing.

In the field of printing, for example, the West prides itself on the invention of printed books and especially the world's first mass-produced book made with movable type. However, these inventions have important and long-overlooked prior art in China, where the Diamond Sutra is a printed book with the date of AD 868[10] and where numerous copies of the massive *Nong Shu*, or *Book of Farming*, were printed with movable type by the inventive Wang Zhen in AD 1313, more than a century before Gutenberg's Bible.[11] These and many other breakthroughs of Chinese origin remain largely unknown to many in the West.

Today innovation is becoming an increasingly important priority in China and throughout Asia. Many Asian nations are investing heavily in research and in systems that will support and encourage innovation, including robust intellectual property systems. In fact, as of 2011, China exceeded the United States in the number of patents filed and has now become the top patent-filing nation in the world.[12] The nation in general is recognizing that it is time to switch gears from low-cost imitation to value-added innovation and advanced technology. Spending on R&D is growing rapidly. Tax incentives for companies qualifying as "high-tech" are significant. Many new skills are gradually being added to the capabilities of Chinese companies and entrepreneurs that will lead to new Chinese brands, new design competence, and new marketing skills at an international level, although for many the Chinese market is large enough for many years to come. In general, there is a surge in innovation capabilities in China, perhaps even a renaissance of innovation of IP.

Significant voices in the West downplay the changes in China, viewing innovation and IP there as largely irrelevant and easily ignored. For example, some Western IP pundits have derided the Chinese patent-filing trend, dismissing these large numbers of patents as being of low quality. It is certainly true that many Chinese patents as filed are of questionable quality.[13] A better gauge of China's innovation prowess may be found in its international filings in the United States and Europe, where low-quality patents are less likely to be filed because of the much higher costs and strict standards for realizing IP success. When international patent filings are considered, China still shows remarkable strength, with two of the top five international patent filers now being Chinese companies (Huawei and ZTE).[14]

In spite of China's impressive international IP efforts, and in spite of aggressive R&D to drive innovation, China frequently does not receive recognition for its innovation. For example, a 2011 report from Thompson-Reuters named the "Top 100 Global Innovators" based on patent activity from 2008 to 2010.[15] The study emphasized international applications, not just filings in one country. The United States had 47 U.S.-based companies in the top 100, followed by Japan, France, Sweden, Germany, the Netherlands, South Korea, Switzerland, and Liechtenstein. Not a single company from China, Taiwan, or Hong Kong made the list. Innovation giant Apple was on the list, naturally, but Foxconn, the Taiwanese company that makes Apple's products in China, was not, in spite of its numerous U.S. and other international patents. In fact, Foxconn (or Hon Hai Precision, its parent) boasts roughly three times more U.S. patents than Apple obtained during the time period of the study, and 50 times more U.S.-granted patents than one of the companies on the top 100 list. The methodology behind the study may have been correctly applied, but I would argue that so thoroughly obscuring China's intense patent activity makes it possible that faulty definitions and filters were used.

Following the Classic Pattern: Ignoring a Disruptive Entry by China?

The relationship between China and the West regarding innovation and IP has parallels with classic disruptive innovation. Insights from Christensen at the level of products and companies can be applied to macroscopic patterns involving nations and economies. Consider China as the newcomer whose initial offering, in terms of both innovation and IP, is easily ignored by the incumbents, especially North America and Europe, because of perceived low quality (based on established metrics of the incumbents for their markets). The incumbents can ignore the newcomer on the low end, not noticing that the newcomer is rapidly developing its capabilities and improving its quality through sustaining advances. Furthermore, as is often the case in disruptive innovation scenarios, the newcomer is developing a different business model, with skills and know-how that will be difficult for the West to learn later when the real pain comes. The business model at this macroscopic level includes rapid market-based innovation in which products are released quickly, without lengthy studies and years of planning. Chinese companies can learn quickly from the market and rapidly iterate designs and business models to achieve success. But they are also learning principles of design and market research to help them be more successful earlier. As Chinese companies and innovation engines hone their skills in the evolving and increasingly sophisticated Asian markets, Chinese innovation and IP prowess will be hard to ignore. It may take five to ten years, but when the West finally recognizes how important Chinese IP and innovation have become internationally, large portions of the economy may be unprepared for the changes that follow. What could have been viewed as an opportunity by the visionary may be felt only as a threat by the unprepared. Attempts to block the fruits of Chinese innovation and IP with trade war tactics as Western companies emphasize higher-end products and markets will only make things worse in the long run.

Preparing for Disruption

The rise of innovation and the growth of IP in China and elsewhere can be good news for those who recognize these trends early and adapt to them. The ability to cooperate with outside innovators will be increasingly important. Partnerships with Chinese innovation engines, including universities, design firms, and consumer products companies, will become important. The use of disruptive intellectual asset strategy will also be valuable in maintaining an edge and in providing reasons for rising companies to be your partners. Currently, though, very few Western companies are looking to China for its innovation and IP, apart from very limited efforts to run Western-style R&D in Asia or to recruit local talent. Few seem to grasp the power of Chinese business models and the strength that they can bring when coupled with skills in the West. There is a need for the West to understand China more deeply, develop relationships more thoroughly, and tap the power that is emerging in innovation and IP creation. Unfortunately, Western companies operating in China often fail to recognize and understand even their largest competitors, let alone their prospective partners with potentially disruptive concepts and business models. This is a time for proactive preparation on multiple fronts. Disruptive intellectual asset strategy must become a part of your future in an increasingly disruptive global economy.

In addition to accumulating intellectual assets, a company's basic approach to innovation should be strengthened. The literature on disruption reveals the need to look beyond technology and new products per se to understand the barriers that are leaving the real but often unexpressed needs of nonusers and low-end users unfulfilled. We must consider innovation in business models, services, customer experience, and so on to provide new levels of convenience, access, and cost-effectiveness—often at the expense of high-end features that overshoot the needs of many who would welcome a "worse" product that made life better for them. By considering and pursuing broader disruptive opportunities, game-changing innovation can be introduced in the marketplace with a lasting advantage. Finding disruptive opportunities will often be easiest when cooperating with outside partners with different business models and different approaches to innovation. Looking to the new Asia to better understand and explore disruptive innovation may be a wise step. The focus on convenience, low cost, and rapid iteration to meet (and discover!) unmet needs is an important characteristic of innovation in China and much of Asia, and as further skills are developed, innovators in that part of the world may become increasingly valuable resources for visionaries elsewhere in the world.

SUMMARY

Disruptive intellectual asset strategy must become a part of your future in an increasingly disruptive global economy. New competitors may arise with new competencies, new business models, and entirely new approaches that may, over time, take away a large portion of your market. If you ignore their entry because their offerings seem inferior and irrelevant based on your existing metrics, you may be setting yourself up for disruption. Proactive early response is needed, and visionary intellectual property can be one of the most practical tools to deploy. Both publications and patents can be used with an eye to preserving your future freedom to operate as well as owning exclusive territory where your own future products and services may find protection or where you may limit disruptive competitive inroads into your territory. Disruptive intellectual assets can overcome some of the natural barriers that tend to keep corporations from pursuing disruptive opportunities or recognizing disruptive threats.

Disruptive intellectual asset strategy must also consider the innovation and IP of others that could be part of future disruptive pain or, in healthier scenarios, resources for creating one's own more successful future. We urge companies to avoid discounting the emerging IP and innovation from nations such as China, for example, and instead prepare early to respond, adapt, or tap their emerging power of innovation and IP as part of a healthy approach to innovation.

CHAPTER 21

What Makes
a Great Invention?

There is a big difference between something that is patentable and a truly great invention. Many great discoveries aren't patentable. On the other hand, some minor variations may be easily protected. When you are deliberately creating new inventions, it's important to understand the difference between what can be patented but isn't of much value, and what really makes a valuable invention. It's often hard to know ahead of time which patents will be the most useful, but there are criteria that can help to focus your inventive efforts on areas that are more likely to create significant value (fitting our definition of a great invention).

In Part 1 of this book, we discussed the basic components of patentability: novelty, nonobviousness, utility, and statutory subject matter. In addition, patent applications are required to enable the invention and disclose the best mode of practicing the invention. While these are general requirements for obtaining a patent, having a granted patent is not the same as creating a valuable invention with substantive patent protection. Many (if not most) patents are simply not valuable—perhaps because they don't protect the right technology, or because equivalent alternatives already exist, or because there isn't a means for detecting infringement, or because the patent is granted too early or too late in the product cycle.

There is also an important distinction between great research and a great invention. These are not mutually exclusive categories, of course, but there are important distinctions between these groups. The requirements for having a patent granted are different from those of scientific research. Many scientific discoveries are tremendous breakthroughs in terms of knowledge and benefit to society—but they are not patentable. On the other hand, if you sort through a stack of granted patents, you will find all manner of absurd trinkets and fanciful products of dubious value. One reason may be that when it comes to ideas and invention, value lies in the eye of the beholder. One man's oxygen helmet filled with cacti (US 4,605,000) is another man's iPad (US 7,688,306 et al.). However, there are criteria that can be used to help characterize great inventions, and to help identify these inventions when they occur.

RESEARCH VERSUS INVENTION

Scientific research often encompasses a new discovery about the natural world, an increase in understanding and knowledge, proving or disproving a theory, or characterizing principles of naturally occurring phenomena. These categories of research generally are not patentable, even though they may lead to patentable inventions. Importantly, many forms of research lack statutory subject matter in that knowledge and natural phenomena are not patentable. Discovering something about nature can be extremely valuable to society, but it is often not patentable. The discovery of the double-helix structure of DNA is not patentable, for example.

Newton's discovery of the laws of gravity was a tremendous contribution to science, but it would not be patentable until someone invented a novel process or apparatus making use of (or based on) those laws. For example, a device for aiming a cannon more accurately based on an understanding of gravity would be a patentable invention (subject to the prior art of the day, of course). In other words, great inventions can result from great research, even though the fundamental research may be unpatentable. Many aspects of what we consider research are patentable because they are closely tied to a product or process that provides utility beyond simply characterizing natural phenomena. For example, searching for drugs to cure disease, identifying functions of genes and related predictive tests, and the discovery of new materials with useful properties are all categories of research that are likely to be patentable.

In the category of research, we also need to mention research into consumer needs, or market research. Unfortunately, identification of a consumer need is not in and of itself patentable. However, addressing that consumer need with a new product or process is likely to be patentable. The knowledge that the need exists is not patentable, but the way in which the need is satisfied by a novel product probably is.

In a nutshell, good research is not always patentable, but practical applications of good research usually are.

THE INTERSECTION OF RESEARCH, INVENTION, AND STRATEGY

Furthermore, truly valuable inventions will usually be found at the intersection of research, invention, and strategy. Within the space of patentable inventions, most of these creations will not be valuable. However, inventions are more likely to be valuable when they coincide with meaningful progress in some form of scientific research. In other words, if we were to seek out the most likely areas to identify future great inventions, investigating groundbreaking research would be a good place to start. However, we also need to consider the impact of the corporation's business strategy. Some of your company's strategies are likely to involve patented products, but some of them will not. In fact, there are many great business strategies that don't involve patents—customer service, sales techniques, marketing strategies, retail sales, real estate transactions, and so forth, are relatively unlikely to involve patents. These are certainly valid and profitable business strategies (they just happen not to be the focus of this book).

Research developments and patentable inventions will be of particular value only if they are closely aligned with the corporation's overall strategies. It is this intersection, as shown in Figure 21.1, which provides the most fertile opportunity for great inventions.

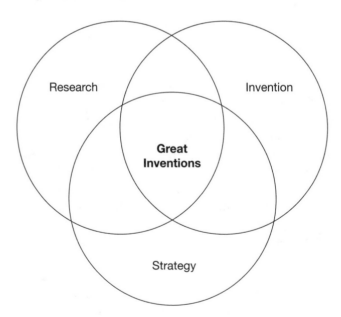

Figure 21.1   Great inventions are usually at the intersection of research, strategy, and invention

If there are significant patentable breakthroughs that *aren't* aligned with the corporation's business strategy, they would be excellent candidates for out-licensing. The difference in alignment may also result from changes over time. For example, it will be three to five years before patents related to research conducted today are granted. In the intervening time, it's quite possible that your company will change its business objectives and focus on different opportunities. In these situations, the patents are usually just abandoned. If there are particularly valuable inventions, however, they may be ripe for out-licensing to other companies—perhaps even companies that would have been your competitors for that product or technology.

One of my own inventions involves a method of printing ink onto paper that involves a very peculiar process. I discovered that applying a little bit of water just before the printing process resulted in brighter colors, better adhesion, and the appearance of higher quality. One of the first experiments involved standing in front of a printing press with a garden hose. The results were quite unexpected, to say the least. Initially, not many people believed the results. Eventually, though, patent applications were filed, and what I perceived to be a significant innovation was created. Unfortunately, this invention never quite aligned with the strategy for the related products, and to my knowledge it has never been implemented. This is one of my favorite inventions (US 6,477,948), but it couldn't be considered a truly great invention because it didn't align with the company's strategy and wasn't implemented.

Another key aspect of a corporation's strategy is the competitive landscape. Competitive products and technology dictate the value of any particular invention for the corporation's strategy, in that patents and inventions derive their value from the nature of the best alternative. As previously mentioned, the best alternative to the new invention (BATNI) is the option that competitors will be forced to apply if they are kept from using your invention entirely. Is the lack of the patented invention noticeable by the consumer—either directly, as in a significant difference in performance, or indirectly, as in a reduction in cost? If it isn't, your competitor will simply rely on its BATNI, with minimal negative consequences.

In summary, the opportunity for great inventions usually occurs at the intersection of research, invention, and strategy. This isn't to suggest that valuable opportunities can't exist elsewhere, only that this should be the primary target when focusing one's resources.

ATTRIBUTES OF GREAT INVENTIONS

In addition to the broad criteria just mentioned, a great invention must also include claims that are written broadly enough to create a significant competitive advantage. The claimed invention will encompass differentiating features which deliver a valuable benefit to the consumer. Also, these claims should be readily testable and enforceable. Ideally, there will be granted claims that encompass these differentiating features in an easily enforceable manner.

In order to identify potential infringers, some means to detect infringement is required. This may not be a significant hurdle for most product claims, though it is frequently a challenge for method claims. Method claims are much stronger if the process leaves a "fingerprint" in the resulting product that can be used to identify infringement. Frequently, it is assumed that product claims have greater value because of this enforcement issue: the product is usually available for inspection and testing against the claims, whereas the process used to make it is usually hidden behind closed doors. While this is not always true, it does highlight the need for claims that can be tested and enforced.

A final component of enforcement is the validity of the underlying patent. Protection of a great invention, even with broad claims, is only as strong as the validity of the underlying patents. If there are questions about inventorship, novelty, ownership, or undisclosed prior art, these will diminish the value of the patent. This reinforces the need for good record keeping, maintaining confidentiality, and proactively managing information transfers with outside collaborators.

To summarize, the intersection of research, invention, and strategy is where you will find the truly great inventions. These inventions will *create value* in the marketplace. They will be based on a *substantial differentiation* from your competitors' technology. And these differences will be result in *testable* and *enforceable* claims, in patents of unquestionable validity.

What If Vitamin C Cured Baldness?

Consider this hypothetical and hyperbolic example: what if you discovered that vitamin C cured baldness? You've conducted a phenomenally brilliant experiment that demonstrated that bald mice could be shown to grow back hair by administering an oral dose of vitamin C at precisely 2:00 in the afternoon. Encouraged by your results, you go to the medicine cabinet every day at 2:00 p.m. to take some vitamin C yourself, and you are astounded by the amount of hair you've begun to grow on your previously balding cranium. You quickly recruit a larger study panel, and a few months later, you have nearly a 100 percent success rate with no negative side effects (it is vitamin C, after all).

Let's evaluate.

Is it great research? It's not quite on the scale of the discovery of the gravity, but it certainly would be a great discovery. As a somewhat balding man, I can assure you that there is a tremendous need for such an invention.

Is there a patentable invention? I'm no expert in this art field, but the results certainly seem novel and nonobvious to me. Clearly, they rank high on the unofficial "unexpected result" criterion as well. Of course, given that vitamin C is well known in the art, the compound per se would not be patentable. However, the method of curing baldness by administering vitamin C at precisely 2:00 p.m. would appear to meet the basic criteria for patentability.

But is this a great invention? Unfortunately, no. The wide availability of vitamin C would allow anyone to use your method, leaving you with essentially no means of enforcing your claims. Once the information is known, there are no elements of the process for the patented invention that can be readily precluded from use by the consumer. The net result is that your invention, however wonderful it might sound, is probably not worth much at all.

While this is a lighthearted example, it does illustrate at least one potential shortcoming of what otherwise might seem to be a great discovery. For readers with a more devious nature, I pose the challenge: what would be your patent strategy based on such an invention? Potential mechanisms do exist for establishing a competitive advantage, although they would require a more creative approach and distinctly strategic inventing.

WHY BOTHER CHARACTERIZING GREAT INVENTIONS?

Strategic inventing must be done with an objective in mind, so that inventions better align with the strategic needs of the corporation, create more significant differentiation, and result in valid and enforceable claims. By knowing the objective, the inventor can improve the value resulting from the invention process. The inventor's target is at the intersection of research, invention, and strategy. The inventor can identify signficant inventions because they create value for the consumer, are based on a substantial differentiation from the competition, and can be protected by testable and enforceable claims.

Furthermore, inventions that are already "good" can be improved through focused efforts. For example, changing the product or invention to provide greater strategic focus might move an invention up toward the center of our diagram. Or, perhaps additional research is needed to broaden the scope of the claims. Or, perhaps new methods of characterizing the product need to be developed so that it can be patented with definite claims. Or, perhaps competitive technologies need to be analyzed and compared with the invention to define quantitative numerical ranges for the claims in order to improve detection and enforceability.

Never let the initial invention be the end of the inventing process. Mediocre inventions can often be made greater through additional effort and focused development. Some of this effort may precede the filing of the first patent application, such as research to broaden the scope of the claims. However, the value can also be strengthened after the initial filing. For example, if the initial patent isn't sufficient to provide meaningful competitive advantage on its own, work to develop a portfolio of individual cases that will collectively protect your technology.

One important caveat to remember is that just because an invention isn't "great" by these standards doesn't mean that it shouldn't be pursued. The strategic value of a particular application is often not known until years after it is filed. A portfolio is made up of patents with a wide distribution of value—some of them great and some not so great. However, the value of an individual patent may shift over time as the competitive landscape changes, business strategies evolve, or new products are developed.

Furthermore, in some research organizations with an emphasis on scientific achievement—perhaps having a significant number of researchers who have spent time in academia—the hurdle for patentability is thought to be very high. Researchers are constantly aiming for developments that will be seen as significant by the scientific community. This is clearly too high a bar for determining when something might be an invention. Seeking academic significance can have the unwanted side effect of filtering out inventions that may be valuable, even though they are not significant from a technical or scientific perspective.

Aiming for a great invention should be a target for all inventors, but it is not a minimum standard. Many inventions, great and small, will be required if you are to maintain a robust patent portfolio.

CHAPTER 22

STRATEGIC INVENTING TECHNIQUES

Clearly, strategic inventing is not the only source of new products or for developing a patent strategy. However, this approach has advantages in some situations. The greatest opportunities for strategic inventing usually occur in highly competitive industries with significant prior art. The prior art makes achieving broad protection for each successive product cycle relatively difficult. As a result, more deliberate strategic techniques are required to create a sustainable competitive advantage. If your latest breakthrough creates a tremendous new paradigm, far outside any previous claims, these techniques are likely to offer less benefit, if only because the claims you are likely to be granted will probably be sufficiently broad with a more straightforward approach.

In more complex situations, strategic inventing techniques like the examples that follow may be used to suggest alternative options for product development, as well as to strengthen the portfolio of patents that supports your overall patent strategy. The goal is to build your "toolbox" to create options for many different circumstances. Any individual tool will be used relatively infrequently, but the collective set of tools creates a problem-solving mechanism for enhancing your overall patent strategy.

DESIGN-AROUND STRATEGIES

The term *design-around* (or *invent-around*) means to intentionally achieve an objective similar to that of another patented invention, but without infringing on any of the patent's claims. When your competitor has a new product with patented features, your strategy may lead you to attempt to deliver the same features while avoiding any related patents.

In general, imitation is frowned upon by the innovators in industry. However, designing around competitive patents is actually encouraged by the patent system. One of the basic tenets of the patent system is that the information needed to practice the invention is available to anyone, increasing "the store of public knowledge." Once a patent expires, anyone may freely practice the patented invention. But even during the patent's life, using this information to develop new—and often better—alternative approaches is considered a good thing because it moves technology forward. This is *not* trying to cheat the system, as is sometimes inferred. Designing around, by definition, means creating something that is different from the claimed invention.

Recall from our discussion of claims that in order to infringe, the potential infringer must practice *every* element of the claim. If one element is missing, the product or process does not infringe. Adding an element, on the other hand, usually won't get your product outside of a claim.

Here is a general outline for working on a design-around invention. Keep in mind that this can be a complex issue, and that developing a product that is close to your competitor's claims is likely to require significant guidance from your attorney.

1. Collect all of the relevant independent claims, including granted patents and pending applications. Recall that the independent claims will be the broadest. Read these first, because if your product is outside of the independent claims, it is also outside of the dependent claims.
2. Make sure to identify any applications that are still pending, as the claims may later be modified (recall our discussion of continuation practice and "submarine" claims). These may require an evaluation of the entire specification to identify unclaimed subject matter, which might support claims added in prosecution or in future continuations.
3. Discuss the interpretation of the claims with your attorney. Do the words mean what they seem to say at face value? Are there unique definitions that have been written into the specification? Are there testing methods needed to measure properties specified in the claims?
4. Break the claims down to separate elements and evaluate each element independently. In other words, if the invention comprises Elements A, B, C, and D, and the prior art includes Elements A, B, and C, then Element D should be the prime target for removal from your product.

5. Search for alternatives that already exist in the prior art. Can you deliver the same benefit by substituting known technology? Is there technology from recently expired or abandoned patents that could be used?
6. Consider inventing functional alternatives for each of the elements, with an emphasis on any elements identified in Step 4 as being particular sources of novelty. Use creativity techniques such as TRIZ to construct alternative solutions that may have radically different or fewer elements.

PREDICTIVE INVENTION AND THE NINE-BALL CONCEPT

One of the most interesting difficulties with using competitive information from patents is that while they are very detailed, publication trails the actual inventive activities by at least 18 months. Likewise, if you start work on a product or invention today, it will probably be months, if not years, before the product is commercialized. Furthermore, it will be years before the patents are actually granted.

While patent strategy might be like a chess game in some respects, it is something like having to commit to your move three moves ahead, even though the last two of those moves won't be realized for two more turns. This would create an interesting lag in the game—instead of responding to a competitor's actions immediately, you would have to wait three moves before you could make a change. In many ways, this is the situation with patents—each resource must be committed long before its use.

If you'll pardon an additional analogy, Nine Ball is a pool game in which the balls must be contacted starting with the lowest number on the table and progressing toward the nine ball. Whoever sinks the nine ball wins. A beginning player will concentrate on sinking the ball he is required to hit in order to ensure another shot. A mediocre player will plan how she will sink the ball after the one she is currently trying to sink. An excellent player will plan out the entire game, from one to nine, in advance. Anticipating each successive shot requires more expertise because the position resulting from the first shot will dictate all of the possibilities that follow. The further ahead shots can be planned and executed, the more likely the player is to win.

Furthermore, each successive shot will influence the opportunities for and consequences of future shots. This is similar to the way in which any patent filing will influence future patent strategy by establishing claims for the current invention, but also by creating prior art that will make future filings more difficult.

Most of the time, we focus on solving the problems of today—the first ball. However, there is also the opportunity for planning ahead. We can potentially predict the next round of problems and associated inventions. The further out you can predict the problems and solutions, the more effective your patent strategy will be.

Unfortunately, this isn't easy. There are certainly opportunities for predictive invention based on technology trends, emergence of new technologies (e.g., how will RFIDs affect your industry?), and emergence of new consumer needs (e.g., how do we manage virtual assets online?). As you fix today's problems, what will be next? Can you predict the next competitive battleground? Can you invent a solution to tomorrow's problem today? This is a great opportunity for both market intelligence and competitive intelligence, as the degree of your understanding of the future landscape is likely to dictate your success in applying this strategy.

COMPETITIVE INVENTIONS AND PLATFORM TECHNOLOGIES

One of the most common situations that corporations and researchers face is the focus on solving internal problems and patenting internal products. This isn't a problem as long as your competitors choose to imitate exactly what your company is producing. However, most competitors with imitative strategies will have some differences in their resources, processes, relationships, or strategies that may enable them to get around your internally focused filings. Perhaps your process is more sophisticated than theirs, but theirs is more flexible. Or perhaps there is a difference in scale. Each of these differences creates a potential opportunity for imitation in order to achieve a similar result without using your patented technology. Focusing only on the product that you plan to produce and on the related internal processes and methods is likely to result in a narrow field of view and an overly rose-colored perception of your patent position.

How can you know what your competitors' products and processes entail? Conveniently, patents are a great source of competitive intelligence for this purpose. As mentioned earlier, reading your competitors' patents can be a great way to develop a better understanding of their internal processes and resource allocations; which new technologies they are developing, and what the next generation of products will deliver. Pay particular attention to any technologies that appear to be fundamental to their strategic plans based on their large commitments in capital or marketing (sometimes called "platform technologies"). The larger the commitment on your competitors' part, the longer it will take them to change that element of their offering to consumers.

This competitive intelligence can be combined with your own inventions to create new, competitively focused inventions that will strengthen your strategic position and protect you against imitation. Here are a few questions that are worth considering:

- What elements of the value chain are different for your competitors?
- What processes do they use with installed capital (i.e., "steel in the ground") that is unlikely to change?
- Are there platform technologies that they are likely to incorporate into multiple future generations or products?
- Have they made commitments to the marketplace that dictate the design or function of future products?

DEFINING A NEW S CURVE

Recall our discussion of the "innovation S curve," which suggests that most innovations proceed through a period of slow adoption, followed by rapid expansion and finally by a saturated, low-growth period. As a reminder, we divide the S curve into three general sections: technology-driven, consumer-driven, and price-driven or commoditization. In the third phase, the technology has reached saturation, and the level of competition has increased to such an extent that differentiation among competitive products has been reduced. Competition without differentiation leads to price pressures and the eventual commoditization of the product or technology.

In theory, products and technologies that are currently in the third phase are ripe for disruption by a new technology that defines a different S curve. This next-generation technology may initially have some performance issues that prevent its immediate widespread adoption, but the long-term prospects suggest that it will continue to progress beyond the first technology. Technology-focused companies will usually attempt to shift from one S curve to the next as rapidly as possible, while imitating competitors, and/or cost-advantaged competitors may be happy to compete even in the more commoditized arenas.

As a product or technology approaches the third phase of an S curve, it's worth considering what technologies may disrupt the S curve in the near future. Can you use predictive models from TRIZ or other techniques to extrapolate to future S curves? Can you identify the white space for filing applications that may prevent or delay such disruption? Is there fundamental new research that may shift the core technology of your industry?

In order to be successful, this approach must precede the general acceptance of the new technology. By the time everyone agrees that the new technology will be successful, it's probably too late to establish a strong patent position. Consequently, it's extremely important to be looking ahead and evaluating technologies long before they are commercially viable. Many of these potential new S curves will not occur, but the one that does may dramatically disrupt your industry. Your patent strategy and strategic inventing can help your corporation prepare for these new disruptive technologies.

THE "BLACK BOX" APPROACH

Often, a distinctly new product or process will entail new steps along the way. Some of these steps may be hidden from your competitors' view and therefore be considered for keeping as trade secrets. For example, any process that is entirely internal to your company, leaves no fingerprint in the resulting product, and is unlikely to be independently developed would be a good candidate for keeping as a trade secret.

However, this can cause problems for other aspects of the overall filing strategy. For example, if this potential trade secret is in fact the best mode of producing the product, it must be included in the disclosure of the product-focused applications. Frequently, this results in the default approach of filing both product and process applications.

One way around this problem is to monitor the developments as a function of time, so that any filing includes the best mode at the time of the invention, but does not include final manufacturing developments because they have not been invented yet. For example, if the product is created and tested at bench scale, this is sufficient to support product-focused claims using only bench-scale best mode and enablement. Later-developed techniques for mass-producing the invention could then be kept a trade secret. In this way, a portion of the process could be maintained as a trade secret while the final product is still patented.

Another similar approach would be to compartmentalize the manufacturing process so that claims to products and processes exist within one segment only. For example, if the manufacturing can be segmented into three sequential steps, applications can be written for the product and processes related to Step 1 and Step 3, while not disclosing all of the details of Step 2. This approach would require careful claim construction so that the invention claimed in Step 3 does not require the disclosure of Step 2 as the best mode.

For example, let's imagine a process for making a healthy but tasty aerated chocolate product in which the first step is mixing the ingredients at a fixed shear rate at a set temperature. The ingredients contain an unexpected component (quinoa extract) that makes the product healthier, but also makes achieving chocolatelike consistencies much more difficult. The second step in the process involves compressing the chocolate mixture with supercritical liquid nitrogen, and extruding the chocolate into a mold, where it expands tremendously, leaving a light and fluffy chocolate product.

In this example, product claims to the composition of the quinoa-chocolate mixture that result at the end of the first step may be possible. This mixture, while not ideal to the marketplace, would presumably be novel, unexpected, and useful (it is edible, after all). If we assume it would be nearly impossible to reverse-engineer the supercritical nitrogen process, the second step may be best kept as a trade secret, so no applications are filed that involve the product of this step.

Keeping a trade secret while also having patent protection may be difficult, but it may be possible given enough ingenuity and forethought.

NOVELTY *EX NIHILO*

What if the product that you are making is effectively in the prior art? Or perhaps you've created a significant degree of differentiation and even met a consumer need, but the resulting product is still not patentable in a meaningful way?

If the strategic need is significant enough, it is possible to *introduce* an element of novelty into your product for the sake of enhancing the patentability of the overall product—creating novelty where there was none before. For this task, I often turn to the fabled "squid juice." While I am not an expert in squid-derived products, nearly anything incorporating squid juice would seem to be both novel and nonobvious, since there is almost no prior art. This is primarily a metaphorical illustration, but I've found it to be a memorable way to illustrate the point quickly when brainstorming with scientists and engineers. If your product isn't patentable as first conceived, increase its patentability by introducing novel and unexpected elements, such as squid juice.

Product development often focuses on delivering the greatest functionality with the least amount of complexity. Generally, having more function with fewer parts is desirable for consumers. However, additional elements—particularly new and unusual elements—may have a substantial benefit when it comes to patentability.

Introducing an element of particular novelty, preferably along with consumer-relevant differentiation, is a potential technique for strategically positioning inventions with a sustainable competitive advantage. For example, consistently pairing a patentable feature with an unpatentable feature would associate one with the other, in much the same way as trademarks associate logos with products.

What's to stop a competitor from creating a similar product, but lacking the patentable feature? Nothing. This process does, however, prevent copying in its entirety. As with trademarks, trade dress, or design patents, differentiating patentable features can create value through your customers' perception of their distinctiveness.

What's the most distinctive composition or feature that could be added to your product? Are there changes that could be made that would increase the novelty and nonobviousness of the product without detracting from its benefits? Can you engineer a source of novelty into your product?

ELSEWHERE IN THE VALUE CHAIN

Another important strategic inventing technique involves looking for other places in the value chain to create competitive advantage. We briefly discussed this approach earlier, with regard to the bridge model for visualizing patent scope based on its relevance in the value chain. It may be helpful to refer to Figure 12.4 as a reminder. Most companies are narrowly focused on the segment of the value chain in which they compete. However, significant inventions may also exist in connection with your technology either before or after your position in the value chain.

In general, the goal with this technique is to identify opportunities for filings that are based on your primary new invention, but are outside the scope of your normal day-to-day strategic interests. Importantly, you're looking for opportunities to get different types of claims and to broaden the claim scope beyond the core filings. Here are a few questions to consider:

- If your new product is successful, what other aspects of the value chain may be affected?
- Will it enable your customers or suppliers to change their product offerings?
- Will it solve any problems for your customers or suppliers?
- Will it significantly change the way your customers do business (if your customers are not the end users, for example)?
- Will it change the way the end user interacts with your product?
- Is your product eventually combined with other products before or during its use?
- Would it be easier to detect infringement and enforce patents somewhere else in the value chain (e.g., the final product sold in the marketplace, perhaps)?
- Are your competitors' value chains different from your own? Do these differences create opportunities for design-around inventions or other forms of imitation without infringing on your core inventions?

A good patent landscape will be invaluable, as will a detailed understanding of other points in the value chain—even segments in which you don't normally interact. For example, let's say that you've invented a new material that can substitute for existing materials at a much lower cost. In addition to the core filings around the material itself, you might also consider filing on applications that your *customers* would have for this new material. Perhaps the lower-cost material would expand your customers' applications to new and different markets and enable them to create their own form of consumer differentiation. You wouldn't enforce against your customers, but you could provide them with a competitive advantage through using your product. Your customers will benefit, thereby strengthening the value you provide to them as a supplier.

CHAPTER 23

USING TRIZ FOR STRATEGIC INVENTING

There are many techniques available for focusing your creative insight on a particular objective. Strategic inventing is probably possible using almost any of these methods. However, TRIZ is a favorite of inventors because of its origin and its focus on patents.

The acronym TRIZ stands for the Russian phrase *teoriya resheniya izobretatelskikh zadatch*, or "theory of inventive problem solving" in English. TRIZ is a popular problem-solving methodology for invention because of both its utility and its deep connection with patents. If you have studied TRIZ already, the following may give you a few techniques for combining your knowledge with patent strategy. If not, consider this a brief sample of a much more complex and robust theory. Dozens of books have been written about TRIZ, and there are numerous improvements and variations. The following is a quick snapshot that may whet your appetite for further study.

TRIZ was created by a Soviet inventor named Genrich Altshuller, based on a study of large numbers of patent filings. In his study of patents, he identified numerous trends and principles that seemed to be repeatable, if not predictable. In short, the theory is that by studying solutions developed in previous inventions and related patterns of innovation, future inventions can be more easily identified and improved. TRIZ is a particularly valuable tool when you are deliberately creating inventions, and it fits nicely with the concept of strategic inventing.

THE LAW OF IDEALITY AND TECHNOLOGY TRENDS

One important observation from studying invention trends is that any system tends to increase the amount of function offered, while decreasing the associated negatives or resources required. If we extrapolate far enough into the future, a function will be delivered without any negative consequences, costs, or resource requirements. Of course, this would be an "ideal" product—and as Arthur C. Clarke once stated, "Any sufficiently advanced technology is indistinguishable from magic." One might then express "ideality" as the ratio of function to (negatives + costs). Increasing function and/or decreasing negatives and costs results in a more ideal product. Any given product or invention has a certain level of ideality, even though it is not yet ideal. Previous generations of the same product will, in general, have lower ideality, and successful future products will probably have greater ideality.

In recent times, mobile phones have undergone perhaps the most significant increase in ideality of any household product. Twenty years ago, a mobile phone was the size of a brick and barely made phone calls. Then camera features were added, and even texting and e-mail. In each case, the function of the device increased significantly. It might be argued that many of these devices suffered from increases in complexity (such as keyboards), which would increase the negatives in our ideality ratio, but certainly the net result has been toward more function in less space. More recently, touch interface has increased the function dramatically, while also decreasing the complexity of interacting with the phones. In comparison to the landscape at the time, Apple's original iPhone was dramatically closer to ideal, offering significantly more function with few additional negatives. In other words, the product made a significant step toward ideality.

This approach to predictive invention challenges us to ask what other functions could be added. What negatives could be removed? Could the phone be even smaller? Could we do away with charging?

When using this metric for inventing, the first step is to identify opportunities for product or system improvements that would increase ideality, then use those opportunities to hypothesize future inventions. For strategic inventing, these hypothetical inventions would be evaluated for alignment with white space in the patent landscape, patentability, and fit with overall strategic objectives. Those hypothetical inventions that have the best fit within the overall strategy would then be pursued, either through actual research or, in the case of a purely strategic filing, perhaps as a prophetic application.

TRIZ also suggests that there are trends in technology development that are repeated across industries and can be reasonably predicted from existing inventions. Examples of such trends might include increased segmentation, the introduction of voids, added functionality, increased customization, or increased density of functions. Importantly, these trends need to be at a level of abstraction that allows for reapplication across products and industries. These particular trends may not apply to your product directly, but the key assertion is that there are trends in technology progression that *do* apply to your product. What are the major changes that have affected the products and processes related to your project over the last few iterations? Can you characterize these changes into a small number of abstract categories? If so, can you predict what the product will look like at the next step of the trend for each of these categories?

When you are considering these trends, it is not necessary that every system progress from one step to the next in an orderly way. In fact, multiple versions may exist at the same time, since specific levels may be optimized for certain applications. These are simply generalized trends that may or may not affect your specific product. Let us consider one simple example based on the introduction of voids into a solid system.

Bricks were initially formed as monolithic structures. Later, a few voids were introduced to reduce the amount of material used without a corresponding loss of strength. Now, large numbers of voids can be introduced, providing dramatically different building properties (Google "foamed concrete brick," for example). Futhermore, current research is developing dynamic "healing" concrete that will respond to fractures by automatically exuding an adhesive (i.e., functionalized voids).

Which trends are relevant to your product or system? That's a challenge for you to solve—and recognizing that these trends exist is a key to predicting the next step in the progression. These trends might include increasing customization, more user interaction, reductions in size or materials, or substitutions of better types of materials. Challenge yourself to evaluate the technology trends that have occurred, and then project the next logical step (or two) in the trend. Then use these projections to identify opportunities for future filings.

By evaluating these future opportunities in light of the patent literature, looking for white space and/or competitive activity, you can get an early jump on new technologies and opportunities for filing cases that support your strategic objectives. However, in some cases, these opportunities will result in properties of the product or system that would also have distinct negatives. The improved aspects are closely tied to negative consequences. These situations bring us to our next topic for discussion: contradictions.

Breaking a Contradiction

Another key aspect of TRIZ is the concept of defining key inventive problems as "contradictions." When you are evaluating a system for potential improvements, the attributes that you desire in an ideal product often bring with them undesirable consequences. For example, if you would like a stronger beam to support your building, that beam will also be heavier, because weight and strength are directly correlated (all else being constant). You need stronger support, but the extra weight will cause problems or costs elsewhere in the system. This contradiction might be stated as wanting lighter and stronger at the same time.

While there are solutions to this problem, most of them will involve some sort of compromise. One solution might be to make the beam a little bit stronger and a little bit heavier. Or perhaps you could introduce additional complexity by adding an additional secondary support structure to support the extra weight (increased complexity means decreasing ideality). Neither of these approaches is preferred. A compromise solution may be sufficient, but it is rarely the best possible result.

Solving the contradiction, on the other hand, would mean achieving both objectives—both stronger and lighter. In this case, this could be achieved by developing a beam with a uniquely designed cross section (such as an I beam), where the same material is used, but the overall strength is greater while the weight is lower.

Of course, at this point in time, I beams are well known and have been for many years. However, this example does illustrate another key point: the solutions to problems in one situation can be used to solve similar problems in other situations. In this case, metal I beams were invented in the mid-1800s. However, wood joists retained their traditional rectangular profile for another hundred years. These days, however, you can readily find wooden joists that have been fashioned into I beams in residential houses.

Returning to the mobile-phone discussion, I expect it will soon be possible to make the device extremely small. While this will make it easy to carry, the small size of the device adds a problem—the difficulty of visually interacting with it. Conversely, a big screen would be great to interact with, but hard to put in your pocket. This is a classic contradiction: we want a smaller device for storage but a larger device for viewing. While it sounds unlikely to achieve both in the same device, I can confidently predict that it will be solved in a forthcoming generation of phones—perhaps through flexible and extendable screens, microprojectors, or commandeering local screens. Or perhaps the screen will be physically small but visually large though incorporation into eyeglasses or contact lenses. Whatever solution is adopted to resolve this contradiction, it will likely be a substantial innovation that disrupts the technological, commerical, and patent landscapes.

Importantly, solving a contradiction is often a useful indicator of a patentable invention. Breaking the typical relationships between key properties usually means obtaining a nonadditive or otherwise unexpected result. If your solution has overcome this contradiction, it is most likely not an obvious variation and very likely to be a significant invention deserving of broad claim scope. Furthermore, the implications of breaking a contradiction are usually meaningful to key product attributes and likely to establish the kind of differentiation needed to create a competitive advantage in the marketplace. Conversely, compromise solutions in which previous results are combined to create an "average" solution or that result in additive performance are less likely to be granted a patent or create significant disruption in the marketplace.

When developing your patent strategy, identifying the contradictions of your product or system can be used to identify opportunities for future filings. Furthermore, solving contradictions usually results in patentable inventions that create significant differentiation in the marketplace. As such, this approach can be a great tool for strategic inventing.

The Nine Boxes

Another TRIZ concept that is useful for strategic inventing is considering your product or system in the overall context and associated interactions. This is best illustrated by a three-by-three matrix of categories, as shown in Table 23.1. The top three categories are the past, present, and future, and the left-hand categories are the subsystem, the system (or product), and the supersystem. The subsystem focuses on smaller elements that make up the product, while the supersystem involves the broader view of anything else that interacts with the product.

Many researchers are focused on the product that they have been asked to deliver—which is entirely reasonable. Likewise, patent attorneys will generally focus on protecting the product that is going to be sold. However, a key aspect of a thorough patent strategy is to identify opportunities for filing, then evaluate those opportunities for strategic fit, regardless of whether or not the patents describe the product you actually sell. For example, if a competitor sees opportunities for applying your new product to a different industry, it may be able to get patents granted that would prevent you from participating in that industry. Your competitor

Table 23.1   **The nine-box chart**

	Past	Present	Future
Supersystem	Forest	Distributors and groceries	Keeping the entire house clean
System	Trees	Paper towels	Cleaning in the kitchen by the consumer
Subsystem	Wood pulp	Nonwoven fibrous substrate bound with hydrogen bonds and polymers	Interactions among water, dirt, and surfaces

would also be prevented from participating because of your original patent applications. However, this is certainly not a value-maximizing situation. Preferably, these opportunities either earlier or later in the life of your product, or in supersystems or subsystems, would be identified early on and incorporated into your overall filing strategy.

What other aspects of the value chain will be affected by your new product or invention? Will your customers or suppliers face potential disruption of their current business plan? Will your new invention create opportunities for filing for broader protection anywhere between the beginning of the value chain and the end consumer (compare our earlier discussion of the bridge model)? Can you stagger these filings to maximize the life span of the overall competitive advantage?

Recall that the primary objective of a patent strategy, as well as of strategic inventing, is to protect against imitation. Your patent claims can extend to any element of the value chain, which means that you should consider preventing imitation or substitution at other levels of the value chain as a part of your strategy. You might consider performing a similar exercise by using steps in the value chain in place of the "time" components in the nine-box chart. This might require significantly more than nine boxes, of course, but the fundamentals of the technique remain the same.

THE VALUE OF TRIZ

To summarize, TRIZ is a particularly valuable tool when you are deliberately creating inventions, and it fits nicely with the concept of strategic inventing. It's particularly useful for predicting future product innovations and opportunities for invention based on technology trends, increasing ideality, solving contradictions, and evaluating other elements in the overall system. Furthermore, many of the tools are designed specifically for the problem-solving aspect of inventing using principles distilled from thousands of patents. It is, however, a much larger and more complex theory that deserves to be studied in greater detail. Hopefully, this brief sample will encourage you to seek out additional resources on this topic and apply them in your inventive endeavors. A good place to start would be the book *The Innovation Algorithm* by Genrich Altshuller, or the website www.opensourcetriz.com.

CHAPTER 24

Implementing a Patent Strategy at the Project Level

Implementing the concepts discussed in previous chapters may seem like a daunting task. The following outline provides step-by-step suggestions for creating and implementing a patent strategy for your project. Keep in mind that this is just a general outline that will need to be customized for your project's specific needs.

These steps are presented sequentially, but you may find several iterations are required. Ideally, the framework for your strategy should be created very early in the project's life, but it will need to be updated as new information is uncovered—competitive developments, new inventions in the lab, or shifting objectives. Be sure to communicate with your attorney early and often as you develop your specific patent strategy and as your research and your project progress.

STEP 1: DETERMINE YOUR OBJECTIVE IN SPECIFIC TERMS

While I have frequently used phrases like "maximizing your competitive advantage," this is not a specific enough objective for implementation at the project level. Your objective needs to include the following key elements:

- How will the patents be used? Will they be used to create competitive advantage in the marketplace, for out-licensing and royalty collection, to ensure your freedom to operate through defensive publications, to build a portfolio to discourage countersuits, or for something else entirely? Be as specific as possible.

- Who are your competitors for the purposes of this product and this strategy? What kinds of products and strategies do you expect from them?
- How does the patent strategy support the overall project strategy? Is it tangential to the product (i.e., you'll go ahead even without patent coverage, if necessary), or is it a core necessity (no patents means no project)?
- How broad do your claims need to be in order to provide a competitive advantage? Would narrow claims be sufficient for some needs, such as technology transfer?
- When do the key elements of the patent strategy need to be in place?
- What geographies are likely to be relevant? Are there unique considerations for patentable subject matter or other differences in patent law that would impact the effectiveness of your strategy?

STEP 2: TALK TO YOUR ATTORNEY ABOUT POTENTIAL CLAIMS STRATEGIES AND PORTFOLIO STRATEGIES

Step 1 will involve your attorney as well, but it will also require input from business, marketing, production, and various other areas involved in the larger project strategy. In Step 2, I would consider a short meeting with your attorney to review the key aspects of your potential filing strategies in more detail. Use this time to define which portfolio strategies are likely to be employed, particularly anything that would be time sensitive, such as life-cycle management. Likewise, bring up any questions that might pertain directly to the research plan and would help you identify patentable inventions when they occur. Consider discussing the following, for example:

- What kinds of inventions are likely to be patentable?
- How much data is required to file an application in this subject area— are claims likely to be granted without data?
- What kind of claims scope is likely to be allowed in this technology area?
- Would your attorney consider filing on hypothetical or prophetic inventions?
- What is the typical filing strategy with regard to provisional, non-provisional, and PCT applications? What is the filing strategy in other relevant geographies?

STEP 3: CONSTRUCT A COMPETITIVE LANDSCAPE

While you should have done a bit of searching of the prior art and competitive patent filings already, it is important to construct a more holistic competitive landscape to gain a better picture of the strategic issues that are involved. Developing a patent strategy without a landscape is something like playing chess on a computer that has been set up so that you can see only your own pieces on the board, not your opponent's. It's extremely difficult to select your best strategy without knowing where your opponent's pieces are.

You may be able to construct the landscape yourself, but your company may also have tools or even dedicated analysts to help with this task. Regardless of the techniques applied, be sure that you understand the output, and that the output is meaningful to your project. If your technology categories are too broad, your conclusions may not be actionable. If the wrong key words are used for either the search or the categorization, the information you get may simply be misleading.

Also, don't forget to include information about your own company's intellectual property. You may find patents that can be used to strengthen the project portfolio. You may also find that your competitive position in a particular area is not what you expected.

STEP 4: SET UP SEARCH ALERTS TO CONSTANTLY MONITOR THE COMPETITION

Now that you know what the landscape looks like, it's a good time to construct some searches that can constantly monitor your competitors' filings, potential technology providers, and likely technology disruptors.

As previously mentioned, most of the major search vendors offer some form of alert capability. Usually it's no more difficult than developing the search terms using standard methods and then saving the search, with some options for frequency and content of the e-mailed alert results. Here are a few simple searches you might consider setting as regular alerts:

- Assignee-based searches for filings from key competitors, technology providers, and potential collaborators
- Inventor-based searches for key innovators in your industry
- Key word–based searches for technologies, products, and other topics of interest.

You may not be the person who is responsible for competitive intelligence at your corporation, but keeping an eye on the patent filings related to your project is always a good thing. Your competitors' applications will give you insight into what technologies are working (or not working). Granted patents will give you examples of what kinds of claims are being allowed and potential red space to avoid. Monitoring patent activity doesn't take much time, and it's usually very informative.

STEP 5: IDENTIFY AREAS OF POTENTIAL WHITE SPACE AND RED SPACE

The landscape generated in Step 3 will primarily tell you what areas are already within the prior art—the red space. However, you'll likely need to distill this information further into an actionable analysis. Keep in mind that any written documents should avoid specific discussion of what claims mean and should probably be created directly under an attorney's supervision. A statement like, "There are numerous patents involving similar products with RFID" is usually OK, whereas a statement like, "We would be infringing this patent if we include RFID in the product" would definitely *not* be OK.

It is also important to deliberately identify areas where there isn't a dense prior art landscape—that is, the white space. These areas don't need to be entirely empty of prior art, but the prior art needs to be sparse enough to lead you to believe that there is space left for continued development. They may include emerging technologies that haven't been applied to your industry yet, cross-fertilization from other industries, new materials, or even new consumer needs.

Importantly, this step does not require that inventions be identified to fill the white space yet. Right now, the focus is on identifying opportunities for further research and potential inclusion into the product. These are likely to have greater claim scope allowed and would probably be a great place to explore for opportunities with strong patent positions. Consider making some diagrams as described in Chapter 12 to help visualize the current situation and future opportunities.

STEP 6: DEVELOP A WRITTEN PATENT STRATEGY DOCUMENT

Ideally, this document should be created as close to the beginning of the project as possible. It should include a summary of the following key aspects of project-level patent strategy:

- The objective of the strategy in practical and concrete terms
- A summary of the competitive landscape, including the white space and the red space
- A summary of your company's existing patents and applications related to this technology
- Types of inventions expected to result from the research plan
- Consideration of opportunities for publication or keeping trade secrets
- The geographies of interest, and any specific legal issues associated with those geographies
- Particular timing needs (e.g., coordination with any mandatory publication, life-cycle management, or marketing disclosures), including when particular applications need to be filed
- *If* things go as planned, what you expect to have protected when your product is in the marketplace

As mentioned earlier, in creating this document, it is best to characterize competitive activity objectively by summarizing numbers of filings or generalizations of technology focus, but not to address specific freedom-to-operate (FTO) issues or anything else that might pose a significant problem for your project. Even under privilege, most attorneys will ask you not to write about such issues, since they can have dire consequences in any later legal disputes.

Once this document has been created, it should be updated frequently as research and development progresses—each new problem solved or feature added will provide new opportunities and consequences for the patent strategy, which leads us to the next step.

STEP 7: ACTIVELY COORDINATE THE PATENT STRATEGY WITH THE RESEARCH EFFORT

As the research and/or product development phase of your project proceeds, the results need to be fed back into the patent strategy in a coordinated cycle. Significant developments are likely to cause a reevaluation of some of the earlier steps. FTO, in particular, will need to be evaluated for any particular embodiments that might make it into the final product.

- Can the patent strategy take an active role in directing the research effort?
- Is it possible to target areas of significant white space that were identified in the previous step?

- Is there cheap or easy testing that could be done to compare your results with your competitors' patented inventions?
- Are there ways to characterize the product that would highlight unexpected results?
- Have recent competitive filings created new hurdles in your development path?
- Should you consider designing around or licensing any technologies?

STEP 8: FILE IDFS AND REVIEW POTENTIAL INVENTIONS WITH YOUR ATTORNEY

This step is likely to occur in parallel with Steps 7 and 9 over the life of the project. Invention disclosure forms (IDFs) should be filed and any review process should be conducted as the potential inventions are developed. Keep in mind that the recent patent law changes have put increasing emphasis on the filing date, as opposed to the inventive date, as the key date for comparison with the prior art so timely filing of the applications will generally be preferred.

Depending on the process for reviewing invention disclosures at your company, individual inventors may not be directly involved in the decision to file or not to file a particular application. In some instances, this is left to the attorneys and management or even a review board of some kind. In general, I would argue in favor of direct inventor involvement because the discussions and reasoning help to educate new inventors about the criteria for filing, policies, or other corporate strategies that will affect the overall filing strategy.

If you, as the inventor, are not directly involved, it is usually worthwhile to meet with your attorney to discuss the outcome of any invention disclosure you have filed—especially when the decision is not to file on something that you think is important. There may be good reasons not to file, but you should be made aware of these reasons so that you can improve your invention disclosures in the future. On the other hand, there may be reasons to file that the attorney didn't recognize—perhaps the technical landscape is extremely complex, or perhaps you see value in this particular invention that is not readily apparent.

STEP 9: ENGAGE IN STRATEGIC INVENTING AND BUILDING THE PORTFOLIO

Once the key aspects of the product have been defined, there may still be a need to bolster the core patents with additional, strategically positioned applications. These new inventions may amount to building a blocking portfolio to prevent design-around efforts, filings that focus on your competitor's likely strategy for imitation, the Nine Ball strategy, life-cycle management, or any of the other strategies we've discussed.

Consider mapping out your portfolio using some of the methods we've discussed. Are key components of the product likely to be protected against imitation by a competitor? Are there easy routes to design-around inventions? What's your competitor's best alternative to the new invention (BATNI)? Are there opportunities for filing elsewhere in the value chain?

Inventors who are too focused on research results may have trouble making inventions of this type unless they make a focused effort. Consider applying some of the techniques we've discussed in Part 3 of this book to identify opportunities for new inventions that can strengthen the overall patent portfolio. Furthermore, this shouldn't be a one-time event, but rather an ongoing process of constant portfolio building.

STEP 10: EVALUATE YOUR POSITION RELATIVE TO YOUR OBJECTIVE

One problem that often occurs when developing a patent strategy and filings to support that strategy is that the process usually takes place over a long time—months or years. Each application will take time to file, and the scope of granted claims probably won't be known until much later. Projects that have long life spans may suffer from the lack of a formal review process as a mechanism for identifying gaps and new opportunities.

Hopefully you've kept your patent strategy document up to date along the way, so you'll be able to readily compare your progress against the objectives and review your progress over time.

• How does your resulting position compare with your initial objective?
• Are there steps you can take to remedy any shortcomings?
• Do you expect to be granted enough claim space to establish a meaningful competitive advantage?
• Are there new technologies that have emerged in the interim that should be added to the patent strategy?
• Has the competitive landscape shifted in a meaningful way? Should you develop a response to the competitive activity?
• What have you learned that could be applied to future projects?

EPILOGUE

The foregoing chapters probably covered some topics either more or less extensively than you had hoped. Unfortunately, each technology area often has unique approaches to patent strategy, so a general book of this type cannot cover every industry in great detail without becoming a weighty tome. On the other hand, the concepts, tools, techniques, and frameworks that we've discussed will provide a solid foundation for creating a sustainable competitive advantage through patent strategy in any industry, increasing the value of individual inventions as well as portfolios of intellectual property.

Here's a brief summary of highlights from the topics we've discussed:

- Learning the basic terminology and key elements of the patenting process will illuminate these topics, which may otherwise be obscured by peculiar words and legalese.
- Inventors should be involved throughout the patenting process, including the formulation of patent strategies that extend beyond a single invention.
- The claims of a patent dictate the value of the patent. Having a patent granted doesn't create value unless it protects valuable features from imitation or design-around by competitors.
- Basic searching can be extremely useful for learning about competitors, what's typically patentable, and common claims styles for a particular technology field.
- Landscape and visualization techniques can be helpful in identifying white space and red space, and in laying the foundation for formulating a patent strategy.

- Significant innovations often involve multiple inventions that result in portfolios of relevant patents and opportunities for a more complex, portfolio-size strategy.
- An understanding of patent strategy issues and opportunities can be used to inform the research and new product development process, leading to better protection for your products and inventions.
- Proactive management of the patent strategy process can be combined with other business strategies, collaboraitons, product differentiation, and innovation cycles to increase the value created.
- Inventions can be created as part of a deliberate strategy and don't necessarily have to flow from traditional discovery-driven sources.
- There are many different techniques and strategies that can be employed, but no single approach is right for every situation.

Combining the knowledge, skills, and techniques from each of the preceding chapters will provide a foundation from which you can extend your technical expertise into the realm of patents, strategy, and competitive advantage.

Many scientists and researchers find the realm of patents to be overly complex, suffering from obscure terminology and arbitrary rules. Unfortunately, nearly all challenges are complicated by necessary rules, whether physical laws or patent laws. The complexity deepens the challenge, but it does not diminish the opportunity. Formulating patent strategies, much like conducting research and creating new products, can be an intellectually rewarding endeavor.

I encourage you to actively apply the information you've learned when the opportunity arises: ask questions of your patent attorney, participate in patent strategy discussions, learn basic searching skills to investigate the landscape and competitors, and open your toolbox of more advanced techniques from time to time. As you develop new products and inventions with meaningful competitive advantage, your appreciation for these topics—and your enjoyment of them—will grow.

NOTES

Chapter 15

1. http://en.wikipedia.org/wiki/Turtles_all_the_way_down.
2. Nikoleta Panteva and Justin Molavi, "Top 10 Most Profitable Industries," Special Report, October 2011, www.ibisworld.com.
3. Richard Razgaitis, *Valuation and Pricing of Technology-Based Intellectual Property* (Hoboken, NJ: John Wiley & Sons, 2003), also *Valuation of Intellectual Property and Intangible Assets* (Smith and Parr, 2000).
4. Uniloc USA, Inc. v. Microsoft Corp., 632 F.3d 1292 (Fed. Cir. Jan. 4, 2011).

Chapter 20

1. Clayton M. Christensen, *The Innovator's Dilemma* (Boston: Harvard Business School Press, 1997).
2. Clayton M. Christensen and Michael E. Raynor, *The Innovator's Solution* (Boston: Harvard Business School Press, 2003).
3. Clayton M. Christensen, Scott D. Anthony, and Erik A. Roth, *Seeing What's Next* (Boston: Harvard Business School Press, 2004).
4. V. Grovindarajan and P. K. Kopalle, "The Usefulness of Measuring Disruptiveness of Innovations Ex Post in Making Ex Ante Predictions," *Journal of Product Innovation Management* 23, no. 1 (2006): 12–18.
5. Ted Leavitt, "Marketing Myopia," *Harvard Business Review* 38 (July–August 1960): 24–47.
6. Jeffrey D. Lindsay, Cheryl Perkins, and Mukund Karanjikar, *Conquering Innovation Fatigue: Overcoming the Barriers to Personal and Business Success* (Hoboken, NJ: John Wiley & Sons, 2009).
7. John Cronin and ipCapital Group teach "Invention on Demand" as a rapid IA-generation process.

8. Jeff Lindsay and Mike Hopkins, "Disruptive Innovation and the Need for Disruptive Intellectual Asset Strategy," *Journal of Product Innovation Management* 27, no. 2 (March 2010): 283–290.
9. Marshall Phelps and John Cronin, "Mining Patent Gold: What Every CEO Should Know," Forbes.com, September 9, 2011, http://www.forbes.com/sites/forbesleadershipforum/2011/09/09/mining-patent-gold-what-every-ceo-should-know/, accessed March 13, 2012.
10. "Diamond Sutra," Wikipedia, http://en.wikipedia.org/wiki/Diamond_Sutra, accessed March 13, 2012.
11. "Wang Zhen (official)," Wikipedia, http://en.wikipedia.org/wiki/Wang_Zhen_%28official%29, accessed February 25, 2012.
12. Lee Chyen Yee, "China Passes U.S. as Top Patent Filer in 2011," *Globe and Mail*, December 21, 2011, http://www.theglobeandmail.com/news/technology/tech-news/china-passes-us-as-top-patent-filer-in-2011/article2279047/, accessed February 29, 2012. See also http://www.reuters.com/article/2011/12/21/us-china-patents-idUSTRE7BK0LQ20111221.
13. "Quality Is China's Biggest Patent Challenge," *Intellectual Asset Magazine*, (IAM blog), January 20, 2011, http://www.iam-magazine.com/blog/Detail.aspx?g=e81c5421-bccc-4eb5-9895-f347443cf73e, accessed March 13, 2012.
14. Yee, "China Passes U.S."
15. Thompson Reuters, "Top 100 Global Innovators," 2011, http://top100innovators.com/top100.

INDEX

About the Author

Nicholas Nissing graduated *summa cum laude* from Washington University with a degree in chemical engineering. He began his industrial experience at Procter & Gamble, where he worked as a corporate inventor in paper goods and cosmetics. After leaving P&G, he founded the consulting firm Luminosity LLC, where he focused on new product development and patent strategy for large corporations in a variety of industries. Currently, he is the biotechnology competitive strategy lead at Monsanto, as well as an adjunct professor at Washington University and a registered patent agent. At the university, the topics of his classes include new product development and intellectual property. His inventions have been applied to successful new products with annual sales in excess of $100 million, and they span a variety of industries ranging from novel printing techniques to cosmetics and molecular genomics.